POLITICAL TV

Political TV serves as an accessible critical introduction to the broad category of American political television content. Encompassing political news and scripted entertainment, the book addresses a range of formats, including interview/news programs, political satire, fake news, drama, and reality TV. From long-running programs such as Meet the Press to more recent offerings including Veep, The Daily Show, House of Cards, Last Week Tonight, and Scandal, Tryon addresses ongoing debates about the role of television in representing issues and ideas relevant to American politics. Exploring political TV's construction of concepts of citizenship and national identity, the status of political TV in a post-network era, and advertisements in politics, Political TV offers an engaging, timely analysis of how this format engages its audience in the political scene. The book also includes a videography of key and historical series, discussion questions, and a bibliography for further reading.

Chuck Tryon is Associate Professor of Film and Media Studies at Fayetteville State University. He is the author of On-Demand Culture: Digital Delivery and the Future of Movies and Reinventing Cinema: Movies in the Age of Media Convergence.

D0878736

Routledge Television Guidebooks

The Routledge Television Guidebooks offer an introduction to and overview of key television genres and formats. Each guidebook contains an introduction, including a brief history; defining characteristics and major series; key debates surrounding themes, formats, genres, and audiences; questions for discussion; and a bibliography of further reading and watching.

Science Fiction TV
J. P. Telotte

Political TV
Chuck Tryon

Lifestyle TV
Laurie Ouellette

Forthcoming in 2016:

The Sitcom
Jeremy Butler

Reality TV
Jonathan Kraszewski

POLITICAL TV

CHUCK TRYON

NEW YORK AND LONDON

First published 2016
by Routledge
711 Third Avenue, New York, NY 10017

and by Routledge
2 Park Square, Milton Park, Abingdon, Oxon OX14 4RN

Routledge is an imprint of the Taylor & Francis Group, an informa business

© 2016 Taylor & Francis

The right of Chuck Tryon to be identified as author of this
work has been asserted by him in accordance with sections
77 and 78 of the Copyright, Designs and Patents Act 1988.

All rights reserved. No part of this book may be reprinted
or reproduced or utilized in any form or by any electronic,
mechanical, or other means, now known or hereafter
invented, including photocopying and recording, or in any
information storage or retrieval system, without
permission in writing from the publishers.

Trademark notice: Product or corporate names may be
trademarks or registered trademarks, and are used only for
identification and explanation without intent to infringe.

Library of Congress Cataloging in Publication Data
Tryon, Chuck, 1970-
Political TV / Chuck Tryon.
pages cm. — (Routledge television guidebooks)
Includes bibliographical references and index.
Includes tv videography.
1. Television programs—Political aspects—United States.
2. Television in politics—United States. I. Title. II. Title:
Political television.
PN1992.6.T755T79 2016
791.45'6581—dc23
2015034066

ISBN: 978-1-138-83999-1 (hbk)
ISBN: 978-1-138-84000-3 (pbk)
ISBN: 978-1-315-73309-8 (ebk)

Typeset in Joanna MT Std
by Swales & Willis Ltd, Exeter, Devon, UK

Printed and bound in the United States of America by Publishers Graphics,
LLC on sustainably sourced paper.

CONTENTS

ILLUSTRATIONS

ACKNOWLEDGMENTS

Writing this book was very much an unexpected detour, but it also proved to be an incredibly rewarding experience, one that was made even more enjoyable thanks to the advice, encouragement, and suggestions I received while working on it. First, I'd like to express my gratitude to Jennifer Gillan for encouraging me to write a book on political television in the first place. Conversations with Tim Anderson, Jonathan Gray, Daniel Marcus, Jason Mittell, Brian Faucette, Derek Kompare, Dan Herbert, Ethan Thompson, Nick Marx, Chris Becker, Evan Elkins, Amber Day, Elana Levine, Michael Newman, Avi Santo, David Gurney, Jim Hansen, and Josh Braun proved incredibly helpful, especially when this project was in its formative stages, and Richard Edwards's collaboration with me on our article on political mashups played a crucial role in sparking my interest in political entertainment. My colleagues at Fayetteville State University, particularly Eric Hyman, Ed McShane, and my chair, Trela Anderson, have proven incredibly supportive and in many cases have challenged me to think differently about Washington's political culture. I'd also like to raise a pint to the crew at Drinking Liberally, especially Kevin Flanagan, Sean Balkwill, and Jerimee Richir, who never tired of talking about politics (and television) at our weekly gatherings. I am also grateful to the editorial staff at Routledge, especially Erica Wetter, who provided helpful suggestions, especially during the project's earliest stages, and Simon Jacobs, who has provided valuable support and encouragement. Perhaps most crucially, I have to give credit to Andrea Biondi, who not only recommended that I write a book on political television but also once again demonstrated remarkable patience when I needed time to write. This book wouldn't have been possible without her, and I'll always cherish our hours of watching *The Daily Show*, *The Colbert Report*, and *Saturday Night Live* together. I can't begin to describe how much I appreciate the life we've carved out together. Finally, I'd like to dedicate this book to the memory of my mom, Glenda Drum Tryon, who always provided quiet but unwavering support for me but who also was one of the first people to inspire my curiosity about politics. She also pretty much single-handedly turned me into a writer when I was eight years old when she handed me a spiral-bound notebook and said I was supposed to write in it. For once, I don't have the words to express my gratitude for what you gave.

INTRODUCTION: POLITICAL TV AND MEDIATED CITIZENSHIP

It is undeniable that there is a large audience for political entertainment. Responding to the popularity of politically themed shows such as *The Colbert Report*, *The Daily Show*, and *Real Time with Bill Maher*, Jeffrey P. Jones explains that, "popular media outlets discovered that political content could be its hottest commodity."[1] Although the audience for network news shows has been in a prolonged decline, cable news shows continue to garner a relatively large, if politically fragmented, audience. Meanwhile, Comedy Central and HBO have built significant chunks of their original programming around political content, whether that entails the fake news and comedic public affairs shows, such as *The Daily Show*, *The Colbert Report*, and *Real Time with Bill Maher*, or sketch comedy shows that prominently feature political content, or even sitcoms based within Washington's political culture, such as *Veep* or *The Brink*. Meanwhile, political dramas, including *Scandal*, *House of Cards*, *Homeland*, and *The Good Wife*, have appeared across the televisual landscape, all of them shaping how we think about our wider political culture. However, despite the popularity of these shows, much of the appeal of them seemed based on the fact that American politics itself was so universally disliked. This distaste for Washington's political culture seems to take one of two forms. First, politics, as most people experience it, appears to be inauthentic, an artificial site that bears little connection to citizens' everyday concerns. Second, Washington has also become widely associated with various forms of corruption and greed, a place dominated by scandals and abuses of power.

In this context, I use the term "political spectacle" to broadly describe the role of politicians and the media to construct idealized images of democratic engagement and national identity. Thus, heavily scripted events, such as political debates, party convention speeches, presidential inaugurations, and other ceremonial media events serve to create a romanticized image of Washington's political culture. The aversion to corruption in Washington was perhaps put most succinctly by comedian Nick Offerman during a speech at the 2014 Radio and Television Correspondents Association dinner, where he described Washington as a "noxious stinkhole where very little actually gets done because of backstabbing, deceit, and greed." Similarly, as longtime Democratic strategist Donna Brazile argues, the dysfunctional behavior of politicians "makes fodder for a Hollywood script. People like the sleaze."[2] But in many ways, these perceptions of Washington leave us attempting to make sense of how the city's political culture continues to disappoint us. In this sense, political TV engages us as potential participants in the political system, whether as voters, activists, or even as observers hoping to come to a greater understanding of processes that often seem beyond our control or comprehension. Thus, even if many political TV shows appear cynical, they are also often involved in the process of making sense of our wider culture. These texts provide ways of reading Washington's political culture, of evaluating the political stories that dominate our nightly newscasts, and allowing us to develop a language for thinking about our utopian aspirations for how politics should work.

RETHINKING POLITICS

This book focuses primarily on television that depicts American political culture. By looking at political television through the lens of American social, political, and industrial contexts, we can begin to consider how all genres and modes of political television—whether news or entertainment programming—provide a way of understanding the beliefs and values about the political realm. Political culture goes beyond individual politicians, parties, or elections. Instead, as John Corner and Dick Pels define it, political culture entails "the realms of political experience, imagination, values, and dispositions that provide the settings within which a political system operates, shaping the character of political processes and political behavior."[3] Thus, instead of looking at whether or not political news and entertainment programming informs the public, this book instead focuses on how political TV structures the way in which we think about the broader political system. In this sense, political television provides a way of "making sense" of politics.

Although this book focuses on political television, it is important to acknowledge that most people encounter political content through a variety of media forms, including television, radio, newspapers and magazines (whether in print or online), books, and social media, often coming across that content informally or even inadvertently. Given the diversity of media that depict aspects of political culture, Jeffrey P. Jones has suggested the term "mediated citizenship" to describe our relationship to politics and our perceived ability to participate in political dialogue. That said, it is worthwhile focusing on how TV functions when it comes to mediating our understanding of political culture.[4] These questions are linked to larger debates about the relationship between media and democracy itself, and historically, television has been central to debates about whether the media are promoting or discouraging political participation and other forms of active citizenship. In fact, TV is often blamed for promoting passivity and cynicism, whether due to the content itself or due to assumptions about TV as a medium. To some extent, complaints about TV's effects on our politics rely upon a narrow set of indicators. For example, some critics have pointed to trends that showed decreased political turnout as an indication of political indifference or apathy, often blaming cable news media and, in some cases, political satire shows for contributing to a widespread cynicism about politics. However, after a brief dip beginning in the 1970s, voter turnout returned to historic norms in the early 2000s. More crucially, voter turnout is an incomplete measure of involvement in a wider political and media culture that affords more avenues for participation than in the past.

Others have expressed concern that entertainment programming has supplanted the news as a source for political information. Many of these fears coalesced around the results of a 2009 poll by *Time Magazine*, in which respondents named Jon Stewart, host of the satirical Comedy Central fake news show *The Daily Show*, as "the most trusted newscaster" in America, easily outpacing the network news hosts Katie Couric, Charlie Gibson, and Brian Williams, taking 44 percent of the overall vote. While the results were likely skewed by the fact that Stewart was the only entertainer listed alongside three network news anchors, the survey also provided fodder for critics who worried that traditional forms of journalism, ostensibly marked by objectivity and sobriety, were losing their power.[5] However, despite concerns about younger audiences obtaining information from these nontraditional sources, research also indicated that most consumers of political entertainment were often more knowledgeable about politics than people who claimed to get their news from more traditional sources. In fact a Pew Research study from 2012 found that regular viewers of *The Daily Show* and *The Colbert Report* tended to score higher on a news knowledge quiz than people who watched CNN, Fox News, or MSNBC and significantly higher than people who reported watching the national network news or local network newscasts.[6] This should not necessarily be taken to indicate that *The Daily Show* is necessarily more informative than the national news. Many people who watch political comedy do so because of a pre-existing interest in that material, whereas someone who consumes local or national news may do so inadvertently or ambiently, as background noise while doing other things. That said, fake news shows often fulfill a valuable pedagogical function by framing complex issues in ways that are easier to understand or more narratively compelling.

RETHINKING TELEVISION

These discussions of television's role in politics are shaped by assumptions about what, exactly, counts as television in the current moment, one that Henry Jenkins has associated with "media convergence."[7] As Lisa Gitelman explains, a medium entails not only the technological components that make communication possible but also the social and cultural "protocols" that inform how a technology is used.[8] Thus, TV entails more than a box in a room receiving a signal, whether from an antenna, a cable wire, or a satellite dish (or even a Wi-Fi connection). It also includes the regulatory apparatus (the laws that govern TV broadcasters) and the production cultures responsible for making shows or making decisions about what shows will be broadcast, as well as the practices of TV users who make choices not just about what to watch but how to watch or even how to talk about the content of the shows they watch. Many of us now access TV programs via cable or satellite subscriptions or through subscription video-on-demand (SVOD) services, such as Netflix or Amazon Prime, that enable us to choose from a menu of programs on our schedule. As a result, most households now have a significantly wider selection of channels, providing us with a diversity of entertainment and informational choices that may not have been available in the past, allowing viewers to make more purposeful decisions about what they watch.

The changes in the television industry have contributed to a steep decline in ratings—and influence—for the broadcast networks. As Jeffrey P. Jones reports, the network audience share for the nightly news declined from 90 percent of those viewing television to 46 percent between 1980 and 2005.[9] By 2012, the audience share had dropped to 29.3 percent, meaning that less than one third of TV viewers were watching the network news shows that had once been central to American political culture.[10] Instead, there has been a significant fragmentation of the viewing audience into niches, whether for news or entertainment content, a transformation that not only changes the ways in which audiences are informed about politics but also how concepts of nation, political authority, and citizenship are understood. In order to explain this historical shift, Amanda D. Lotz has argued that television has moved through three distinct eras, the network era, the multichannel transition, and what Lotz calls the "post-network era."[11] The network era, which ran from the 1950s to the early 1980s, was dominated by the three major networks ABC, CBS, and NBC, which defined, through their programming choices, not only what counted as television but also established assumptions about the role of news in a democratic society.[12] By the early 1980s, as cable television became increasingly accessible, the dominance of the networks began to fade, as viewers could choose from a menu of approximately 40 to 50 channels, including several 24-hour news and informational channels. Finally, beginning in the early 2000s, Lotz documents the emergence of the "post-network era," one that is marked by the end of network dominance. This post-network era is characterized by rapid change and unstable broadcast models but also by fragmented audiences whose experience of television may have very little in common with others outside their taste culture or community. In fact, when teaching courses on television, I find it increasingly difficult to identify a shared set of TV programs that all—or even most—of my students have seen. Thus, as Elana Levine observes, the shift in TV's industrial and institutional practices means that it is "increasingly difficult to study or teach television as a unified object, even within a single national context."[13] Instead, we are now greeted with a multiplicity of viewing options, a seemingly unlimited array of choices in terms of when, where, how, and what we watch.

These forms of media convergence raise a number of questions about mediated citizenship and political participation. What does it mean, for example, that many people encounter political news primarily through short, often decontextualized, clips embedded in their news feeds on Facebook or Twitter? These questions are pertinent not just for political news but for entertainment programming as well. In fact, the hit Comedy Central show *Inside Amy Schumer* was viewed far more often in on-demand formats than it was on linear television. For the first seven episodes of season three, the show was streamed 27 million times on YouTube and another 1.2 million on Hulu. It was also streamed on Facebook and Snapchat over 4 million times each, while approximately 1.4 million people actually watched the show on linear TV. Similarly, a typical episode of Comedy Central's *Key & Peele* will usually have about 2 million viewers, but the show's episodes have been streamed hundreds of millions of times on YouTube.[14] In my case, I usually watch segments of the show on social media after friends have recommended them. Then, in some cases, I will share a clip, adding a brief comment that might encourage others to watch. As these viewing habits suggest, these shifts in programming models have changed the way in which we understand television as a medium. As Viacom's Doug Herzog, who oversees much of that media conglomerate's entertainment programming, acknowledged, it no longer made sense for Comedy Central to "think of ourselves as a TV network anymore—we're a brand."[15]

POLITICS OF THE TELEVISION INDUSTRIES

The politics of television doesn't stop with the programs themselves, but we must also consider questions of media ownership. Even while the technologies we use to access television have changed, the rules of media ownership have changed alongside of them. Given the vast proliferation of cable channels, it is easy to forget that most of these channels, and the cable and satellite services we use to access them, are owned by a small number of giant media conglomerates, making it less than fully clear whether this vast expansion of choices has truly democratized television. As Jennifer Holt has documented, beginning in the 1980s, a massive structural transformation of the media industries began to take hold, one that reduced regulations on media ownership. Companies were given the freedom, for example, to engage in the practice of what is called *vertical integration*, allowing them to own companies at all levels of the supply chain. Thus, in the world of film production, major studios could own production studios, distributors, and movie theaters, while companies such as Comcast may own television stations (such as NBC and MSNBC), the production facilities where TV shows are produced, and the cable companies (Comcast's cable and Internet services) that enable us to access these shows. In turn, these conglomerates also were permitted to integrate horizontally—that is, to own properties across industries, bringing together film and television with distribution pipelines such as cable and satellite TV providers, a move that allowed a small group of media "empires" to control much of our entertainment culture.[16] These questions of media ownership shape debates about whether television has been truly democratized by the vast expansion of television choices in the post-network era, questions that are vital to discussions of political media, and the ability to cover news or depict narratives that might be critical of corporate interests. For example, as Robert McChesney explains, the consolidation of the cable industry has been particularly notable, resulting in a dramatic reduction in competition that has also led to monthly cable bills that have increased at three times the rate of inflation. Perhaps even more crucially, because Comcast controls such a large share of the cable TV market, they are in a position to have enormous leverage when it comes to negotiating with cable TV channels that wish to be carried on their service, making it increasingly difficult for smaller, independent stations to survive, a situation that could result in less popular points of view becoming even further marginalized because they don't serve the interests of cable providers, as when Time Warner Cable initially refused to carry Al Jazeera America.[17] Thus, as Holt explains, the recent history of media ownership is tied up with questions of what she calls "empire building," the process of "amassing power and centralizing control," a scenario that potentially works against the needs of both consumers and citizens.[18]

Although media consumers are often aware of the lack of competition among cable and satellite TV providers—especially when we look at our monthly cable bill—less attention has been directed toward the issue of the concentration of ownership of so-called affiliate stations, the local stations that contract with networks to air broadcast network programming. While a handful of these stations are locally owned and operated, most others are owned by larger media organizations, such as the Sinclair Broadcast Group (SBG), which owned and operated 164 local affiliates, as of July 2015, and has used its reach to support conservative causes and political candidates. Days before the 2004 election, for example, SBG required its local affiliates to pre-empt their primetime programming in order to show a documentary, *Stolen Honor: Wounds that Never Heal*, that criticized Democratic presidential candidate John Kerry, accusing him of extending the Vietnam War because of his anti-war protests.[19] More recently, SBG produced two infomercials timed to coincide with the 2010 and 2012 elections, including *Breaking Point: 25 Minutes that Will Change America*, which alleged that Barack Obama had received campaign funding from the terrorist group Hamas, even though the Obama campaign claimed it had returned the money. In all cases, SBG sought to use its position as an owner of a significant number of local affiliates to influence political views days before an election by showing a documentary that did not provide both sides of the issue equal time to explain their positions. Whether these documentaries had any effect on the outcome of the elections they attempted to influence is not clear—Obama clearly won both presidential elections handily—and not necessarily relevant. What matters most is the fact that media consolidation has resulted in a small number of corporations framing debates about what issues are most relevant to the viewing audience.

The Federal Communication Commission (FCC) is responsible for regulating the media industries, and historically, it has been expected to enforce the mandate that television should serve the public interest, in part by requiring that broadcast channels, as a condition of keeping their broadcast license, provide content that served local needs, that provided a diversity of viewpoints, and that served the public interest. These questions about media ownership—and the implications for consumers—re-emerged when Rupert Murdoch, owner of News Corp. and the Fox News Channel sought to purchase rival cable news channel CNN in 2014. Similarly, in April 2014, the cable giant Comcast made a bid to purchase Time Warner Cable, a deal that would have given Comcast access to over 30 million cable subscribers— or about two-thirds of the market. Comcast ultimately abandoned the deal when the Department of Justice began preparing an antitrust suit to block the merger because it would reduce competition. But as these examples illustrate, it's not just the content of television that is political. Instead, politics is at the very core of the industry and is shaped by questions about media ownership and government regulations.

A similar concern is raised when it comes to political television advertising. The landmark 2010 Supreme Court ruling *Citizens United vs. The Federal Elections Commission* (FEC) prohibited the government from restricting political spending by both non-profit and for-profit corporations, a decision that reversed prevailing rules that prevented corporations from directly endorsing political candidates. Although there is some debate about the changes that *Citizens United* introduced to the rules governing political donations, there is little doubt that the flow of money into politics has dramatically increased. The millions spent during a midterm election will likely be dwarfed by the amount of money raised for the 2016 election. Charles and David Koch announced that they intended to raise a total of $889 million on the 2016 elections, at all levels, a number that would be more than double the amount spent by the Republican National Committee during the 2012 Presidential election. Regardless of whatever political messaging the Koch brothers might promote, the underlying message of this announcement is that when it comes to political participation—at least when it comes to donating to a political candidate—the real statement is that donors must plan to "go big or go home," lest their voices get drowned out by bigger donors. More crucially, these donations also provide the donors with more direct access to the politicians they are supporting, allowing them to shape legislation in ways that might exclude other, less powerful voices.[20] *Citizens United* does not preclude other forms of political participation. In fact, numerous citizens' groups have formed with the goal of seeing the *Citizens United* ruling overturned, a form of activism that is deeply invested in protecting more democratic forms of participation. However, in its current form, unregulated campaign spending does potentially distort the process, providing some participants with a much larger and more influential voice.

As these examples illustrate, there is still a clear sense that political television matters. It is important not only because of its role in informing the public—a task that remains crucial to our role as citizens—but also because it helps us to make sense of the social and political concerns that inform our everyday lives. One of the tools we use to make sense of politics, as we consume it on television, is genre. Genre expectations guide how we evaluate and understand programming, whether that entails entertainment genres such as the melodrama or informational genres such as the news or political talk show. Although news programming is often treated as "natural," Geoffrey Baym astutely recommends that we treat news as a genre, one that relies upon conventions and expectations. These decisions play a powerful role in determining not only what stories get covered—or treated as relevant or worthy of attention—but also how they are covered.[21] Thus, the news media tend to rely on what Stuart Hall et al. refer to as "primary definers," political and corporate leaders who can define the parameters of a topic and set the agenda for what topics are worthy of attention and how those topics should be covered.[22] Although Hall et al. were writing before the fragmentation of the TV news audience associated with cable television, the concept of "primary definers" still applies in many ways, in that relevant political issues continue to be defined by a Washington media consensus that is dependent on official sources—elected officials and party leaders— for information. In some rare cases, provocative or dramatic events can provoke journalists to turn to nontraditional sources, as we saw with the deaths of Michael Brown, Freddie Gray, Sandra Bland, and several other African- American men and women during interactions with white police officers. And, as Lance Bennett, Regina Lawrence, and Steven Livingston have shown, videos and photographs taken by smart phone cameras and other recording devices have provided reporters with material that allows for more rigorous forms of inquiry.[23] But even with these powerful forms of evidence, members of the mainstream press can also concoct narratives that define and limit the meaning of these forms of visible evidence when it comes to raising serious questions about the militarization of the police or the devaluing of black lives.

By comparison, entertainment programming can take the raw material of politics and can allow users to sort through these political meanings. A useful model of thinking about this process comes from TV scholar John Ellis, who proposes the idea of entertainment television as a device for providing viewers with a way of "working through" complex political content that might be too difficult to absorb otherwise. For Ellis, these complex or difficult ideas sometimes require further time in order for viewers to fully make sense of them. In this sense, Ellis sees television as providing a "vast mechanism for processing the raw data of news reality into more narrativised, explained forms."[24] For example, a March 5, 2015 episode of the ABC melodrama *Scandal* addressed many of the concerns about police brutality through a narrative in which Olivia Pope was forced to balance her position as a guardian of the interests of the political elite with her awareness of the mistreatment of black youth at the hands of the police. By watching Pope's moral choices, viewers of the show could also begin to reflect on similar ongoing storylines that were circulating in the news media. Thus, rather than dismissing entertainment television, we should instead recognize its value in producing narratives that can be used to make sense of the role of formal politics in shaping our everyday lives.

POLITICAL TV AND INTERTEXTUALITY

In this context, I will now turn to two distinct "reading strategies" that provide audiences of political television with techniques for making sense of politics. The first strategy, intertextuality, can be associated with most any genre of television and is, in fact, central to television itself. Intertextuality, quite simply, refers to the fact that all textual meanings depend upon meanings cultivated in or proposed by other texts.[25] The second reading strategy I wish to highlight is melodrama. While the melodrama has typically been associated with the idea of emotional and aesthetic excess, more recent scholarship, led by the groundbreaking arguments of Linda Williams, has made the case that melodramatic narrative can serve a vital role in political sense-making, in part through its role in playing out conflicts between heroes and villains as a device for engaging with larger issues of justice.[26] Each of these "reading strategies" can be aligned with specific genres of political television, whether comedy or drama, and both strategies invite forms of active engagement with questions of political justice, whether this engagement takes place in informal conversations or in the more public formats of political talk shows.

In the most general sense, intertextuality describes the central condition that guides all of our interpretations of texts, wherever we encounter them. Concepts such as genre, aesthetics, and ideology only become legible through one text's relationship with a wider body of texts.[27] We must acknowledge that reception of a text is invariably embedded in a wider discursive environment, a network of texts—other TV programs, movies, books, op-ed pieces—that shape and inform our interpretation and use of that text. Political TV programs—like other texts—constantly overlap or intersect with other texts that we have encountered in our daily lives. However, as Keren Tenenboim-Weinblatt contends, intertextuality can refer not only to the ways in which TV texts refer to other sources but also to the social uses of particular texts by different audiences. While there is an incredibly rich strain of scholarship that has looked at the practices of fan communities, political activists, and online discussion forums, these practices also include the role of media professionals in evaluating and discussing media texts. In this regard, journalists, political commentators, and politicians simply function as specialized audiences that contribute to shaping the meaning or significance of a text.[28] Thus, a binge viewer of Netflix's cynical political melodrama *House of Cards* isn't really watching the show alone. Instead, her viewing of it is likely to be shaped by reviews, whether by TV critics, technology journalists, or even political professionals who might comment on whether the show is an authentic portrayal of what Washington is "really" like. These articles allowed *House of Cards* to enter a larger cultural conversation, one that was attentive both to changing models of television and cultural perceptions of DC's political culture.

In order to describe how intertextuality functions on television, Jonathan Gray identifies two modes or strategies used to engage with other texts. The first category is what Gray describes as "supportive intertextuality," which refers to texts, which serve primarily to promote or support other texts, such as advertisements, trailers, interviews, and promotional articles. As Gray explains, these texts can help to provide public knowledge that will shape expectations and begin to prepare the process of shaping its meaning. The second category involves texts that function to attack or subvert the meaning or power of an original text, a mode that Gray describes as "critical intertextuality." For the most part, outrage discourse relies on this strategy, attacking an original text, often by taking words or phrases out of context, in order to make a political opponent appear ridiculous.[29] However, the most significant form of critical intertextuality involves the use of parody. As Gray points out, parody can function to "talk back to more authoritative texts and genres, to recontextualize and pollute their meaning construction processes."[30] Thus, parody—in genres such as fake news or political impersonations—can operate as a powerful rejection of political authority, working to undermine media genres and modes that serve to reinforce power. Parody becomes a device for critical reading, teaching us how to read ostensibly more serious and sober forms of political media more critically.

That being said, the oppositional forces of parody are also caught within what Gray describes as the dilemma of "economic complicity."[31] Although fake news shows offer powerful critiques of a wide range of commercial television, they are also big business. Shows like *The Daily Show*, *The Colbert Report*, and *Saturday Night Live* generate millions of dollars in advertising revenue alone. In fact, Comedy Central's brand is largely structured around its late-night political parody shows. On a similar note, these shows may also participate in what amounts to a "textual complicity" with the news sources they criticize. Even while Jon Stewart and Stephen Colbert offer their parodic—and often highly encoded—critiques of Fox News, pundits on that channel will show clips from these shows, often as a means of amplifying the very outrage that they are attacking. Similarly, blog posts from websites such as Daily Kos or Talking Points Memo also drive up page views (and potentially advertising revenue) for the outrageous comments they are criticizing. These forms of complicity arguably open up fake news shows—and the project of political parody in general—to claims that they are cynically and hypocritically playing to politically jaded audiences, even while becoming complicit with that media culture. However, parody's positive effects as a device for holding politicians and the political media accountable are far more significant.

POLITICAL TV AS MELODRAMA

The second major "reading strategy" builds upon the tropes of the televisual melodrama. Typically, the term melodrama has been treated negatively, especially when it comes to depictions of politics, given its association with tropes such as emotional and aesthetic excess and its relationship to traditionally feminine genres such as the soap opera. However, a number of recent scholars, influenced by Linda Williams, have made the argument that serial television has succeeded in adapting the melodramatic mode to tell powerful stories about politics. Williams isolates four major components of melodrama. The first is the use of suspense, the sustained anticipation produced as audiences await the resolution of a dangerous situation, whether the seemingly endless sinking of the cruise ship in *The Titanic* or the real-time suspense produced by melodramas of national security, such as 24, in which entire seasons are structured around ticking time-bomb scenarios. The second quality is what she describes as the issue of moral legibility, which addresses the question of who the viewer will conclude deserves to survive the storyline.[32] Of course, as Williams acknowledges, serial TV melodrama, with its long-running narratives that can sprawl out over several seasons, resists the simple beginnings and endings associated with classical narratives.[33] Instead, these serial narratives provide the time for characters to change and evolve in response to new circumstances, while also potentially providing for greater complexity when it comes to making sense of issues of electoral politics or national security. In this context, Jason Mittell explains that serial TV melodrama uses suspense, or what he calls "anticipation," to generate "an engaging emotional response to *feel* the difference between competing moral sides as manifested through forward-moving storytelling."[34] Thus, an expansive melodrama, such as *Scandal*, could allow viewers to engage emotionally with the show's narrative threads about political power to address questions of justice. Williams's third category entails what she calls the "space of innocence," the need to believe that some kind of moral good can be located and restored. Thus, although a show such as *Scandal* seems to portray the political world as hopelessly cynical and corrupt, honest and well-intentioned characters continue to provide some form of hope that our politics can be better. Finally, Williams cautions against reading melodrama in terms of excess, both in its emotional and aesthetic forms, and instead aligns it with the more realist genres that are central to serialized storytelling. With that in mind we can rethink melodrama, recasting it as a form that opens up larger questions about social and political justice.

Williams develops these arguments about the melodrama in her book-length study on the HBO show *The Wire*. In analyzing *The Wire*, Williams powerfully illustrates how the melodramatic form can be used to engage with questions of justice within the so-called war on drugs, particularly as it has played out in the post-industrial city of Baltimore, questions that have gained new relevance in the light of the death of Freddie Gray while in police custody. Thus, *The Wire* serves as what she calls a "melodrama of dysfunctional systems," an analysis of the failures of low-level institutions such as city hall, the police force, the news media and the educational system, all organizations that are largely responsible for ensuring the stability and safety of a community. Williams is attentive to the role of what she calls "lower-level villains," bureaucrats and politicians who reinforce the status quo, whether out of apathy or out of a more acute desire to profit from the misery of others.[35] The show acutely illustrates the fact that devoting resources to a war on drugs has been a monumental mistake, one that fails to alleviate the real social problems that have affected cities such as Baltimore, where thousands of blue-collar jobs have been eliminated, for decades. For Williams, melodrama therefore becomes an attempt to use narrative techniques to bring to the surface questions about social and political justice. As she explains it, the essential point of melodrama is to make explicit "the contrast between how things are and how they could be, or should be."[36]

Through melodrama's use of serialized storytelling, viewers can feel the weight of past episodes, of characters' histories, and the larger narratives that surround them. With that in mind, I have isolated two significant (though by no means exclusive) categories of political melodrama. The first category, *melodramas of political process*, deals with dramas that depict aspects of political governance: the business of passing legislation, holding elections, conducting trials, or otherwise managing the affairs of running a government. The seminal show in this category is *The West Wing*, a show that depicted the daily activities of the president's staff members as they worked to support his legislative agenda. The show was deeply concerned about the ethics of political power, especially as it plays out in the corridors of the White House, and while many narratives were resolved in the space of a single episode, narrative cycles, such as President Bartlet's admission that he concealed the fact that he had been diagnosed with multiple sclerosis (MS) prior to running for his first term as president, often took place over the course of multiple episodes over several seasons. Such storylines could speak to questions about whether (or how) Bartlet's deception should be punished but also questions of whether his disability should disqualify him from holding political office.

The second major category, *melodramas of national security*, includes series such as *24* or *Homeland* that engage with the moral and ethical questions that emerge for individuals or groups who are tasked with protecting the nation's citizens from attack, in most cases by external threats such as terrorism. Although *24*'s ticking time-bomb cliffhangers and depictions of Middle Eastern terrorists have inspired many critics to dismiss the show, it provided a compelling forum for thinking about the political cultures of national security organizations. More recently, the FX series *The Americans* complicated these notions of national security by inviting viewers to identify narratively with Soviet spies during the height of the Cold War in the 1980s who are working to overthrow the U.S. government. Because the show is set in a "safe" moment in the past, *The Americans* is able to use the tropes of national security melodrama to develop a de-familiarizing narrative that allows us to view the U.S. security and political apparatus from a critical perspective. To be sure, melodramas of political process can address issues of national security—several episodes of *The West Wing* address issues related to the war on terror; these categories can be used to speak to specific moral questions about the wider political system. Thus, while these two categories of political melodramas are by no means exhaustive or exclusive, they do provide a useful way of thinking and talking about political cultures.

POLITICAL TELEVISION AND CITIZENSHIP

In addition to the challenges of redefining television in the on-demand era, we also face the difficulty of defining how political television fits into larger concepts of citizenship. This question runs up against discussions within media and television studies about the role of the audience—and even who "counts" as the audience. For many observers, entertainment television has frequently been characterized as being harmful to the practices associated with political citizenship, as cultural pessimists such as Neal Postman, Jeffrey Scheuer, and Robert Putnam have argued. In his influential book *Bowling Alone*, Putnam worries that watching television is a passive activity, one that gets in the way of the ostensibly more important forms of civic engagement. Even those who use television to consume the news are at risk of becoming "socially withdrawn" and therefore less involved in civic, political, and even social activities that create a sense of community. But a bigger concern for Putnam seems to be the amount of time devoted to watching entertainment TV. Putnam summarizes data that suggest that people devote hours daily to consuming TV, presumably at the expense of other, more social activities, building to the conclusion that "TV steals time" and contributes to lethargy and passivity.[37] Putnam goes on to argue that certain genres—namely, morning talk shows or dramas featuring beloved characters—were likely to produce a false or deceptive sense of community, making us "feel engaged with our community without the effort of actually being engaged."[38] In the same vein, Scheuer characterizes television as a leading force in what he calls a "sound bite society," in which political messaging has become increasingly simplified, with TV "filtering out complex ideas in favor of blunt emotional messages that appeal to the self and to narrower moral-political impulses."[39] Like Putnam, Scheuer worries that TV promotes a "narcotizing passivity," as viewers become seduced by the charisma of individual politicians, rather than becoming engaged with more complex ideas. While Scheuer is writing in 1999, somewhat before the emergence of the complex serial melodramas that became increasingly popular with the commercial and critical success of shows such as *The Sopranos* and *The Wire*, similar anti-TV sentiments continue to hold enormous sway. By comparison, Neal Postman, writing in the 1980s, expressed concern that political culture had been utterly swamped by the visual biases of television, turning politics into just another component of a shallow entertainment culture, in which substantive political and social issues are swamped by inane talk shows and comedies. Building from Marshall McLuhan's assertion that a medium has essential properties that ultimately shape its content, Postman was convinced that TV audiences would contribute to increasing superficial thinking. However, while Postman's account seemed enticing to network-era viewers who were accustomed to lowest-common-denominator programming, it also failed to grasp the ways in which entertainment programming provided audiences with the tools to make sense of the political culture they inhabited.[40]

However, as the discussion of parody and melodrama suggest, political television offers viewers a space in which they can negotiate or engage with a wide range of texts "about the formal political process of government and political institutions as they conduct their daily lives," a process that Jones associates with the concept of "mediated citizenship."[41] Thus, instead of treating fictional or entertainment television as a distraction from politics, we should understand it as the very essence of political activity, as a means of making sense or working through political decision-making, at all levels of government. In addition to these attempts to make sense of social and cultural issues, television has often provided the building blocks for other forms of political self-expression and activism. For example, clever video editors have created political mashups, short video montages that mix clips of politicians with scenes from movies and TV shows, to comment on a politician or issue through a process Richard Edwards and I, following Jonathan Gray, called "critical digital intertextuality."[42] However, although Edwards and I initially celebrated political mashups as being aligned with a progressive critique of the political status quo, it is important to note that the production of political memes is not aligned with a specific political ideology. In fact, as Henry Jenkins, Sam Ford, and Joshua Green have more recently documented, conservative Tea Party activists appropriated the iconic Joker images from the 2008 Batman film *The Dark Knight* to recast liberal politicians such as Barack Obama and Hillary Clinton as super-villains.[43] In any case, these examples suggest that audiences can play a vital role in contributing to wider discussions about politics.

THE ROAD AHEAD

One of the goals of this book is to challenge many of the assumptions that guide scholarly research on political television. As Geoffrey Baym points out, much of this research reinforces "obsolete distinctions" between news and entertainment programming. These distinctions often carry with them assumptions about the value or importance of certain kinds of programming. News, we are told, should fulfill the function of informing the public, providing us with knowledge that we can bring with us to the ballot boxes when we carry out our civic duties to vote, while entertainment shows have often been blamed as a fictional distraction from those responsibilities.[44] In many cases, this distinction is based on legacy media forms, such as the public affairs show or the network-era news broadcast aligned with sober analysis and objective reporting, that continue to serve as important sites for expressing a vision of politics. However, in a more fragmented media environment, fictional and nonfictional depictions of American political culture provide materials for audiences to engage with. Political storylines circulate across genres, with fictional narratives and entertainment programs serving as fodder for cable news shows, such as when storylines from the national security melodrama 24 were used as touchstones for debates about national security during the Republican and Democratic presidential primaries, as when Republican candidate Tom Tancredo linked his vision for defending against terrorism with the aggressive interrogation practices used by Jack Bauer.[45] Meanwhile those same cable TV personalities lend their credibility to fictional programming, making cameos as themselves on shows like *House of Cards*. However, these genres continue to retain enormous power in shaping the ways in which we think about politics. Therefore, this book will use genre as an organizational category, one that can help us to make sense of what amounts to a highly dispersed category of television. In focusing on genre, I follow Jason Mittell's productive argument that "genres are cultural products, constituted by media practices and subject to ongoing change and redefinition."[46] Thus, rather than treating genre as an unchanging formalist idea, Mittell proposes that we recognize the cultural, political, and industrial factors—such as scheduling choices and branding practices—that contribute to the production and evolution of genres. In turn, as Mittell illustrates, a "cultural" definition of genre also allows us to treat televisual trends such as reality television as genres that can play a vital role in negotiating questions about citizenship and political participation.[47] Finally, by treating news as a genre, we can begin to recognize how political news has evolved in the face of changing industrial and political conditions and also to acknowledge how our assumptions about the news are often shaped by a nostalgic set of expectations associated with the network era.[48] With these questions in mind, I now turn to a range of TV genres and categories that help to define politics as it is represented in U.S. television.

Chapter 1, "Selling Politics," starts with the assumption that American television is predominantly a commercial institution, one that is heavily dependent on advertising as a source for revenue. In turn, U.S. politics, especially in an era of virtually unlimited campaign financing, has seen a dramatic uptick in the amount of money spent on elections, with most of that money being directed to purchasing political advertisements. Thus, this chapter looks at the implications of this new political advertising model at both the state and federal level.

The second chapter of the book, "Political News in the Post-Network Era" will focus on the most commonly accepted category of political television, the news. This chapter engages with ongoing debates about the role of cable news in shaping American political culture. Specifically, I draw from arguments that describe cable news as a form of branded political entertainment that may only be loosely related to traditional expectations that the news serve the purpose of creating informed citizens. At the same time, these cable news channels often play a significant role in promoting a Washington consensus, policing both what counts as a legitimate news story and who can serve as an authority on a given issue.

The following two chapters focus on political comedy. Chapter 3 focuses on the role of "fake news" in engaging with contemporary political discourse. Although a large body of scholarship now acknowledges that political satire can serve a vital function within a democracy, in part by providing filters that viewers can use to read political news more critically, one strain of scholarship still maintains the perspective that political satire contributes to increased cynicism. However, political satire has instead functioned to provide a language for engaging in critical readings of the media and political discourse more generally. Shows such as *The Colbert Report* and *The Daily Show* parody the tropes of cable news in order to show their excesses. In addition, by quoting news sources, these shows can also help to document the emotionally manipulative and misleading rhetoric that has shaped political culture. In this regard, the label "fake news" often proves to be somewhat misleading, in that these shows use parody and satire to get to a more authentic truth not just about current events, but also about the wider political system.

Chapter 4, "Comedy and the Political Spectacle," focuses on two categories of scripted political comedy: sketch comedy shows and political sitcoms. Although these are relatively distinct categories, both use scripted storylines to parody aspects of American political culture. Sketch comedy shows such as *Saturday Night Live* and *Key & Peele* have often functioned as instantaneous comedic responses to current events, calling attention to the foibles of public figures, often within days of a major event. By comparison, serial and episodic comedies can develop extended storylines that explore political culture through both the oppositional force of parody and satire and the more reflective techniques of narrative and character.

While comedy has satirized aspects of the political process, melodramas, as I have suggested, perform the role of enabling viewers to negotiate difficult moral questions about politics. With that in mind, I have divided political melodrama into two distinct categories that address different aspects of Washington's political culture. Chapter 5 focuses on what I am calling melodramas of political process. These shows use melodrama to engage with the ethics of aspects of the political process, often through backstage programs, such as *The West Wing*, *Scandal*, and *House of Cards*, that focus on the everyday activities of Washington's political culture, especially issues related to passing legislation. At the same time, many of these shows also engage with the role of the press as the so-called Fourth Estate that is meant to serve as a check against potential abuses of power. Further, as the example of *The Wire* suggests, melodramas of political process are also ideally situated for addressing the local, for depicting local political challenges, such as the post-industrial environment of Baltimore or the corrupt political culture of Chicago, Illinois, in *The Good Wife*.[49] Chapter 6, "Surveillance Culture," focuses on what I am calling melodramas of national security, shows such as *24*, *Homeland*, or *Madame Secretary*, that address or depict the efforts of national security organizations to protect the country from both internal and external threats. These shows are also deeply invested in ethical and moral questions about the use of power, in this case as it pertains to defending the United States against potential threats, especially in the face of terrorist threats. Both types of political melodramas also continue to play a crucial role in shaping how policy questions are framed in the news media.

NOTES

1 Jeffrey P. Jones, *Entertaining Politics: Satiric Television and Political Entertainment*, 2nd ed. (Lanham: Rowman & Littlefield, 2010), 4.

2 Quoted in T. A. Frank, "America's Least Favorite City Has Become TVs Favorite Subject," *The New Republic*, November 25, 2013, http://www.newrepublic.com/article/115690/washington-tv-politics-scandal-homeland-veep.

3 John Corner and Dick Pels, "Introduction: The Re-Styling of Politics," in *Media and the Restyling of Politics*, ed. John Corner and Dick Pels (London: Sage, 2003), 3.

4 Jeffrey P. Jones, "A Cultural Approach to Mediated Citizenship," *Social Semiotics* 16.2 (June 2006): 366–383.

5 Megan Garber, "Shocker of the Day: Stewart (Still) Most Trusted Newscaster in America," *Columbia Journalism Review*, July 23, 2009, http://www.cjr.org/the_kicker/shocker_of_the_day_stewart_sti.php.

6 "In Changing News Landscape, Even Television is Vulnerable," *Pew Research Center*, September 27, 2012, http://www.people-press.org/2012/09/27/in-changing-news-landscape-even-television-is-vulnerable/.

7 Henry Jenkins, *Convergence Culture: Where Old and New Media Collide* (New York: New York University Press, 2006).

8 Lisa Gitelman, *Always Already New: Media, History, and the Data of Culture* (Cambridge: MIT Press, 2006), 7.

9 Jeffrey P. Jones, "I Want My Talk TV: Network Talk Shows in a Digital Universe," in *Beyond Prime Time: Television Programming in the Post-Network Era*, ed. Amanda D. Lotz (New York: Routledge, 2009), 14.

10 Emily Guskin, Mark Jurkowitz, and Amy Mitchell, "The State of the News Media 2013," *Pew Research Center*, 2013 http://www.stateofthemedia.org/2013/network-news-a-year-of-change-and-challenge-at-nbc/network-by-the-numbers/.

11 Amanda D. Lotz, *The Television Will Be Revolutionized* (New York: New York University Press, 2007).

12 Geoffrey Baym, *From Cronkite to Colbert: The Evolution of Broadcast News* (Boulder: Paradigm Publishers, 2010), 9.

13 Elana Levine, "Teaching the Politics of Television Culture in a Post-television Era," *Cinema Journal* 50.4 (Summer 2011), 177.

14 Jonah Weiner, "Comedy Central in the Post-TV Era," *New York Times Magazine*, June 21, 2015, http://www.nytimes.com/2015/06/21/magazine/comedy-central-in-the-post-tv-era.html.

15 Quoted in Weiner, "Comedy Central."

16 Jennifer Holt, *Empires of Entertainment: Media Industries and the Politics of Deregulation, 1980–1996* (New Brunswick: Rutgers University Press, 2011), 2–3.

17 Robert McChesney, *The Problem of Media: U.S. Communication Politics in the Twenty-First Century* (New York: Monthly Review Press, 2004), 179.

18 Jennifer Holt, *Empires of Entertainment*, 4.

19 Alison Dagnes, *Politics on Demand: The Effects of 24-Hour News on American Politics* (Santa Barbara: Praeger, 2010), 73.

20 Kenneth P. Vogel, "The Kochs Put a Price on 2016: $889 Million," *Politico*, January 26, 2015, http://www.politico.com/story/2015/01/koch-2016-spending-goal-114604.html.

21 Geoffrey Baym, *From Cronkite to Colbert*, 7.

22 Stuart Hall, et al., *Policing the Crisis: Mugging, the State, and Law and Order* (New York: Holmes & Meier, 1978), 61–62.

23 W. Lance Bennett, Regina G. Lawrence, and Steven Livingston, *When the Press Fails: Political Power and the News Media from Iraq to Katrina* (Chicago: The University of Chicago Press, 2007), 77.

24 John Ellis, "Television as Working-Through," in *Television and Common Knowledge*, ed. Jostein Gripsrud (London: Routledge, 1999), 55.

25 Jonathan Gray, *Watching with The Simpsons: Television, Parody, and Intertextuality* (New York: Routledge, 2006), 3–4.

26 Linda Williams, *On The Wire* (Durham: Duke University Press, 2014).

27 Jonathan Gray, *Watching with The Simpsons*, 4.

28 Keren Tenenboim-Weinblatt, "'Where is Jack Bauer When You Need Him?' The Uses of Television Drama in Mediated Political Discourse," *Political Communication* 26 (2009), 371–372.

29 Jonathan Gray, *Watching with The Simpsons*, 37.

30 Jonathan Gray, *Watching with The Simpsons*, 4.

31 Jonathan Gray, *Watching with The Simpsons*, 8–9.

32 Linda Williams, "Mega-Melodrama! Vertical and Horizontal Suspense of the 'Classical,'" *Modern Drama* 55.4 (Winter 2012), 524–526.

33 Linda Williams, "Mega-Melodrama," 532.

34 Jason Mittell, *Complex TV: The Poetics of Contemporary Television Storytelling* (New York: New York University Press, 2015), 244.

35 Linda Williams, *On The Wire*, 82–83.

36 Linda Williams, *On The Wire*, 83–84.

37 Robert Putnam, *Bowling Alone: The Collapse and Revival of American Community* (New York: Simon & Schuster, 2000), 238.

38 Robert Putnam, *Bowling Alone*, 242, emphasis Putnam's.

39 Jeffrey Scheuer, *The Sound Bite Society: Television and the American Mind* (New York: Four Walls Eight Windows, 1999), 10.

40 Neal Postman, *Amusing Ourselves to Death: Public Discourse in the Age of Show Business* (New York: Penguin, 1985).

41 Jeffrey P. Jones, "A Cultural Approach to Mediated Citizenship," 378.

42 Richard L. Edwards and Chuck Tryon, "Political Video Mashups as Allegories of Citizen Empowerment," *First Monday* 14.10 (October 2009), http://firstmonday.org/article/view/2617/2305.

43 Henry Jenkins, Sam Ford, and Joshua Green, *Spreadable Media: Creating Value and Meaning in a Networked Culture* (New York: New York University Press, 2013), 28.

44 Geoffrey Baym, "Political Media as Discursive Modes: A Comparative Analysis of Interviews with Ron Paul from *Meet the Press, Tonight, The Daily Show*, and *Hannity*," *International Journal of Communication* 7 (2013), 490.

45 Keren Tenenboim-Weinblatt, "'Where is Jack Bauer When You Need Him?'" 368–369.

46 Jason Mittell, *Genre and Television: From Cop Shows to Cartoons in American Culture* (New York: Routledge, 2004), 1.

47 Jason Mittell, *Genre and Television*, 196–201.

48 Geoffrey Baym, *From Cronkite to Colbert*, 9.

49 Fredric Jameson, "Realism and Utopia in *The Wire*," *Criticism* 52.3–4 (Summer & Fall 2010), 359.

1

SELLING POLITICS: ADVERTISING AFTER *CITIZENS UNITED*

The chief currency of television is time. And for politicians seeking to attract attention in the midst of a fragmented and cluttered media environment, the easiest way to ensure airtime and to craft a narrative that is beneficial to them is through advertising. This chapter addresses three major themes associated with political advertising. First, I consider the economic role of advertising in shaping elections. Specifically, I focus on the creation of a so-called "shadow primary" during the 2016 election, where candidates attended a variety of events that focused not on winning votes from Republican primary voters but on the billionaire donors who would be supporting their campaign. Although these donations have a powerful effect on federal elections, I also discuss their implications at the state and local levels. Second, I discuss the role of political advertising in creating narratives about individual candidates. Third, this chapter addresses the fact that political advertisements are rarely read in isolation. In fact, advertisements can actually have a multiplier effect through the creation of controversy. When a provocative ad attracts the attention of cable news, the advertisement will get replayed—often repeatedly—across a wide range of cable channels, allowing the ad's argument to get replayed as well. Even if the advertisement is broadly criticized, the cable news discussion serves to provide increased visibility for that message, especially in an era where audiences may be more likely to shield themselves from advertisements through time-shifting technologies such as DVRs or streaming video. Thus, although most analysis of television focuses on the programs themselves, I argue that political advertisements play an important role not just in shaping political messaging but also in shaping wider perceptions about political culture.

CITIZENS UNITED AND THE SHADOW PRIMARY

As I explained in the Introduction, the *Citizens United* ruling has resulted in a mass influx of money into politics, to the point that both major political parties are likely to see billions of dollars spent on the campaigns, with much of that money going to advertising. Although complaints about political advertising often focus on presidential races, the most significant effect of increased spending has been at the state level, where political candidates have fewer opportunities to define themselves to a wider voting public. In presidential elections, voters are more likely to encounter information about candidates from news coverage, debates, or televised speeches, but statewide campaigns rarely receive the same level of attention.[1] The exponential rise in political spending has come at a time when TV advertising revenues have decreased dramatically. As one general manager of a local affiliate in Las Vegas admitted during the 2010 election cycle, "political advertising has been a gigantic Band-Aid" for television broadcasters. In fact, during the 2010 election, in particular, some estimates suggested that political advertising would account for as much as 11 percent of spending at local TV affiliates.[2] But the floodgates opened even more dramatically during the 2 election, with local television revenue growing by $500 million to a whopping total of $2.8 billion, money that likely went a long way to offset declining advertising revenue due to streaming video and other entertainment options. More crucially, outside spending—money that came from political groups not associated with the campaigns—was far more likely to be focused on negative advertising and far less likely to receive the detailed fact-checking and critical analysis directed toward national political ads. At the same time, voters are significantly less likely to watch a debate between candidates for a statewide audience than they would be for the presidential election, making it more likely that low-information voters in particular will be affected by ads. A study by *Public Citizen* noted that of the

$600 million spent during the 2012 election, $520 million—nearly 86 percent—went to so-called negative advertisements that expressed opposition to a candidate. As the *Public Citizen* report went on to point out, these groups are essentially unaccountable, allowing them to do most of the dirty work, when it comes to tarnishing a candidate's reputation.[3]

In addition to dramatic increases in federal spending, these campaign war chests have also had a profound effect at the state level, where local elections could cost tens of millions of dollars. In fact, in the hotly contested 2014 Senate race in North Carolina between the incumbent Democrat Kay Hagan and Republican challenger Thom Tillis, there was a combined $82 million of outside spending, more than tripling the total of $25 million spent when Hagan won the seat in 2008.[4] Because many political observers felt that the North Carolina race could be pivotal in determining which party would have a majority in the Senate, it became, in many ways, a national race. This spending was used to purchase—among other things—over 114,000 television ads that blanketed the airwaves in North Carolina for months.[5] As a resident of North Carolina, I found it virtually impossible to watch any television, whether news, sports, or entertainment, without encountering multiple ads for Hagan or Tillis, the vast majority of which were incendiary attack ads that all but threatened the collapse of the nation if their rival candidate was elected. Most of this spending was by outside organizations such as Crossroads GPS, the PAC (political action committee) run by Republican operative Karl Rove, the National Rifle Association, and the National Education Association. North Carolina was certainly not alone when it came to costly elections. The 2014 Senate race in Colorado reportedly cost $70 million, while the Senate race in Iowa cost about $61 million. Another measure of how much money was spent can be gleaned from looking at the Alaska Senate race where $41 million was spent in a race where about 245,000 total votes were cast, about $167 per vote for the Senate race alone. In addition to these legislative races, *Citizens United* has also opened up the flow of campaign donations to judicial races, creating the potential for significant conflicts of interest as judges may find their impartiality called into question when they address cases involving corporations or industries that have donated to their campaign. Political donations can have an even more pernicious effect on judge's elections. Although the Supreme Court has upheld state rules that ban political contributions to judicial candidates, these donations are legal in a number of states, and as one study by the American Constitution Society concluded, there is a statistically significant correlation between interest group donations and judicial rulings.[6]

By the early stages of the 2016 election, the role of unregulated money in politics was undeniable. In fact, David and Charles Koch, co-owners of Koch Industries, the second largest privately owned company in the United States, announced their intentions to make up to $889 million available to the presidential candidate they intended to support during the 2016 election. This public declaration would initially appear to be shocking; however, their announcement could have the effect of silencing or discouraging smaller donors from giving money to candidates, providing the brothers with even more control over the political process. Thus, although some forms of political media, such as satirical news shows and even partisan cable news shows, have been blamed for contributing to political cynicism, a more notable factor might be the huge increase in political spending. In fact, the Koch brothers' projected influence on the 2016 election was so substantial that many observers claimed that Republicans were involved in a "shadow primary" or "Koch primary" focused not on collecting votes but on securing their endorsement—and the hundreds of millions of dollars in support that came with it. This Koch primary was structured around a private donor meeting held in August 2015, days before the first Republican presidential debate, in which five hand-picked candidates were invited to make their pitches for the Koch money. The majority of the summit was off-limits to the press, and reporters could only cover the event on the condition that they not reveal who was present without their permission. The Koch brothers' political organization even came with its own data and analytics firm, as well as grassroots organizations targeted at attracting Latino voters and veterans. Although political observers breathlessly waited to see who would win the Koch's support, their network also announced their intentions to support advocacy groups that promoted causes that were central to the Kochs's interests, including lower taxes, reducing environmental regulations, and repealing the Affordable Care Act.[7] As a result, Republican presidential candidates faced pressure to embrace these positions in order to garner the support of the Koch brothers' donor base, whether or not those positions were in the interest of the wider public.

INFLUENCE OF POLITICAL ADVERTISING

Political advertising, as one of the most visible components of a larger election campaign, largely involves the creation of a narrative, one that positions a candidate as providing a solution to the problems confronting the nation at a given time. As Paul Waldman explains, presidential campaigns succeed because "the winner tells a coherent, appealing story, while the loser tells a bad story, or more often, no story at all."[8] Thus, during his 1980 election campaign, speaking to a nation shaken by a hostage crisis in Iran, high unemployment, and rising inflation, Ronald Reagan masterfully crafted a narrative around the promise of "restoring America's greatness." Four years later, against the backdrop of American success at the 1984 Olympics Reagan embraced a triumphalist account of national unity that could assure voters that things were improving. This narrative was encapsulated in Reagan's "Prouder, Stronger, Better" advertisement, in which pastoral images of small-town American life (a paperboy on his bicycle, white picket fences, farm workers on tractors) appeared while a voice-over assured audiences that it was "morning in America." During the 2008 election, Barack Obama's campaign used the keywords "hope" and "change" to position the youthful Senator from Illinois as the face of a new kind of politics that was less cynical.

Of course, while positive ads can help to define a candidate, negative advertising also plays a crucial role in shaping perceptions of the opposing candidate. An effective controversial ad may be successful in redefining a political candidate or reshaping a political narrative. Notably, controversial ads can allow candidates to acquire what amounts to "free" airtime as the news media replays an advertisement in the guise of analyzing it. In fact, what is considered the first political attack ad on U.S. television, Lyndon Johnson's "Daisy," was shown on television only once. The advertisement shows a young girl in a field counting the petals of the flower, her counting gradually replaced by the ominous sound of a booming male voice counting down before a nuclear warhead goes off. The implication of the ad was unmistakable: elect Johnson's opponent, Republican Barry Goldwater, and face the possibility of nuclear war. For voters who had just endured the threat of the Cuban Missile Crisis, these dangers were certainly palpable. Republicans immediately responded with outrage, and while Johnson had the ad pulled from circulation, "Daisy" was shown dozens of times on the nightly news by journalists who dutifully reported the story while objectively presenting both sides. Thus, even if Johnson's campaign was scolded for its excessive portrayal of Goldwater, the message that he was a danger to innocent children repeatedly came across loud and clear.[9]

Another notorious example of this attempt to foment outrage was a 1988 advertisement produced by George H. W. Bush's campaign manager, Lee Atwater, used to depict his opponent, Massachusetts governor, Michael Dukakis as being soft on crime. The ad told the story of Willie Horton, a convicted murderer who committed a series of violent crimes while on furlough from a Massachusetts prison and prominently featured a threatening mug shot of Horton, who is African-American, staring menacingly into the camera. The ad explicitly played to white fears and seemed to imply that a vote for Dukakis would be a vote for allowing violent criminals to roam our streets.[10] A similar strategy was used at the state level in North Carolina during a competitive 1990 Senate election between the white Republican incumbent Jesse Helms and the African-American Harvey Gantt. The ad, "White Hands," depicted a blue-collar white worker crumpling up a job rejection letter, while a voice-over explained that the company had been forced to hire a black worker because of mandatory quotas, a narrative that played to perceptions of white victimhood. Like the "Willie Horton" advertisement, "White Hands" used dog-whistle politics to play to white fears while also dramatically misrepresenting Gantt's position on affirmative action. Thus, both advertisements not only played to political fears but also helped drive policies such as tougher crime laws and the elimination of affirmative action programs that shaped legislation for years.

Negative advertisements can also play a crucial role in shaping perceptions of government policies as well. One of the most effective negative advertising campaigns focused not on an individual candidate but on the health care plan promoted by Bill Clinton. The "Harry and Louise" campaign featured a white suburban couple in their 40s, and faced with increased costs and bureaucracy that were attributed to Clinton's plan. The most famous ad in this cycle featured the couple sitting at their kitchen table, where they struggled to navigate a giant stack of bills and other documents associated with a recent hospital visit, but later advertisements showed the apparently healthy couple—Harry is playing basketball and Louise has returned from a bike ride—complaining that everyone with health insurance would pay the same rate, regardless of their health. All of the advertisements encouraged viewers to contact their representatives in Congress to express opposition to the bill.

More recently, soon after Barack Obama announced a treaty in which Iran agreed to stop trying to produce nuclear weapons in exchange for the United States and several other countries agreeing to drop economic sanctions, a number of political organizations immediately sought to undermine the deal. To some extent, these efforts took place in the usual settings of Congressional press conferences, in which a number of Republicans— and some prominent Democrats—announced that they would oppose the treaty. But alongside this more public attack on the deal, a group called the American Security Institute also began running advertisements that sought to turn public opinion against it. The advertisement uses many of the fear tactics common to political advertisements, playing to concerns that Iran will attack the United States, even while offering little evidence that Iran would violate the terms of the agreement signed with the United States and several other countries. In the ad, a woman's voice dramatically asks, "If Iran has nothing to hide, why does it feel like they are hiding something?" This question is posed over images of political protests and bombs exploding intercut with a stereotypically Middle Eastern "shell game," in which someone (who is presumably Iranian) hides a ball under a shell in a game that we know to be rigged, suggesting again by insinuation that Iran is playing a shell game with the American people. The advertisement helped to reinforce the perception that Obama is naïve, while also neglecting the fact that several other world powers, including the United Kingdom, Russia, China, Germany, and France, had all agreed to the treaty. More crucially it created a sensationalized narrative, which reinforced stereotypes of Iranians as duplicitous. As the advertisement concludes, it urged viewers to call their Congressional representatives to speak out against the bill. In this sense, the advertisement served as a powerful tool for creating fears that could be exploited, even while failing to offer a clear reason that the treaty placed the United States or Israel in specific danger.

The power of creating a negative narrative was also illustrated powerfully during the 2012 election when the Obama campaign used a secretly recorded audio track of Mitt Romney taken at a private Florida fundraiser. The "My Job" advertisement consisted almost entirely of audio of Romney explaining to his wealthy supporters that 47 percent of the population paid no taxes and was "dependent on the government" and therefore would support Barack Obama no matter what. Romney went on to claim that this group considered themselves "victims" who believe themselves to be "entitled" to health care and other government services. Romney's comments play over a video track of still photographs of retirees, veterans, and blue-collar workers while key phrases from Romney's speech were displayed on screen. Thus, instead of a divisive discourse that segmented the population into groups, Obama's advertisement offered an image of inclusiveness. As a result, the advertisement played a crucial role in reinforcing a narrative about the campaign, one that positioned Mitt Romney as being concerned only with the interests of the wealthy, with several keywords from the ad—most notably the phrase "47 percent"—becoming some of the more memorable phrases from the 2012 election.

In this regard, Robert W. McChesney and John Nichols worry that "TV news increasingly publicizes TV ads, especially controversial ones, and assesses how much political impact the ads are having as the basis of their political journalism."[11] McChesney and Nichols further explain that this form of coverage is relatively cheap to produce and that politicians can use controversy to drive news coverage. In the midst of an increasingly complex election process, in which candidates can continue to stay afloat in a race on the strength of a small number of wealthy donors, there is a great deal of validity to this concern. As candidates increasingly compete for scarce airtime on cable news, controversy has become a crucial method to gain attention from the media, as negative political advertisements continue to play to political fears and resentments. However, in a competitive political news argument, controversial attack ads are often subjected to careful critique. For example, during the 2008 election between Barack Obama and John McCain, MSNBC's Andrea Mitchell took McCain campaign spokesperson Nancy Pfotenhauer to task over the campaign's notorious "Celeb" ad, which visually compared Obama to celebrities such as Paris Hilton and Britney Spears. The advertisement, which was originally an online-only ad, sought to imply that Obama had accomplished little other than giving a few speeches and was part of a larger Republican strategy to paint Obama as politically inexperienced and unprepared to lead. But the subtext of the ad—which associated Obama with extremely sexualized white women—was hard to miss. In her analysis of it, Mitchell noted that the ad could be read as "demeaning" to Obama and challenged Pfotenhauer to defend charges that Obama had accomplished little other than giving a few speeches.[12] Notably, even Paris Hilton got into the act of criticizing the ad, producing her own web video through the Funny or Die website, condemning McCain as a "wrinkly, white-haired guy" whose condescending depiction of Hilton was a cheap shot. Thus, although the ad did receive a significant amount of attention, much of the discussion of it was negative.

VIRAL POLITICS

Finally, although television advertising has played an important role in influencing political discourse, online videos have become increasingly important not only in shaping the outcomes of election but also in promoting new forms of political activism. The power of online video was originally illustrated when Virginia Senator George Allen was captured on video during his 2006 election campaign using a racial slur to describe his opponent's oppositional researcher, S. R. Siddarth. In the video, Allen is seen speaking to a group of voters in rural Virginia, when he glances at the camera, spots Siddarth and calls him "macaca," before inviting the audience to welcome him to the "real" state of Virginia. Siddarth quickly posted the video to YouTube, where it circulated wildly, first among liberal activists before eventually gaining national attention on cable news. At the time, Allen, who was the son of a famous Washington football coach, had been seen as a potential Presidential candidate, but after the video surfaced, his image became increasingly tarnished, and he ended up losing a narrow election to his opponent, Jim Webb, essentiallly ending his political career.

A second powerful example of a citizen-generated video that helped to fortify emerging campaign narratives was Phillip de Vellis's "Vote Different" advertisement, a mashup of an iconic Apple Macintosh advertisement and Hillary Clinton's presidential announcement video. The Macintosh ad famously restaged a scene from the film version of *1984*, in which futuristic

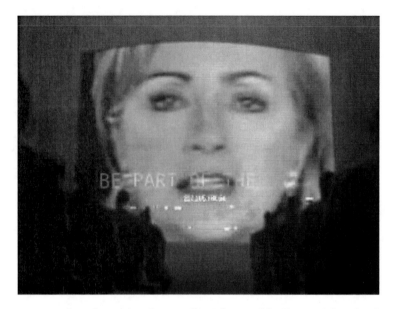

Figure 1.1 The video mashup "Vote Different" powerfully illustrated the role of citizen-generated videos

workers stare blankly at a giant screen that looms above them, but rather than an image of Big Brother, Hillary Clinton has been superimposed onto the screen, linking her visually to the notion of an autocratic leader offering progressives a false choice. The original advertisement culminates in a female athlete running into the auditorium and shattering the screen, suggesting that computer buyers could rebel from their mindless dependence on IBM computers, or in this case, could support an inspiring young candidate in Barack Obama.[13] While it would be difficult to measure the precise effect the video had in shaping perceptions of either candidate, the real impact of "Vote Different" seemed to be its promise that everyday citizens now had access to a more powerful form of political participation. Rather than being dependent upon commercial media culture for defining the images of candidates—the Big Brother of dominant media—video producers (and even the people who shared the videos on social media) could participate in the meaning-making process. In this regard, Amber Day locates within these videos a great deal of earnestness as the videos enticed younger viewers to become more involved in the political process, a sense of participation that the Obama campaign itself effectively tapped through its appeals to hope and change.[14]

Perhaps the most influential example of this use of viral media took place when Rick Santelli, a CNBC reporter, went on an extended diatribe in which he bemoaned the news of the Homeowners Affordability and Stability Plan (HASP), a planned incentive program, which used financial incentives to encourage banks to reduce homeowners' mortgage payments to less than 31 percent of their income. The segment, which took place on the floor of the Chicago Board of Trade, has been attributed with being the launching point for the Tea Party movement, a conservative anti-tax movement that was fanned by a number of special interest groups. Santelli's rant deliberately invoked populist, anti-government discourse that pitted one group of citizens against another in order to fan outrage against Barack Obama's proposed stimulus package. Santelli began by pushing the idea that the bailout was "promoting bad behavior" by encouraging people to make purchases they couldn't afford. He went on to mock the Obama administration's investment in online media by challenging them to "put up a website to have people vote on it as a referendum to see if we want to subsidize the losers' mortgages or would we like for people to buy cars and houses that might have a chance to prosper down the road?" Santelli went on to push this antagonism further, creating an opposition between "people that can carry the water instead of drink the water." This initial monologue laid out a worldview in which one group of Americans had played by the rules, while others had been living beyond their means and would have to be bailed out by those who could "carry the water," or fulfill their responsibilities as hard-working citizens. Santelli consistently referred to the Chicago Board of Trade workers behind him as "Real Americans" and even invoked Richard Nixon's highly charged concept of the "silent majority" to suggest that these workers' voices had somehow not been heard during the 2008 election, despite the fact that Obama had won the election handily. From there, Santelli proposes the idea of a "Chicago Tea Party" that would fight back against the bailout. The "Tea Party" metaphor referred to the Boston Tea Party, a Revolutionary War protest in which patriots led by Samuel Adams, led a protest against excessive taxation by America's British rulers. Notably, the hosts in the CNBC studios immediately began to frame the moment as a "revolutionary" one, joking in one case that Santelli was provoking "mob rule," while another referred to him as a "revolutionary leader." But rather than merely being the spontaneous response to a specific piece of legislation, Santelli's rant was part of a much longer history, led by groups such as the Heritage Foundation and Americans for Prosperity, of efforts to dismantle government programs such as Medicare and Social Security in favor of massive tax cuts for the wealthy.[15]

Thus, although Santelli's rant was seemingly spontaneous, it was amplified by a conservative political infrastructure that sought to create an opposition movement to fight back against the newly elected President Obama. The afterlife of Santelli's rant as a rallying cry for the Tea Party illustrates the work of the outrage industry in mobilizing anti-tax and anti-Obama activism. In fact, the video circulated widely on YouTube, where it was posted by several users, including the Heritage Foundation, a conservative think tank that opposed the bank bailouts. The video was also cited affirmatively by Fox News hosts Sean Hannity and Glenn Beck, where it served as a narrative that could be used to create opposition to Obama's fiscal policies, and Fox News even posted instructions for how to organize a Tea Party on its website even though the clip had aired on a rival network.[16] Thus, although the original live show was likely seen only by a small audience, it became a powerful tool used to advocate for Tea Party policies, one that was not a spontaneous or grassroots movement but one that was clearly executed in a collaboration between anti-tax think tanks and members of the conservative media. In fact, much of the funding for the Tea Party came indirectly from the Koch brothers, who gave $12 million to FreedomWorks, a group that organized a number of the most significant Tea Party rallies.[17]

CONCLUSION

There is little doubt that political advertising has, for the most, polluted the electoral process and, by extension, contributed to increasing confusion about politics, often by playing to low-information voters who may take an advertisement's claims at face value. Writing about this aspect of political culture, McChesney and Nichols emphasize that "the U.S. electoral system is wallowing in a sea of money, idiocy, and corruption precisely at the moment the nation's growing problems demand solutions that work to the benefit of the vast majority of Americans—the 99 percent—who have no role in the current regime except to be manipulated and exploited."[18] While I share the concerns of McChesney and Nichols about the importance of informed citizenship and the role of trustworthy and responsible journalism to evaluate the credibility of political advertisements, it is also important to note that contemporary political advertising circulates within a more complex media culture, in which citizens may encounter political messages in a much wider context, and to suggest that viewers are manipulated by ads assumes passive viewers who take the information they encounter at face value. Mediated citizenship allows for the possibility that advertisements will not be encountered in isolation. This does not guarantee that viewers of advertisements will be able to decode all of the false or manipulative political messages they encounter. More crucially, while I share McChesney and Nichols's concerns about income inequality, their argument seems to imply that voters—once they are made aware of how the system is rigged and how ads use manipulative techniques—will automatically vote in their economic interests. Finally, beyond the persuasive effects of political advertisements, *Citizens United* has opened up spending to astronomical levels. Thus, rather than specific concerns about the persuasiveness of these ads, we should instead look at what the political donors are buying when they contribute to a campaign: access to the legislative, and in some cases, judicial process. As the 2016 "Koch primary" seemed to illustrate, donors could keep moribund political campaigns alive and, with them, circulate a set of political values. In all cases, campaign narratives play a crucial role in shaping perceptions about Washington's political culture, and as this chapter has implied, political news plays an important role in facilitating that process. With that in mind, we now turn to a more extended discussion of the role of the news in cultivating narratives about Washington's political culture.

NOTES

1 For a discussion of this issue, see Darrell M. West, *Air Wars* (Washington, DC: CQ Press, 2010), 89.

2 Quoted in Andrew Vanacore, "Sick of Campaign Ad Avalanche? TV Stations Aren't," *Cleveland Plain Dealer*, October 29, 2010, http://www.cleveland.com/tv/index.ssf/2010/10/sick_of_campaign_ad_avalanche.html.

3 "*Citizens United* Fuels Negative Spending," *Public Citizen*, November 2, 2012, http://www.citizen.org/documents/outside-groups-fuel-negative-spending-in-2012-race-report.pdf.

4 Jim Morrill, "Outside Spending, 'Dark' Money Fuel N.C. Senate Race," *Charlotte Observer*, July 4, 2014 http://www.charlotteobserver.com/news/politics-government/article9138026.html.

5 Jason deBruyn, "How Much Did Hagan and Tillis Spend on Their U.S. Senate Races in N.C.?" *Triangle Business Journal*, November 5, 2014, http://www.bizjournals.com/triangle/news/2014/11/05/hagan-tillis-us-senate-campaign-spending-nc.html.

6 Maggie Clark, "Do Campaign Donations in Judicial Races Influence Court Decisions," *Pew Charitable Trusts*, June 11, 2013 http://www.pewtrusts.org/en/research-and-analysis/blogs/stateline/2013/06/11/do-campaign-donations-in-judicial-races-influence-court-decisions.

7 Ashley Parker, "'Koch Primary' Tests Hopefuls in the G.O.P. Primary," *The New York Times*, January 20, 2015, http://www.nytimes.com/2015/01/21/us/koch-seminar-is-early-proving-ground-for-gop-hopefuls.html.

8 Paul Waldman, "The Power of the Campaign Narrative," *The American Prospect*, July 17, 2007 http://prospect.org/article/power-campaign-narrative.

9 Drew Babb, "LBJ's 1964 Attack Ad 'Daisy' Leaves a Legacy for Modern Campaigns," *Washington Post*, September 14, 2014, https://www.washingtonpost.com/opinions/lbjs-1964-attack-ad-daisy-leaves-a-legacy-for-modern-campaigns/2014/09/05/d00e66b0-33b4-11e4-9e92-0899b306bbea_story.html.

10 Notably, Fox News President Roger Ailes worked as a media consultant on this campaign, as well as previous election campaigns involving Republican presidents Richard Nixon and Ronald Reagan.

11 Robert W. McChesney and John Nichols, "The Bull Market: Political Advertising," *Monthly Review* 63.11 (April 2012), 24.

12 Lyndsi Thomas, "MSNBC's Mitchell Defends Obama against McCain Ad," *Newsbusters*, July 30, 2008, http://newsbusters.org/blogs/lyndsi-thomas/2008/07/30/msnbc-s-mitchell-defends-obama-against-new-mccain-ad.

13 Richard Edwards and Chuck Tryon, "Political Video Mashups as Allegories of Citizen Empowerment," *First Monday* 14.10 (October 2009), http://firstmonday.org/article/view/2617/2305.

14 Amber Day, "Why More Americans are Being Informed and Entertained by Satire than Ever Before," *The Huffington Post*, February 16, 2011, http://www.huffingtonpost.com/amber-day/why-more-americans-are-be_b_824064.html.

15 See Mark Ames and Yasha Levine, "Exposing the Rightwing PR Machine: Is CNBC's Santelli Sucking Koch," *The Exiled*, February 27, 2009, http://exiledonline.com/exposing-the-familiar-rightwing-pr-machine-is-cnbcs-rick-santelli-sucking-koch/; and Eric Zuesse, "Final Proof the Tea Party was Founded as a Bogus Astroturf Movement," *The Huffington Post*, January 23, 2014, http://www.huffingtonpost.com/eric-zuesse/final-proof-the-tea-party_b_4136722.html.

16 Jeffrey M. Berry and Sarah Sobieraj (New York: Oxford University Press, 2014), *The Outrage Industry*, 157.

17 Frank Rich, "The Billionaires Bankrolling the Tea Party," *The New York Times*, August 28, 2010, http://www.nytimes.com/2010/08/29/opinion/29rich.html.

18 Robert W. McChesney and John Nichols, "The Bull Market," 25.

2

POLITICAL NEWS IN THE POST-NETWORK ERA

When we think about the category of political TV, we are most likely to focus initially on the news. One of the principles most often associated with a functioning democracy is the idea of a free and independent press that fulfills the obligations of informing citizens about vital political issues. With that in mind, when television was first institutionalized as a medium in the United States, a central concern was how to ensure that broadcasters would use this resource to serve the public interest. And television's perceived failures to do this have provoked some of its harshest critics to speak out, as when former FCC chair Newton Minow famously described television as a "vast wasteland" during a speech before the National Association of Broadcasters in 1961. What is often forgotten about Minow's speech is the fact that he also saw TV's vast potential to educate and entertain; however, the speech was also a bracing call for accountability, especially when it came to serving the public interest.[1]

To fulfill this task, the three major broadcast networks (ABC, CBS, and NBC) produced nightly national newscasts, along with a smaller number of weekly public affairs programs, such as *Meet the Press* and *Face the Nation*, that could, in principle, provide viewers with the information they needed about political affairs. Notably, this news programming was initially strictly separated from the networks' entertainment divisions, ostensibly protecting news programming from the need to make a profit and from the potential conflicts of interest that could arise from sponsorship, although in the latter case, there are numerous examples of networks killing or downplaying stories because of their connections to advertisers. Most famously, 60 Minutes temporarily killed a story that implied that the CEOs of several major companies had perjured themselves when they claimed not be aware that nicotine use was addictive. However, despite these potential conflicts, network news was aligned with a high-modernist belief in the principle of politically neutral and objective reporting that could be used to inform the public, an ideal that was expressed in Walter Cronkite's reassuring promise to his viewers as he was signing off for the night, "that's the way it is." As Geoffrey Baym has observed, such a claim not only assumes the accuracy of the content but also reinforces the belief that the news content was universally relevant to the sizeable audience that tuned in every night.[2] It also arguably provided viewers with confidence that everything had been covered, a promise that would become increasingly complicated by the 24-hour news cycle introduced by cable news.

However, beginning in the 1980s, as cable TV led to increasing competition and media deregulation led to the consolidation of ownership, the division between news and entertainment became increasingly eroded. As a result, news has become reconceptualized not just as a potential profit center but more notably as a form of branded infotainment focused less on informing viewers about the day's events than on keeping them tuned in to a community around shared political values and concerns. In this regard, former CNN president Jonathan Klein urged his staff to produce "emotionally-gripping, character-driven narratives."[3] Thus, rather than an emphasis on objective, rational news designed to inform the public, post-network news focuses instead on producing content that will attract and maintain an audience. With that in mind, Jeffrey P. Jones outlines two overlapping strategies cable news channels have used to retain viewers: channel branding and community-building. To keep audiences watching, Jones argues, "it is necessary for cable channels to craft intensive relationships with their viewers, connections that will encourage routine and repeated viewing."[4] The practices of community-building can take place through inclusive discourse (referring to audience members as "real Americans") or, more commonly, by excluding groups (liberals, Democrats) who don't uphold a shared set of values. While Fox News has been most successful at this form of branding,

MSNBC, to a lesser extent, created a format where progressive and liberal voices could be heard. In turn, CNN has tended to promote itself as a non-partisan source, a brand identity that may make the production of a sense of community more complicated.

Thus, instead of describing cable news programming by the network-era standards of objective journalism, Jones proposes instead that we treat these channels as "*television* productions" that are driven by business imperatives that "use politics as the central identifying mark of their brand."[5] Cable news channels, by this logic, are driven by the business of television, which is to produce programming that will keep audiences engaged. As Jones points out, cable news channels continue to align themselves with the network-era discourses of journalistic integrity (as evidenced by Fox News's slogan "Fair and Balanced"); however, both Fox News and MSNBC, in particu-lar, have sought to brand themselves along partisan lines, although MSNBC began revising its brand in the summer of 2015, complicating the idea that two or more cable news networks can serve as ideological counterweights for each other.[6] Meanwhile, CNN continues to promote itself as upholding more traditional modes of journalism, highlighting its nonpartisan engage-ment with the politics, even while emphasizing its high-tech use of digital graphics and other new media formats. This branding becomes more than just a way of presenting information. Instead, for many viewers, it serves as an important means of developing a sense of identity and community. As Laurie Ouellette observes, these niche news audiences are often linked through wider taste cultures and practices of consumer citizenship, par-ticularly on Fox News, where celebrity hosts such as Sean Hannity and Bill O'Reilly have websites primarily devoted to promoting products—books, t-shirts, coffee mugs—associated with the brand.[7] Thus, rather than simply being a source of news, where the public can become informed about the important news stories of the day, cable news offers a branded experience, one that can even offer a sense of immersion in a wider culture of mediated citizenship, in which media texts enable viewers to cultivate an identity associated with their chosen political tribe.

With this background in mind, this chapter describes the role that con-temporary cable news serves in making sense of political culture. Although cable news may associate itself with the informational aspects of the news, it more readily functions as a form of branded political infotainment, whose primary purpose is to create dramatic and ongoing political narratives that will keep audiences engaged. One result of this evolution of the news genre is the production of scandals designed to provoke outrage, as when Fox News dedicated days of coverage to the deaths of four civil servants in Benghazi, Libya. By this logic, post-network era news becomes, as Baym argues, another form of "reality TV," a device for using the raw material of politics to weave powerful melodramatic narratives, complete with heroes and villains. And given that these stories are often produced by news channels that have been branded along ideological lines, they invite viewers to take sides. To make sense of how this process works, this chapter focuses on two major types of stories. First, I will discuss the role of cable news in engaging with and, in many ways, producing Presidential election narratives. Although we traditionally understand the news media as simply reporting what happens, it has become increasingly clear that cable news channels, in many cases, actually produce the news, creating narratives and events that become part of the political culture itself. This role of "producing" the news was in clear evidence during the first Republican primary debate of the 2016 election cycle, which was hosted by Fox News. Although partisan cable channels had held a number of debates in the past, Fox's role in orchestrating the debate, of establishing the rules of who would get invited, and in promoting the debate as a "must-see" event very much made the cable channel part of the story. Second, the chapter addresses disruptive events that unsettle Washington's political consensus. During the course of writing this book, there were several incidents of police violence against African Americans, events that provoked significant questions about whether blacks were adequately represented by their local and national elected leaders. These stories, in some cases, did allow journalists room to raise challenging questions and to introduce experts who lived outside of Washington's political culture to define how these stories were told.

THE EVOLVING GENRE OF THE NEWS

In order to examine these issues, this chapter offers a brief timeline that traces the history of televised news. This timeline is structured around three key technological moments in the history of television distribution. Following Amanda Lotz, it starts with the network era, the period in which many of the standards of television news were established. During this era, networks were regulated by the Federal Communications Commission (FCC) and were expected to give over at least some of their daily programming to shows that served the public interest, which was generally understood to include informing the public, providing access to a diversity of voices, and ensuring that broadcasters serve the interests of their community, a principle known as localism.[8] As a result, broadcasters were required to provide equal time to parties on all sides of an important political or social issue. This doctrine, of course, did not require that both sides get equal treatment, but it did ensure a modicum of balance when it came to major political issues.

The second phase took place during what Lotz calls the "multichannel era," a brief transitional period beginning in the early 1980s, in which cable was first becoming popularized. Initially, cable television was greeted with enthusiasm, in part because the introduction of cable seemed to offer the utopian promise that additional channels could be used to inform the public and to provide space for more diverse perspectives that were frequently ignored or marginalized in the network era. It was during this early phase that C-SPAN was introduced as a public service resource for covering Congressional deliberations and other important political events, such as the annual White House Correspondents Dinner. Ted Turner launched CNN with the promise of offering 24-hour coverage that would create a global community, an ideal that seemed especially enticing in the waning years of the Cold War. However, cable television's emergence also provided the initial challenge to the scarcity models that had guided the FCC policies that required broadcast networks to produce content that served the public interest. The Fairness Doctrine was eliminated during the Reagan presidency of 1987 under a larger trend towards deregulation of the media industries. Finally, beginning in the late 1990s, a third phase has begun to take form with the emergence of what Amanda Lotz has called the post-network era.

This third phase is marked by an even larger selection of television channels and sources for political entertainment, with most cable or satellite subscription services offering viewers a choice of well over 100 stations. This era is also marked by the growth of on-demand programming, in which viewers can watch programs on their own schedule, on the devices of their choosing; but as these on-demand alternatives continue to flourish, the dominance of both traditional broadcast news and cable news programming is becoming increasingly contested, as many younger viewers are opting not to pay for cable or satellite TV subscriptions. As a result, the current moment is marked by increasing instability, making definitive claims about cable news contingent and subject to rapid change. However, the practices of branded television news targeted toward specific political tribes continued to dominate cable news well into the 2016 election cycle.

NEWS IN THE ON-DEMAND ERA

Perhaps the most widely shared belief about news in the on-demand era is the observation that news has increasingly become a niche product. As Amanda Lotz defines it, the on-demand era provides a "vast expansion in economically viable content," making it possible for viewers to select from a wide range of content choices, including a significant number of news channels.[9] Those viewers who continue to subscribe to cable or satellite TV now have far more channels than they did in the multichannel era. In 2005, the typical household averaged 18.8 television channels, but by 2008, households received 130.1 channels on average.[10] These numbers do not take into account the innumerable online news and entertainment sources now available to those households with broadband Internet connections.

Although the post-network era has been characterized by instability and flux, several key characteristics of political news can be identified. First, the fragmented viewing environment has led to niche news channels. Most often, this discussion focuses on the role of Fox News and MSNBC in seeking to appeal to conservatives and progressives respectively. Fox News, for example, has successfully branded itself as the "fair and balanced" alternative to a mainstream media that they characterize as biased against conservative values. However, rather than simply offering a conservative alternative to more traditional media, Fox News also provides what Kathleen Hall Jamieson and Joseph Cappella have referred to as a "safe haven" where conservative audience members are shielded from views that contradict their own (or are provided with the ammunition to resist those opposing views). Fox News also plays a significant role in holding Republican politicians accountable to maintaining what it defines as conservative ideals.[11] Notably, when these ideological narratives are contradicted by undeniable factual data, it can lead to a breakdown in the representative codes that uphold those storylines. One example of this failure took place on election night during the 2012 presidential election when it became clear that Barack Obama would be re-elected. As Fox News host Megyn Kelly announced that Fox News's Decision Desk had determined that Obama had won Ohio—making a Mitt Romney victory mathematically impossible by the logic of the Electoral College—conservative political consultant Karl Rove immediately questioned her, offering a tepid explanation about exit polls. Kelly retorted by asking, "Is this just math that you do as a Republican to make yourself feel better or is this real?" Other Fox pundits, including Chris Wallace, and members of the Romney campaign immediately seized upon Rove's narrative, prompting Fox to send Kelly out from behind the anchor desk, past a bank of cameras and lights, and off the soundstage to the Decision Desk, which was located down a long hallway, where Kelly interviewed several polling experts who all confirmed and explained the announcement. Although a relatively unscripted moment, it showed how Fox's narrative about the election—and the evidence it had used to support this narrative—had collapsed.

When MSNBC first launched in 1996 as a joint venture between Microsoft and NBC, it was planned as a "smarter" cable news source that would provide analysis from across the political spectrum, and many of their hosts at this time reflected this commitment to ideological diversity. MSNBC also included several shows that focused on the dotcom and technology cultures associated with Microsoft. However, as the political context evolved and Microsoft withdrew its involvement in the network, MSNBC became increasing focused on Washington's political culture, a focus that was expressed in the channel's slogan as "the place for politics." Beginning during the waning years of the Bush administration, MSNBC's primetime pundit Keith Olbermann became an important figure for channeling liberal outrage when he delivered a series of scathing monologues attacking the Bush administration for its role in selling the war in Iraq. During his show, Olbermann also featured a regular segment in which he identified "the worst person in the world," often a member of the Bush administration or a pundit from Fox News, whose offenses he would describe in meticulous detail in an extended lecture punctuated by a grand gesture in which he would toss his cue cards toward the camera in contrived frustration. As Olbermann's commentaries began drawing an audience, the network began the process of rebranding itself as a liberal alternative to Fox News, promoting emerging stars such as Rachel Maddow and Chris Hayes from frequent guests to hosts of their own primetime commentary shows.

The network's liberal identity was encapsulated in its "Lean Forward" branding. Commercials promoting the brand, many of them directed by film auteur Spike Lee, featured MSNBC's hosts articulating their political philosophies. Chris Matthews, for example, cast America's history as a "battle" between groups who wanted to expand freedoms versus those who would restrict them, language that was only slightly more muted than Fox's staging of an agonistic conflict between conservatives and progressives. Meanwhile Chris Hayes argued for the need for universal health care. In all cases, the hosts espoused progressive policies of government while positioning viewers as active agents in facilitating change. Embedded within this brand is a tone that Kelefa Sanneh of The New Yorker aptly described as "earnest, upbeat, and perhaps a little wonky."[12] In this sense, MSNBC, much like Fox News engages in the production of politicized narratives that address audiences' values, tastes, beliefs, and emotions. This branding, like Fox's, seems designed to produce a sense of community built around not only shared political views but also other points of identification associated with a shared stance toward the news media and its role in a wider political culture.

IMPLICATIONS OF NICHE NEWS

There is little debate about the fact that cable has provided a home for partisan media. Fox News, in particular, has been successful at promoting a conservative ideology, whether that grows out of Fox News President Roger Ailes's political beliefs or a broader commitment to corporate branding. What seems less clear, however, is what effects these forms of "niche news," to use Natalie Jomini Stroud's phrase, have on a broader political culture. For some critics, including Kevin Arceneaux and Martin Johnson, niche news "threatens the functioning of American democracy as politics increasingly becomes two strongly opposed ideological camps talking past each other rather than deliberating toward sound public policies."[13] Underlying almost all of the analyses of partisan media is an implicit assumption that they are contributing to increasing polarization, and in most cases, this divergence is seen as facilitating a decline in deliberative democracy. There is certainly some legitimacy to these concerns; however, while MSNBC has served as a useful foil for Fox News as a liberal counterweight, its ability to drive policy and to shape perceptions of Washington's political culture are not as clear, especially given the channel's somewhat ambivalent relationship to its partisan branding. Thus, when evaluating claims about partisan media effects, we must be attentive to differences between these cable channels. Stroud offers a number of useful explanations for how partisan media may be responsible for changes in how citizens think about and participate in politics. In particular, Stroud is attentive to the fact that partisan media can actually invigorate political participation. Notably, she points out that citizens can become motivated to donate money to candidates or pledge support to a cause based on their reactions to partisan media events. In some cases, cable news channels have become directly involved in the political process, as when Fox News provided instructions on their website in 2009, soon after Barack Obama was inaugurated, for people interested in organizing Tea Party rallies that would protest government spending, helping to amplify the voices of a small, but admittedly significant, minority of the population. In fact, Stroud is attentive to the fact that partisan media may invigorate participation in politics but only for those who are already active in politics.[14] Like Stroud, Matthew Levendusky is attentive to the fact that partisan media have the potential to polarize citizens, reinforcing existing beliefs or values. Levendusky adds that although a tiny minority of the population consumes cable news, the people who do watch tend to be more engaged, and therefore more likely to engage in protests, to contact their representatives, to donate to campaigns, or to engage in other behaviors that will make their voices heard by politicians, meaning that cable news (and other partisan media) can have an indirect, but often very powerful, effect on the political process.[15]

Stroud also expresses concern that "partisan selective exposure," the practice of seeking out news media that reinforces a single political perspective, can affect political knowledge, preventing voters from making informed decisions. The implication here is that the public may understand arguments supporting their party's position on an issue but may be oblivious to opposing views, and in many cases polling questions have shown that many voters appear to be unaware of basic facts about politics. However, recent evidence suggests that people may be aware of opposing views but instead find ways to deny their validity. Instead, what seems to be happening is a crisis in institutional authority that often splits along partisan lines. In fact, Chris Mooney has identified what he calls a "growing left-right split over the validity of scientific information," a divide that was particularly evident when it came to the issue of global warming. As Mooney points out, a Pew study found that most conservatives knew the scientific consensus associated with the "theory" of global warming (almost as well as liberals); however, they also stated that the do not trust scientists on the issue. Although the cause-effect relationship is likely far from simple, Mooney identifies a correlation between climate change skepticism and doubts about the validity of the theory of evolution and viewership of Fox News.[16] While Mooney attributes these expressions of distrust for the scientific community to exposure to Fox News, it is equally likely that many of the viewers who already have these beliefs are likely consciously choosing to consume conservative media where their political beliefs are endlessly and vociferously reinforced. A more persuasive argument is that poll answers may not reflect political misinformation at all. As Levendusky explains, many people who claimed to believe that Barack Obama is a Muslim, for example, were manipulating the poll question in order to engage in an "expressive political act," one that served in this case as an expression of defiance against Obama's legitimacy as president.[17]

Perhaps more crucially, partisan media have the effect of creating narratives that can set the agenda for other forms of political coverage. Levendusky, for example, points out that Fox News was largely responsible for directing attention to the efforts of the Swift Boat Veterans for Truth to undermine John Kerry's military record during the 2004 Presidential election, a story that went largely ignored by national network news until Fox began covering it so relentlessly.[18] More recently, Jeffrey P. Jones has outlined Fox News's ability to manufacture outrage over perceived (but utterly artificial) threats such as the "War on Christmas." For Jones, many of these narratives actually have no real relationship to the truth; instead, they produce it by presenting opinion—often grounded in a narrative of ongoing political struggle in which conservative or traditional values are perceived as increasingly threatened—as fact. By declaring that there is a "war" on Christmas being led by liberals who are imposing politically correct values from above, we suddenly find that such a war exists.[19] Thus, as Jones implies, political media do significantly more than just report on politics. They are a vital part of Washington's political culture, and in many ways, actively help to create it.

Although there is little doubt that partisan media continues to exercise an effect on politics, it is also important to acknowledge the role of a Washington political consensus that serves to frame issues and to set a political agenda. In fact, as Kathleen Hall Jamieson and Paul Waldman argue, reporters tend to be shaped by "professional" biases, not political ones, noting that they typically depend on "official sources," especially given that these sources are readily available.[20] In this context, political news coverage becomes increasingly reliant upon official sources, such as representatives of the political or entrepreneurial class in determining what issues are worthy of attention and how they should be covered. As Shanto Iyengar explains, issues that receive attention from the media tend to become the issues that viewers themselves become most concerned about.[21] Thus, political media, regardless of partisan affiliations, can serve an important role in defining the stakes of political debate, of determining what issues are relevant to voters and what political candidates might best address those concerns. As a result, political media plays an important role in defining candidates and shaping the storylines that guide the electoral process. As Lance Bennett explains, these ongoing narrative arcs have become increasingly covered as if they are an alternative form of reality television. Specifically, Bennett seems to be talking about the so-called "gamedocs" or competition reality shows, such as Survivor, Fear Factor, or Big Brother, in which contestants are forced to undergo various challenges in order to win the competition of appearing presidential.[22] For Bennett, such "candidate challenges" actually obscure substantive policy considerations, instead focusing on more superficial storylines that are instead focused on the candidates' techniques and personalities rather than what they said, reporting that is often characterized as a form of horserace journalism. This perception of election coverage as a form of reality television has become so internalized that the early stages of the 2016 election were often covered almost entirely in these terms. In fact, much of the election coverage focused on the role of the political media in imposing "rules" of decorum about how elections should be conducted and what types of language should be used when talking about rival candidates and, more broadly, Washington's political culture. Predictably, many of these debates coalesced around the outsider candidacy of billionaire businessman and reality television star Donald Trump, whose rise in the polls threatened to unsettle that consensus. In this context, discussions of events, such as the first Republican debate, hosted by Fox News in August 2015, helped to illustrate the role of the political media in policing campaign discourse. Similarly, Washington insiders such as Chuck Todd could frame the race during his post-debate analysis in terms that focused on personality and performance, rather than on policy, arguing that Wisconsin Governor Scott Walker needed to act "more alpha," that is, to appear tougher, in order to win the Republican nomination. With that in mind, this chapter now turns to a discussion of the campaign narratives that were used to frame candidates from the earliest stages of the 2016 election.

NEWS AND ELECTION NARRATIVES

Cable news plays a vital role in both shaping and amplifying political narratives. Because news talk shows function, in large part, to police the appropriate language of Washington's political culture, they work to define not only the candidates involved in the race for political office but also the boundaries of who counts as a legitimate or serious candidate for office. More crucially, as Lance Bennett argues, "elections may be our most important storytelling ritual, a time when we remind ourselves, with the help of candidates, what we stand for as a people, what our challenges are, where the next chapter of our national saga is heading, and who may best lead us there."[23] As Bennett's comments suggest, elections serve as narratives that can be used to make sense of where we are as a nation. During the 2016 election, cable news's role in determining political relevancy was notable, both in terms of how pundits worked to create narratives about specific candidates and in terms of how the cable networks fought to control aspects of the political process through their participation in early campaign events.

In particular, Fox News played a crucial role in negotiating who would count as a relevant contender for the Republican nomination for president by establishing rules about which candidates would be allowed to participate in the first Republican primary debate, scheduled for August 6, 2015, more than a year before the general election and about six months before the Iowa caucuses, the first statewide vote to decide who would be the nominee for each party. Responding to the massive field of Republican candidates, Fox News faced the prospect of either allowing sixteen candidates to face off during the debate—a scenario that would have prevented presidential contenders from speaking at any length—or find some way to artificially winnow down the number of viable competitors. The result was a decision to allow the top ten candidates in national polling to appear during the debate, a move that was widely criticized for excluding more marginal voices within the party and for nationalizing the election much earlier than in past elections, when statewide primaries played a more crucial role in evaluating candidates. Fox News eventually tweaked the process, creating a second debate for candidates outside the top ten, but the earlier debate was not shown in primetime, when most viewers would be watching, and was derided by many participants as the "kids table," worthy of lesser attention than the main event.[24] Of course, the debate itself was very much the product of political hype as Fox News sought to promote it as potentially the "most watched" debate ever, and even while many Fox News pundits were openly critical of Trump, they used his presence at the debate to hype it as something completely unpredictable.

Because the debates were framed as such a crucial event, low-polling candidates faced the unusual prospect of having to build their national audience well in advance of the first primary in order to ensure that they would qualify for the primetime debate, with the result that some candidates, including New Jersey governor Chris Christie, invested heavily in national advertising, much of it on Fox News, in order to attract enough attention—whether directly through the ads themselves or indirectly through discussion of the ads on news talk shows—so that they would qualify for this first debate. As a result, Fox News could benefit enormously from fostering a highly competitive Republican primary by both generating speculation about who was winning the race at any given time and by shaping the rules that govern the process. In other cases, candidates produced provocative videos with the hope of attracting attention from TV, as when South Carolina Representative Lindsey Graham made a video of himself destroying his cell phone after Trump gave out his phone number during a public speech or when Kentucky Senator Rand Paul used a chainsaw and wood chipper to destroy the U.S. tax code. While both videos ostensibly had political points—Paul, in particular, wanted to reinforce his libertarian *bona fides* by literally cutting through one of the most potent symbols of Washington's bureaucratic culture—their primary purpose was to buy some free attention from Fox News, CNN, and MSNBC, as well as the fake news satirists Jon Stewart and Stephen Colbert.

More crucially, these modes of analysis often served to create candidate narratives that served two functions. First, they often function to create artificial obstacles for candidates, whether out of a desire to actually damage that person's reputation or out of a desire to create conflict that could justify excessive attention to the election. Second, these narratives played the larger role of defining what counts as a "legitimate" contribution to Washington's political culture. Of course, Trump, perhaps more than any other candidate, understood both the power of narrative associated with reality TV and the power of free media attention. Even during his career as a businessman, Trump deliberately crafted a strategy of attracting media attention by making himself available to the media for TV, radio, or even newspaper interviews. As Trump explained it in his autobiography *The Art of the Deal*, a full-page print ad in *The New York Times* might cost $40,000, but an interview or story in the paper's op-ed pages was significantly more valuable. Thus, as Chris Cillizza recognized, Trump's strategy of reaching out to the press provided him with hours of free publicity, even while the press stood to benefit by amassing more page clicks or higher ratings that, in turn, contributed to their bottom line.[25]

These definitions of candidates emerge in news talk formats where pundits engage in different forms of election analysis. Often, that involves examining advertisements, policy positions, or other candidate comments to determine whether those statements are beneficial to the candidate's campaign. Although I am skeptical of the false binary of politics and entertainment crafted by Jay Rosen and others, Rosen is correct to raise doubts about the potential conflicts involved when political journalists become infatuated with covering the process, rather than focusing on matters of political policy.[26] Rosen, drawing from Lindsay Tanner, argues that political reporting will focus on a "titillating" story—a verbal gaffe or some other trivial event—and exaggerating that moment's importance, distracting audiences from what "really" matters. Instead, this form of reporting also serves to reinforce a Washington consensus of what is (and isn't) worthy of discussion during a political campaign, questions that can have clear implications for what kinds of policies and what types of candidates get their voices heard throughout the process.

Of course, in a fragmented political media environment, in which voters get political information from a variety of sources, the narratives produced by the dominant political news sources are no longer definitive when it comes to shaping public perceptions of the candidates. In fact, during the early stages of the Republican primaries, Donald Trump's candidacy seemed to upend all of the common wisdom about how elections should be conducted. During his presidential announcement speech, for example, Trump made inflammatory comments about illegal immigration, asserting that "When Mexico sends its people, they're not sending the best . . . . They're sending people that have lots of problems and they're bringing those problems. They're bringing drugs; they're bringing crime. They're rapists and some, I assume, are good people, but I speak to border guards and they're telling us what we're getting." Trump's comments were widely condemned by the traditional cable news media, as well as by the dominant Latino news sources. NBC Universal and Univision both cut ties with the Miss Universe pageant, while several of Trump's endorsement deals, including a clothing line sold by Macy's, were also terminated. Even the conservative Fox News initially sought to diminish the power of Trump's early popularity, by calling attention to the apparent incompetence of Trump's campaign staff. On the July 29, 2015 episode of Fox's late-morning news show, *America's Newsroom*, the hosts pointed to yet another apparent "gaffe" by Trump's lawyer to argue that the campaign needed an official spokesperson and faulting Trump for not having a campaign infrastructure. However, despite this widespread condemnation, Trump's poll numbers continued to rise, making clear that television's role as a "gatekeeper" may be waning in an era of hyper-mediated citizenship, as more people find information online. Instead, Trump could appeal to a populist anti-politics sentiment to provide people with the sense that someone was finally speaking out about the frustrations they were feeling. In this sense, Trump's candidacy, from its earliest stages, proved to be a disruptive force, one that challenged the norms of Washington's political culture and one that also unsettled the efforts of the political news media to police these norms and to maintain consensus.

This mode of disciplining Donald Trump also appeared on Fox News's rival MSNBC during *Morning Joe*, the network's influential morning show that explicitly brands itself as the bipartisan source for articulating the day's political agenda. Although Joe Scarborough, a former Republican Congressman, is a political conservative, the show fits other aspects of MSNBC's brand as "the place for politics" and also largely serves to prop up the Washington, DC establishment. These practices were evident during the July 20, 2015 episode, which aired the Monday after Republican Presidential candidate had made comments disparaging Senator John McCain's military service, suggesting that McCain "was not a hero" because he had been captured and held captive during the Vietnam War. Most of the last hour of the program was devoted to scrutinizing the implications of Trump's comments, largely in terms of how they would affect his presidential campaign. To address this question, the hosts began by interviewing McCain himself for a segment that was simulcast on NBC's *Today*, in a moment of corporate synergy, with McCain performing the role of being above the fray by stating that he didn't need Trump to apologize. Later, the hosts immediately defended McCain, while also suggesting that the comments would be politically damaging to Trump. In particular, frequent guest John Heilemann emphasized that the comments had "given everybody free rein" to attack Trump, a claim that was supported by a montage of Republican candidates dutifully condemning the comments and, in some cases, questioning whether Trump should remain in the race. Although other political segments were built into the show—including a discussion of the landmark news story that Cuba and the United States had restored diplomatic ties after fifty years—*Morning Joe* repeatedly returned to Trump's comments during an interview with New York Republican Representative Peter King, insisting that the remarks were "wrong, morally wrong."

Thus, although Morning Joe professes to be calling attention to—and analyzing—the political narratives that dominate political conversations, the show played a vital role in directing those conversations. In fact, one effect of the Trump discussion on Morning Joe was to ensure that people on social media continued to focus on Trump's comments for the rest of the news day, a discussion that would bring attention both to the show and to Trump's destructive and self-aggrandizing political campaign. Thus, as political media scholar Matthew Dickinson argued, the segments—even while criticizing Trump—served his interests both by continuing to give him free publicity and by reinforcing the idea of a political campaign built on attacking the Washington establishment. In short, by playing the role of establishment scolds, Morning Joe was, in many ways, bolstering Trump's outsider status as an authentic, blunt straight-talker, deepening his support that is "coming from that part of the electorate that is increasingly dissatis-fied with what it views as a corrupt political establishment."[27] In this sense, Morning Joe plays several roles that serve the needs of both MSNBC and the political establishment. By weaving political narratives—in the guise of ana-lyzing them—they play the role of setting the agenda for that day's political conversations. But by articulating what kinds of comments are permissible, the show also serves the function of policing political discourse, of com-municating what forms of attacks are permissible or appropriate.

If coverage of the Republican primary faced the challenge of sorting through an excess of candidates, the Democratic primary presented the opposite problem. The party had a relatively clear frontrunner in Hillary Clinton who was also extremely familiar to both news reporters and vot-ers. However, like the coverage of the Republican primary, discussions of Clinton tended to focus on her electability rather than on the policies that she was promoting on the campaign trail. Even when Clinton did intro-duce a new policy, such as her call to end the embargo against Cuba, the proposal was often evaluated in terms of its electoral effects (could Clinton still win Florida despite potential opposition from some Cuban voters?) instead of what implications the policy shift might have on the economy or foreign relations. Many of these questions about the role of cable news in constructing narrative frames were illustrated when former Secretary of State and Senator Hillary Clinton announced that she would be running for president. On Sunday, April 12, 2015, Clinton, following precedent set by many other Republican and Democratic candidates in recent presidential elections, announced via YouTube video that she would be making a second run for the Oval Office. The timing of Clinton's announcement had been predicted for a few days, but on another level, her intentions to run again had been expected for years, a fact that essentially meant that a number of media outlets and political activists already had developed pre-existing narratives in which Clinton's candidacy could be framed. In fact, Clinton's decision to announce was so widely anticipated that *Saturday Night Live* (SNL) actually managed to parody her web video announcement during their cold open even before Clinton's video went online. The SNL sketch specifically parodied the perception that Clinton is somehow both calculating about her ambition to be president and oblivious to the social norms that guide political discourse. These narratives were consistent with what Shawn J. Parry Giles has described as the "news frames" through which the political news media construct and perpetuate images of public figures.[28] Of course, as the SNL skit illustrates, political entertainment also plays a vital role in both perpetuating and, in some cases, interrogating these frameworks.

In this sense, coverage of Clinton also conformed to the idea of political coverage as a series of reality TV narratives. As Baym adds, the postmodern news formats associated with the on-demand era are most commonly involved in "the business of constructing dramatic narratives—televisual spectacles crafted for public consumption."[29] Linking these narratives to a largely depoliticized public sphere, Baym adds that politics is no longer marked by rational discourse but is instead an "aesthetic performance," one that is marked by largely trivial analyses of the staging of campaign events. Thus, for Hillary Clinton, the "candidate challenge" created by different media outlets, was to assume an almost contradictory set of performances that would meet all of these goals.

It should come as no surprise that the most overt attacks on Clinton's announcement video came from Fox News. For example, Howard Kurtz's *Media Buzz*, which purports to analyze the media frames that are shaping politics, actually served instead to reinforce many of the frames that had been used to evaluate her. In fact, Kurtz's segment openly reinforced several of the existing narratives used to shape Clinton's persona independently of any political views she might have. The segment opened with Fox News contributor Mary Katharine Ham gleefully dismissing the announcement as a "snoozefest," promoting the perception that Clinton is too boring to win the presidency. Similarly, one of Kurtz's guests, *Washington Examiner* columnist Susan Ferrechio, pushed the idea that the video was an example of Clinton "controlling the message" because she made the announcement via social media rather than during a live speech—despite the fact that most Republican candidates announced in a similar fashion. Further, by focusing on perceptions of Clinton's personality, Ferrechio was able to deflect attention away from the actual content of the video, which emphasized (however vaguely) Clinton's expressed desire to fight for working families. Meanwhile Kurtz himself trotted out the frame, also imposed on Barack Obama during the 2008 election, that Clinton might be "covered as a celebrity" even while suggesting, almost in the same breath that she had been "disdainful" of the media. This connection to the trope of celebrity also showed up during Fox News's coverage of the first Republican debate. During the August 7, 2015 episode of *Outnumbered*, for example, the show's hosts devoted a full segment of the show to a discussion of a selfie that Clinton took with reality TV star Kim Kardashian. The segment played to perceptions of Hollywood stars as shallow and uninformed, as one host pointed out that Kardashian had misspelled "presidential" when posting the photo, a discussion that was almost immediately reprised during Fox's midafternoon show, *Happening Now*, in this case to infer (falsely) that Clinton might be having difficulty raising money because of her declining poll numbers. At the same time, the photograph was used to create an entire speculative narrative, in which the hosts of *Outnumbered* asserted that "we" couldn't trust Clinton when she (or her representatives) told us that she wasn't watching the debates. Although there was no evidence that Clinton was watching the debates offered by Fox News, they were able to use insinuation and speculation to posit the idea that Clinton might have been watching and that this might be another example of her attempts to manage a political message. Thus, Fox News continued to use its position to connect Clinton to the hint of scandal and imposing on her a reputation for not being forthcoming with her positions on issues.

As I have argued, cable news plays a significant role in shaping perceptions of political culture. Partisan media serves a major role in setting the agenda of what stories will get covered, how the stories are framed, and who will be given the opportunity to speak about these issues. These news channels also frequently became the story, as was the case with the August 2015 Fox debate. As a result, electoral politics has increasingly become not merely a form of political spectacle but even one that fabricated reality TV narratives that were used to evaluate the electability of presidential candidates, often on the basis of superficial traits, such as whether the candidate had been "alpha" (i.e., tough) enough or whether the candidate had appeared in a picture with a celebrity. In addition, although niche news has often been faulted for reinforcing partisan divides, it is also important to note the role of political news in upholding a Washington consensus. This effort to police language emerged when the hosts of MSNBC's *Morning Joe* show jointly attacked Donald Trump for disparaging Senator John McCain's military service by insinuating that he was not a "hero" because he had been a prisoner of war. But even while this consensus narrative served to limit what issues would receive attention, in some limited cases, urgent news stories could force the news media to challenge this consensus. These pressing news stories—mass tragedies, natural disasters, and other political crises—often forced reporters to deviate from existing scripts and to expand the range of authority figures who would could comment on a story. This challenge became especially acute when a number of news stories came out that documented incidents of violence against African-American men and women, many of them committed by police officers.

PROTESTS AND THE CRISIS OF POLITICAL AUTHORITY

As W. Lance Bennett, Regina G. Lawrence, and Steven Livingston argue, "a typical situation that opens the news gates to underreported versions of events involves some shock to the Washington consensus: a catastrophic event or policy failure, a scandal, an electoral realignment, or a building political opposition that changes the power balance within institutional decision-making circles."[30] When confronted with an event that challenges political norms, journalists may be put in the position of being able to question authorities without concern about being cut off from access to political power. Bennett, Lawrence, and Livingston cite the reporting on Hurricane Katrina as an example of a situation in which the press was able to build a narrative that clearly documented policy failures by the Bush administration that made the hurricane both a natural and a political disaster.[31] Many of these questions were revisited over the course of several months, when several African-American men and women were killed, most of them during altercations with police over relatively minor incidents. The first incident was the killing of Trayvon Martin by George Zimmermann, who claimed that he was acting in self-defense. Zimmermann was also acting in his capacity as the coordinator of the neighborhood watch program of his gated subdivision when he confronted Martin. In defending himself from second-degree murder charges, Zimmermann cited Florida's controversial Stand-Your-Ground law, which gave extraordinary latitude to claims of self-defense. Although the shooting did not involve the police, Martin's death was seen as a powerful reminder of the fact that African Americans still were not treated equally by the legal system, and the incident helped to consolidate support for the Black Lives Matter movement, while journalists were forced to confront a social, political, and economic history in which systemic violence against African Americans was taking place, much of it sanctioned by institutions such as the police or judicial system. Given the wide range of stories and events that brought these issues to the surface, coverage of these events developed through a number of different filters. The most significant incidents typically involved the moments of political crisis, when political protests, particularly the incidents in Ferguson, Missouri, and Baltimore, Maryland, shifted from peaceful marches and chants into violent outbursts that included arson and looting. These events presented a social rupture where cable news channels were confronted with the challenge of making sense of the unfolding crisis. But as the outbursts began to settle, a secondary process, one that attempted to place the crisis into a larger narrative, often began to unfold. In this scenario, the competing partisan news frames associated with cable news channels did come into play.

To some extent, the news coverage of these incidents of police brutality served not just as a way of engaging with the failed policies for alleviating inner-city violence and of aggressive police enforcement, but also as a moment of reflection in which news media outlets were forced to be more self-critical about their depictions of political protests. News coverage of black political protests has a long history, one that frequently cast protesters into stereotypical roles. As Herman Gray argues, "Black people portrayed in news coverage of the civil rights and black power movements appeared either as decent but aggrieved blacks who simply wanted to become a part of the American dream, or as threats to the very notion of citizenship and nation."[32] Many similar framing narratives were at play in the cable news coverage of protests in the aftermath of the deaths of Michael Brown and Freddie Gray, with reporters singling out some blacks as seeking to preserve the American dream, often by finding members of the community who worked to protect or rebuild businesses that had been damaged or destroyed during the protests, and by comparing them favorably to rioters "with nothing better to do," a framing that was also used during the Los Angeles rebellion after the verdict in the Rodney King case.[33] As a result of this history, throughout the coverage of the demonstrations, there was clearly an awareness of how the black community was being portrayed by the media, and many of the main confrontations with the media that emerged during the protests were precisely connected to this issue of representation and of who counted as an expert on these issues.

These attempts to ask critical questions about police brutality and other forms of racial violence were aided by the ubiquitous diffusion of video cameras on cell phones, making anyone who was witnessing a news event into a potential journalist. For example, a witness caught the assault on Eric Garner by members of the Staten Island, New York, police force on camera. In the video, the police applied a chokehold against Garner, who was being detained for illegally selling rolled cigarettes. As the chokehold tightened and Garner struggled against it, his shouts that he was unable to breathe went unheeded, and Garner eventually died in police custody. Similarly, video of police shooting the 12-year-old Tamir Rice, who happened to be holding a toy gun, inspired further investigation into that case. Additionally, in North Charleston, South Carolina, an officer was arrested and charged with murder after shooting the unarmed Walter Scott, who had been pulled over for a nonfunctioning brake light. In this case, cell phone video shot by a witness contradicted the original police report that claimed that Scott had been armed and had been a direct threat to the officer's safety. Finally, in July 2015, an African-American woman Sandra Bland was found dead in her jail cell in what was initially ruled as a suicide, two days after being pulled over by a police officer for failing to signal a change of lanes. The Bland incident was captured by a camera on the dashboard of the police car, and again, the incident raised questions about how the police officer was culpable in escalating tensions by demanding that Bland put out a cigarette and then angrily demanding that she exit the car. As Bennett, Lawrence, and Livingston argue, these videos can force the news media to cover stories that might otherwise go ignored and can provide space for journalists to ask questions that might challenge dominant narratives. The widespread mistreatment of African-American men by the police revived debates about policing practices, institutional racism, and ignited debates about how these actions are framed in the news media, which, as Bennett, Lawrence, and Livingston have argued very rarely use the term "police brutality."[34] These incidents provoked increased calls for police cars and uniforms to be equipped with cameras, but they also helped to illustrate the democratic potential of handheld cameras as tools for documenting incidents of police violence. In fact, some of the most powerful images that were captured in Ferguson did not appear on television at all. Instead, amateur journalists, using consumer-grade cameras or smartphones, captured footage of riot police using rubber bullets and tear gas to subdue protestors and used livestreaming technology to post that material on the web, where it could be shared on social media and, eventually, on television.[35] However, while these videos were often presented as visible evidence that could be used to document events that might otherwise have been ignored or forgotten, they were often interpreted in vastly different ways. In one remarkable example, *Fox and Friends* host Elisabeth Hasselbeck postulated that Sandra Bland could have used a lit cigarette as a weapon against the police officer who had pulled her over for a routine traffic stop.[36] But in almost all cases, TV commentators could identify extenuating factors that could justify the act of violence.

Thus, as with many past uprisings or protests, news anchors and commentators were eventually able to locate narrative explanations that would allow them to place "safer" meanings onto stories that threatened to unsettle a political consensus. Although Bennett, Lawrence, and Livingston cite the example of the video of the 1991 beating of Rodney King as an example of a situation where visual evidence could be used to provoke "an explosive national debate on institutionalized racism," the verdict in the trial—in which all four officers were acquitted—and the shaping of public opinion through deconstructions of the video went a long way toward obscuring over concerns about patterns of police mistreatment of African-American men.[37] In this context, perhaps the most iconic image of the Baltimore protests became the irate mother, Toya Graham, who famously found her son among the Baltimore looters, grabbing and then slapping him as she pulled him away from the scene, with all of these actions dramatically taking place in front of a news camera. Graham's actions were quickly placed into competing narratives that were used to make sense of the protests and to categorize the protesters themselves. Geraldo Rivera, for example, read the situation as an example of a mother taking responsibility for her child, a narrative that could then be used to push the idea that the "failure" that led to the riots was not one of economic inequality or police brutality but one of personal responsibility. On the April 28, 2015 episode of Fox News's The Five, Rivera commented, "the big hero here in Baltimore is that mom yesterday who smacked her teenage son up the side of the head, got that the mask off his face and kicked his butt until he left the protesters, the rioters, the looters and got his—got his teenage fanny home. There needs to be responsibility here."[38] Similarly, Joe Scarborough, the host of MSNBC's Morning Joe, offered a conservative frame for reading Graham's actions, referring to her as a "good, strong mother," based exclusively on her fleeting actions in front of the camera. As Sheena Howard points out, the underlying meaning of this narrative is that if black parents were disciplining their children correctly, then their youth would not be out in the streets protesting. Howard adds that this narrative conveniently omits the fact that black people are protesting because of police violence.[39] Notably, however, even some Fox News hosts openly contested the narrative that the crisis in Baltimore could be attributed solely to the perceived failures of black parents. On an April 27, 2015 episode of Fox News's The Five, an afternoon political forum show in which five Fox News hosts would discuss the day's news stories, Shep Smith challenged the other hosts, making reference to "decades of turmoil" in West Baltimore and a community in which nearly a quarter of the neighborhood's youth was incarcerated. However, the dominant narrative offered on Fox tended to focus primarily on the issues of personal responsibility rather than on the institutional factors of poverty, unemployment, and mass incarceration.

Perhaps the most notable aspect of the protests in both Ferguson and Baltimore was the awareness demonstrated by the protesters of the tropes of political protest coverage. Notably, many of the protesters in both Ferguson and Baltimore directly engaged with the media, questioning their representational strategies and their decision to cover the protests while ignoring years of disastrous policies affecting their neighborhoods. Thus, the protests were connected to the questions of political authority, of who gets to appear on television. In some cases, these attempts to "change the narrative" involved the use of visual elements. While describing the cleanup efforts around the community in the aftermath of the riots and looting on an April 28 episode of MSNBC's *Politics Nation*, Thomas Roberts addressed these questions of political visibility when he reported that Baltimore residents had told him they "wanted America and the world to see that they had rakes in their hands and shovels, not bricks, and they wanted the world to know that they were taking control of their own communities with the cleanup."[40] But, in addition to these efforts to promote positive images of black protest, others focused on the role of the media in manufacturing false narratives about African Americans. In fact, one of the largest protests associated took place in Atlanta, at the headquarters of CNN, where several thousand people, led by student activists, held a rally that, in part, sought to criticize media depictions of the death of Michael Brown and the resulting protests in Ferguson and other cities.

These questions of political authority became even more explicit when protestors were given the opportunity to voice their concerns during interviews. During an interview on MSNBC later the same day, one protestor, Danielle Williams, focused on precisely these representational matters:

> My question to you is, when we were out here protesting all last week, there were no news cameras, there were no helicopters, and there was no riot gear, and nobody heard us. So now that we burned down

buildings and set businesses on fire and looted buildings, now all of a sudden everybody wants to hear us. Why does it take a catastrophe like this in order for America to hear our cry?[41]

Williams's comments function as an incisive critique of the routine coverage of crime news on both local and national news stations, as well as the limited attention given to the peaceful protests that had taken place over the previous few days immediately after Freddie Gray's death. It is only after the "catastrophe," that is after the looting and riots that took place on the night of April 27, 2015, that the question of police brutality and economic inequality began receiving any significant attention. Similarly, when CNN's Wolf Blitzer pushed political activist DeRay McKesson to condemn the property damage associated with the previous night's riots, much of it associated with a CVS drugstore that had been looted and burned, asking him, "There's no excuse for that kind of violence, right?" McKesson directly echoed Blitzer's language in asserting that there was "no excuse for the seven people the Baltimore Police Department has killed in the last year, either, right?" Thus, by recontextualizing Blitzer's language, McKesson was able to challenge the analytical frames that were used to describe the Baltimore rebellion.

In another context, several Baltimore protesters also sought to call attention to the use of language and other framing devices that could serve to dehumanize black inner-city youth and to devalue their experiences. During an April 28, 2015, live broadcast on Fox News featuring Geraldo Rivera, minutes after a 10 pm citywide curfew had been imposed, a protester stood directly in front of the camera, with Rivera repeatedly imploring him, "Stop blocking the camera. Stop it. You're making a fool of yourself." Meanwhile, other protesters could be heard in the background shouting that Fox News was "making money off black pain," a reminder that the news channel was profiting off of contrived conflicts with the protestors. Similarly, representatives from the Baltimore community sought to challenge some of the frames that were being used to describe the rioters. Seizing on Baltimore mayor Stephanie Rawlings-Blake's use of the word "thugs" to describe the looters, CNN anchor Erin Burnett asked Baltimore City Councilman Carl Stokes, "Isn't that the right word?" Stokes quickly challenged that frame, arguing, "No, of course it's not the right word to call our children 'thugs.' These are children who have been set aside, marginalized, who have not been engaged by us. No! We don't have to call them thugs." Later in the same episode, Burnett, seemingly wanting to feel justified in using the term, asks CNN political Van Jones, "Is the word thug the same as the N-word?" Like Stokes, Jones calls attention to the ways in which the term "thug" was functioning as a way to deny the humanity of black youth: "I wouldn't use that term, I don't use that term because it's becoming kind of a fashionable way of almost dehumanizing folks who are doing stuff that I make no apology for what those young people are doing." [42] Thus, once again, representatives from Baltimore are in the position of contesting a media framing, challenging the language used to describe African-American youth. The protests in Ferguson and Baltimore played a vital role in altering media conversations about police violence. Although the cable networks did eventually impose narratives that could be used to make sense of the rebellions in Ferguson and Baltimore, the fact that many of these incidents were unfolding in real time forced TV reporters to go beyond traditional interpretive frames. To be sure, many of these incidents were subsequently placed into narrative explanations that sought to remove these incidents of police violence from the longer history of police violence against black youth. In fact, even the slogan "Black Lives Matter" frequently was co-opted to diminish its political meaning in the context of police violence by the more general formulation "All Lives Matter." Where the phrase "all lives matter" is an undeniable truth, the emphasis on black lives was a pointed reminder that, in too many cases, blacks were dehumanized. But in this case, the partisan media did allow voices that challenged the political consensus to be given time for these voices to be heard. Although these speakers may have been counterbalanced by political experts who sought to build consensus, media coverage of these incidents served as an ongoing reminder that these events were part of a much longer history, one that still remains unresolved.

CONCLUSION

While cable news has been associated with the processes of political polarization, it is also part of a larger commercial television. Therefore, the political branding strategies that guide partisan media are never final, and commercially unsuccessful branding strategies are subject to change. In this sense, articles or books that describe the cable news environment as featuring two equally weighted resources for information may be somewhat misleading. In fact, as I was in the process of completing this chapter, Comcast, the parent company of MSNBC, was in the process of redefining the channel's brand, subtly shifting it away from being a destination for liberal audiences to a source for more neutral forms of politics-driven programming. In July 2015, MSNBC cancelled *The Ed Show*, featuring liberal firebrand Ed Schultz, whose program focused extensively on issues of income inequality and worker rights from an openly pro-union point-of-view. The network replaced *The Ed Show* with a news-driven program hosted by Chuck Todd, who would also continue to host the weekly public affairs program, *Meet the Press*.[43] Similarly, the network jettisoned much of its afternoon lineup, including *Now with Alex Wagner*, in part to appear less partisan. These rebranding efforts reflected MSNBC's failure to maintain its grip on the liberal cable TV audience. In fact, despite MSNBC's sustained efforts at branded programming that would address liberal audiences, liberal viewers rarely named the network as the news source they trusted most.[44] Thus, rather than simply seeing MSNBC as a liberal counterpoint to Fox News, we must look more carefully at how branding functions. In all cases, we must also be equipped with the critical thinking skills necessary to read political news against the grain. While Fox News, CNN, and MSNBC have been used to promote the idea that potential voters are presented with a diversity of voices about politics, in most circumstances, they also reinforce a Washington political culture that places value on the opinions of elite leaders.

NOTES

1 Newton N. Minow, "Television and the Public Interest," National Association of Broadcasters, Washington, DC, May 9, 1961.
2 Geoffrey Baym, *From Cronkite to Colbert*, 13.
3 Quoted in Baym, *From Cronkite to Colbert*, 14.
4 Jeffrey P. Jones, "Fox News and the Performance of Ideology," *Cinema Journal* 51.4 (Summer 2012), 180.

5 Jeffrey P. Jones, "The 'New' News as No 'News,'" *Media International Australia* 144 (August 2012), 147–148.

6 Jeffrey P. Jones, "The 'New' News as No 'News,'" 148–149.

7 Laurie Ouellette, "Branding the Right: The Affective Economy of Sarah Palin," *Cinema Journal* 51.4 (Summer 2012), 188.

8 For a thorough explanation of how the FCC defined the public interest, see Edward Jay Epstein, *News from Nowhere: Television and the News* (Chicago: Ivan R. Dee, 2000), 47–49.

9 Amanda D. Lotz, *The Television will be Revolutionized* (New York: New York University Press, 2007), 5.

10 Natalie Jomini Stroud, *Niche News: The Politics of News Choice* (Oxford: Oxford University Press, 2011), 66.

11 Kathleen Hall Jamieson and Joseph N. Cappella, *Echo Chamber: Rush Limbaugh and the Conservative Media Outlet* (Oxford: Oxford University Press, 2008), x.

12 Kelefa Sanneh, "Twenty-Four Hour Party People," *The New Yorker*, September 2, 2013, http://www.newyorker.com/magazine/2013/09/02/twenty-four-hour-party-people.

13 Kevin Arceneaux and Martin Johnson, *Changing Minds or Changing Channels? Partisan News in an Age of Choice* (Chicago: University of Chicago Press, 2013), 4.

14 Natalie Jomini Stroud, *Niche News*, 9.

15 Matthew Levendusky, *How Partisan Media Polarize America* (Chicago: University of Chicago Press), 139–140.

16 Chris Mooney, "Poll: Tea Party Members Really, Really Don't Trust Scientists," *Mother Jones*, May 20, 2014, http://www.motherjones.com/environment/2014/05/tea-party-climate-trust-science.

17 Matthew Levendusky, *How Partisan Media Polarize America*, 145.

18 Matthew Levendusky, *How Partisan Media Polarize America*, 145.

19 Jeffrey P. Jones, "Fox News and the Performance of Ideology," 184.

20 Kathleen Hall Jamieson and Paul Waldman, *The Press Effect: Politicians, Journalists and the Stories that Shape the Political World* (Oxford: Oxford University Press, 2003), 170.

21 Shanto Iyengar, *Media Politics: A Citizen's Guide*, 2nd ed. (New York: Norton, 2011).

22 W. Lance Bennett, "Beyond Pseudoevents: Election News as Reality TV," *American Behavioral Scientist* 49.3 (2005): 364–378.

23 W. Lance Bennett, *News: The Politics of Illusion*, 9th ed. (Boston: Longman, 2012), 37.

24 Mike Allen, "Fox Lowers Threshold for Early Debate," *Politico*, July 28, 2015, http://www.politico.com/story/2015/07/fox-republican-debate-lowers-threshold-120748.html.

25 Chris Cillizza, "One Thing Donald Trump is Doing Very Right," *The Washington Post*, July 29, 2015, http://www.washingtonpost.com/news/the-fix/wp/2015/07/29/let-me-now-praise-donald-trump/.

26 Jay Rosen, "Why Political Coverage is Broken," *Press Think*, August 26, 2011, http://pressthink.org/2011/08/why-political-coverage-is-broken/.

27 Matthew Dickinson, "Why the Donald Trumps the Media (and What They Should Do About It)," *Presidential Power*, July 19, 2015, http://sites.middlebury.edu/presidentialpower/2015/07/19/why-the-donald-trumps-the-media-and-what-they-should-do-about-it/.

28 Shawn J. Parry-Giles, *Hillary Clinton in the News: Gender and Authenticity in American Politics* (Urbana: University of Illinois Press, 2014), 15.

29 Baym, *From Cronkite to Colbert*, 58.

30 Bennett, Lawrence, and Livingston, *When the Press Fails*, 60.

31 Bennett, Lawrence, and Livingston, *When the Press Fails*, 64–65.

32 Herman Gray, "Remembering Civil Rights: Television, Memory, and the 1960s," in *The Revolution Wasn't Televised: Sixties Television and Social Conflict*, ed. Lynn Spigel and Michael Curtin (New York: Routledge, 1997), 350.

33 John Thornton Caldwell, *Televisuality: Style, Crisis, and Authority in American Television* (New Brunswick: Rutgers University Press, 1995), 303.

34 Bennett, Lawrence, and Livingston, *When the Press Fails*, 105.

35 Judd Legum, "Police Officer Threatens to Shoot Reporter Live-Streaming Protests in Ferguson," Think Progress, August 17, 2014, http://thinkprogress.org/justice/2014/08/17/3472290/police-officer-threatens-to-shoot-reporter-live-streaming-protests-in-ferguson/.

36 Scott Eric Kaufman, "Fox News' Elisabeth Hasselbeck Justifies Sandra Bland Arrest: She Could Have Used Cigarette as Weapon," *Salon*, July 27, 2015, http://www.salon.com/2015/07/27/fox_news_elisabeth_hasselbeck_justifies_sandra_blands_arrest_she_could_have_used_cigarette_as_a_weapon/.

37 Bennett, Lawrence, and Livingston, *When the Press Fails*, 76–77.

38 *The Five*, "Tensions Running High as Curfew Looms in Baltimore," Fox News video, 8:42, April 28, 2015, http://www.foxnews.com/transcript/2015/04/28/tensions-running-high-as-curfew-looms-in-baltimore/.

39 Sheena Howard, "Sheena Howard: Dear MSNBC, Let's Talk about this 'Mom of the Year' Narrative and Police Brutality," *The Trentonian*, April 28, 2015, http://www.trentonian.com/opinion/20150428/sheena-howard-dear-msnbc-lets-talk-about-this-mom-of-the-year-narrative-and-police-brutality.

40 *Politics Nation*, MSNBC.com, April 28, 2015, http://www.nbcnews.com/id/57309975/ns/msnbc-politicsnation/#.VXRaEVxViko.

41 *The Ed Show*, "Protester: 'Why Does it Take a Catastrophe,'" MSNBC.com video, 1:11. April 28, 2015. http://www.msnbc.com/thomas-roberts/watch/protester—why-does-it-take-a-catastrophe—436363843830.

42 Joanna Rothkopf, "CNN Guest Slams Media for Saying Protesters are 'Thugs': 'Just Call Them N***ers,'" *Salon*, April 29, 2015, http://www.salon.com/2015/04/29/baltimore_councilman_slams_media_use_of_thugs_for_protesters_just_call_them_nggers/.

43 Dylan Byers, "Bernie Sanders 'Disappointed' in Ed Schultz Cancellation," *Politico*, July 23, 2015 http://www.politico.com/blogs/media/2015/07/bernie-sanders-disappointed-in-ed-schultz-cancellation-211128.html.

44 Eric Wemple, "Ouch: MSNBC Barely Registers in Media Study," *Washington Post*, June 10, 2014 https://www.washingtonpost.com/blogs/erik-wemple/wp/2014/06/10/ouch-msnbc-barely-registers-in-media-study/.

3

FAKE NEWS AND POLITICAL SATIRE

In the previous chapters, we considered the role of news and advertising in shaping political culture. Specifically, the news chapter focused on the branding practices of cable news channels and their role in constructing political authority—of determining not just what counts as news but also who should be consulted as an expert on pertinent social, political, and economic issues. This chapter examines the role of so-called fake news shows in challenging these claims to authority. By mocking the tropes of political news, especially as it has evolved in the post-network era, fake news shows have played a vital role in equipping audiences to engage with the news in a more critical fashion. In fact, by so relentlessly mocking many of these techniques, fake news shows such as *The Daily Show* and *The Colbert Report* made it difficult to take traditional news at face value. While these shows have often been analyzed correctly as brilliant examples of media analysis that make use of what Jonathan Gray has called "critical intertextuality" to challenge political authority, it is also worthwhile to consider them as a product of a specific historical moment. Jon Stewart's tenure at *The Daily Show* began in the late 1990s, when cable news was becoming an increasingly dominant force within the political media culture, while Stewart himself became a vital media critic at the height of the Bush administration when it was using the political media, particularly Fox News, to prop up its case for war in Iraq. Meanwhile, Stewart's late-night counterpart, Stephen Colbert, mercilessly satirized the "truthiness" found on many primetime political pundit shows, the reliance on belief rather than factual information as a gauge of truth. In both cases, elements of the shows, including set design, graphics, and even the construction of segments replicate the techniques common to able news shows, especially the Fox News shows *The O'Reilly Factor* and *Hannity*. In this context, I am writing this chapter in a moment of profound transition in the genre of fake news as Colbert and Stewart's departures from the late-night Comedy Central lineup have upended what had been a remarkably stable and consistent genre that reliably both challenged and participated in the culture of political media. Thus, in many ways this chapter serves as a historical account of fake news with the goal of contextualizing Stewart and Colbert's shows in a longer narrative of fake news shows and of thinking about how this genre can serve as a flexible format for challenging political authority as it evolves over time.

The Comedy Central fake news block has been celebrated as a kind of antidote to the failures of political news. In particular, the Stewart–Colbert lineup was touted for its ability to engage youth audiences who otherwise were characterized as being turned off by politics. More crucially, watching fake news ironically seemed aligned with political knowledge. In other words, people who watched shows such as *The Daily Show* and *The Colbert Report* almost invariably were more prepared to answer basic current events questions correctly than people who watched other kinds of news programming. Unlike political news shows, Comedy Central's formidable late-night lineup appealed to a comparatively younger audience. In fact, according to a 2015 Pew Research Center study, the median age for a *Daily Show* viewer was 36, while the median age for *The Colbert Report* was 33. By comparison, viewers of CNN's *Anderson Cooper 360* had a median age of 47, while viewers of *The Rachel Maddow Show* and *The O'Reilly Factor* had median ages of 53 and 54, respectively.[1] Notably, surveys also have revealed that *The Daily Show*, in particular, has gained a reputation for being a reliable news source. In fact, a 2007 Pew study found that 47 percent of the content on *The Daily Show* was dedicated to political content, a number that was comparable to cable news shows, while *Time Magazine* famously declared that Jon Stewart was the "most trusted" news anchor on American television.[2] Later, in 2012, viewers of *The Daily Show* performed significantly better on a basic news quiz than people who watched any of the three cable news channels or listened to right-wing commentator Rush Limbaugh's radio show. These numbers should not indicate that audiences for fake news were getting their political news solely from Jon Stewart or Stephen Colbert. In fact, many of the show's jokes would not likely generate laughs for viewers who were unaware of the references they were making. Instead, fake news provided viewers with a wide range of viewing strategies that could enable them to make sense of stories that may have been somewhat arcane and complex. In particular, Stewart and Colbert were incredibly adept at mocking the ways in which powerful people and institutions use the media to reinforce power, providing viewers with what Jeffrey P. Jones has called a "citizen surrogate," who can channel all of the outrage and frustration that viewers might feel about the political media culture. When confronted with examples of deceptive or faulty reporting, Stewart's righteous indignation and Colbert's unflappable mockery provide us with a source of pleasure, media figures who have earned our trust.[3] Finally, these shows benefited significantly from the fact that Comedy Central proved remarkably flexible in allowing viewers to share or embed clips on blogs and social media websites, a strategy that not only allowed viewers to catch the show (or segments from it) on their own schedule but also enabled the shows to more readily enter into cultural and political conversations, as media critics were able to cite the shows as insightful, and often very funny, forms of media analysis.

FAKE NEWS AND INTERTEXTUALITY

By satirizing cable news discourse, in part by embodying it, fake news shows were able to make use of a technique that Jonathan Gray has called "critical intertextuality."[4] The concept of intertextuality refers to the idea that texts of whatever medium constantly refer to, depict, or make use of other texts. Drawing from the Russian literary critic Mikhail Bakhtin, Gray argues that "texts are always talking to each other . . . and any new text as utterance will find its meaning only by adding its voice to the already-existent dialogue."[5] This dialogue can entail references to older texts, that is, remakes or retellings of older versions of the same story. Or it can entail stars who appear across multiple films or TV shows or directors whose past work may have a distinct style. Thus, a viewer might interpret a show made by *Grey's Anatomy* or *Scandal* producer Shonda Rhimes based on aspects of her previous work. Or they might enjoy a *Simpsons* episode based on its parody of domestic comedies such as *The Flintstones* and *The Honeymooners*. As these examples suggest, making sense of a television show then involves a more active form of reading, as we view a text in light of previous episodes of that show, or even other TV shows or movies.[6] In this sense, intertextuality provides a powerful means for viewers to "work through" the raw material of the news, even while in some cases, becoming part of the larger news narrative that was being criticized. As Gray notes, these intertextual strategies can produce promotional or officially sanctioned readings, or in some cases they can produce readings that challenge the original text. Thus, a fake news show such as *The Daily Show* might take a clip from Fox News that is meant to criticize Hillary Clinton, but instead of endorsing that reading, Stewart could, instead, show how the clip uses faulty evidence, overblown rhetoric, or emotional language. Political comedy, especially the fake news shows that engage so readily with the news stories of the previous day, provides a powerful example of this form of critical intertextuality, allowing viewers to develop strategies for reading the news.

FAKE NEWS AND POLITICAL CYNICISM

The role of fake news within a wider political culture has been contested not only within the news media itself but also within media studies scholarship. One of the more significant strains of scholarship on fake news has been whether or not these shows have an effect on their audience, as measured by behaviors such as viewers' attitudes towards politics or their likelihood of voting or by whether or not fake news shows make people more or less informed about politics. Perhaps the most frequent criticism of *The Daily Show* was the belief that it contributed to an increasing cynicism among younger voters, making them less likely to vote or to engage in other forms of political activity. For example, a study by Jody Baumgartner and Jonathan S. Morris claimed to identify a "*Daily Show* effect," in which they found that their subjects viewed candidates for office more negatively after watching the show.[7] Others, such as Roderick Hart and Johanna Hartelius, claim that the show's primary function is to tutor younger audiences in the "language" of cynicism.[8] However, Stewart's critique of political discourse is born out of what appears to be a sincere desire for a better political system. As Jeffrey P. Jones explains it, "The Daily Show is nothing if not a nightly criticism of discourses of power and an attack on the complicity of news media in constructing and circulating such discourses."[9] Thus, one of the continual tasks of The Daily Show has been to point out the ways in which the news media—particularly cable news—have failed in their engagement with and analysis of power and functions instead to highlight these limitations in order to encourage more transparent political dialogue. Similarly, as Amber Day explains, fake news "enables and articulates a critique of the inadequacies of contemporary political discourse, while demonstrating an engaged commitment to the possibility of a more honest public debate."[10] The show frequently offers lessons in rhetorical analysis, pointing out the ways in which news channels repeatedly fail in their role as government and corporate watchdogs. Stewart's cynicism can therefore be seen as a logical response to a wider political culture characterized by a deeply cynical engagement with its citizens.

A more convincing objection is that fake news shows are both economically and ideologically complicit with the discourse they criticize. While fake news shows have engaged in powerful forms of political parody, these shows are essentially dependent upon the excesses of political media they criticize. Baffler writer Steve Almond, for example, argues that Jon Stewart plays the role of a "humble populist" fighting against a political elite even while taking home a multimillion-dollar check from Viacom, one of the largest entertainment companies on the planet. Almond even goes as far as suggesting that Stewart and Colbert, through their comedic attacks on political discourse, might have dissipated energies that would have been better directed at more visible forms of opposition, such as public protests.[11] However, Almond's arguments reinforce the perception that watching political satire shows precludes any other form of activity. In fact, people who consume fake news are far more likely to engage in other forms of political activism.

FAKE NEWS IN THE NETWORK AND MULTICHANNEL ERAS

Although Comedy Central's late-night political comedy block has been the most memorable and enduring version of fake news, there are a number of important precedents that helped to define the genre. One important precedent was the work of the guerilla filmmaking collective, Top Value Television (TVTV), a San Francisco-based group that embraced cheap, portable video technology to produce a number of "do-it-yourself" videos, several of which sought to mock the political spectacle, often by using deliberately crude effects such as abrupt cuts, hand-drawn titles, and natural lighting. The two most significant examples of this were their video productions that documented the 1972 Republican and Democratic conventions, *Four More Years* and *The World's Largest TV Studio*. Both videos focused less on the spectacle that was elaborately staged by the political parties for the consumption of TV audiences watching at home than on the production of that spectacle by the producers and workers who helped to manufacture it. *The World's Largest Studio*, for example, devoted scenes to workers building the stage and preparing the Miami arena where the convention would take place. More crucially, the videos illustrated how the reporters themselves were complicit with producing the spectacle, rather than criticizing it. In *The World's Largest TV Studio*, for example, Dan Rather gleefully explains that for a reporter, attending a convention "is like being a kid in a candy store." Meanwhile, in *Four More Years*, reporters are unwilling to criticize the staging of the convention, acknowledging that the affair is completely "packaged" but that as a news network, they have a "responsibility" to cover it. *Four More Years* also called attention to the limitations of network-era journalism that placed emphasis on objectivity and balance. When asked about his view of journalism that might support a specific point of view, one CBS reporter immediately demurs, saying, "I'm not a fan of advocacy journalism. I'm here to tell what happens." Thus, TVTV helped to establish some of the conventions of fake news, most notably a critique of the real news of its era, in this case, the objective network-era news that helped to reinforce the political spectacle. TVTV also cultivated some of the guerilla techniques that Michael Moore, The Yes Men, and others would use to remarkable effect. In addition, the videos also helped to illustrate how fake news could satirize the news through mocking its techniques for manufacturing narratives about politics.

More recent models for the fake news genre include two shows by documentary raconteur Michael Moore, who produced two magazine-style comedic news shows, *TV Nation* (1994–1995), which originally aired on

NBC before being picked up by Fox, and *The Awful Truth* (1999–2000), which appeared on the cable channel Bravo. Moore, best known at the time for his agitprop documentary *Roger and Me*, used a comedic news magazine style to cover stories that were not receiving attention from the commercial media. The news magazine style evoked syndicated soft news shows such as *A Current Affair*, *Inside Edition*, and *Hard Copy* that arose as cheap infotainment programming during the multichannel era. Moore's show featured segments hosted by younger comedians, including Karen Duffy and Janeane Garofalo, and many segments focused on issues such as income inequality and corporate crime. In one episode, for example, Moore challenged CEOs to go to one of their factories and make or use one of the products created by their company, a guerilla technique in which the filmmaker sought to catch powerful people off guard. Another segment featured Moore visiting Cobb County, Georgia, home of House Speaker Newt Gingrich, who had campaigned on cutting taxes. Moore, however, highlighted Gingrich's skill at passing pork-barrel legislation that would bring back federal money to his district. Moore did this by vainly attempting to wave cars off of a taxpayer-subsidized highway and by trying to close down schools and a senior center that had also received federal funds. Perhaps the most inspired stunt on *TV Nation* was Crackers the Corporate Crime Fighting Chicken, a costumed mascot who was introduced as a parody of McGruff the Crime Dog, to call attention to corporate crime. In his first appearance, Crackers confronted New York Mayor Rudy Giuliani over tax breaks the city gave to First Boston Bank, even after the company had moved its offices out of New York. Later, Crackers visited a suburb of St. Louis where he shed light on a battery factory that may have been improperly disposing of toxic materials that were then seeping into drinking water.

Although *TV Nation* achieved respectable ratings and critical acclaim, even winning an Emmy Award for outstanding informational programming in 1995, the show was moved from NBC to the Fox Network before it was quietly cancelled. However, its most lasting effect may be its role as a precursor for *The Daily Show*, which was launched on Comedy Central with host Craig Kilborn. Like *TV Nation*, early episodes of *The Daily Show* made extensive use of satirical field reports in which "correspondents" would seek out guests who were engaging in absurd behaviors. Although the show's first few seasons under Kilborn tended more toward apolitical absurdist comedy,

The *Daily Show* readily adopted *TV Nation's* skillful parody of the news magazine format. More crucially, it helped to foster the recognition of humor's
pedagogical power, its ability to help disrupt social and political discourses
that viewers might take for granted. Moore's show proved to be too subversive for broadcast television, especially for networks such as NBC and Fox
that were dependent on high ratings and on programming that would not
risk alienating sponsors; however, his influence on future fake news shows
is undeniable. As Jeffrey P. Jones points out, Moore's use of "the news-
magazine format gave license to engage in investigative reporting, while the
fake gave license to satire it."[12] While Moore's shows provided a valuable
service in critiquing the conservative revolution led by Newt Gingrich and
other House Republicans, his most vital role was to map out some of the
potentials associated with fake news.

REAL TIME WITH BILL MAHER

While Michael Moore adopted the news magazine format to challenge political norms, Bill Maher reworked the political panel show to challenge the
authority of public affairs shows such as *Meet the Press* or *The McLaughlin Group*.
Maher's original show actually premiered on Comedy Central, but he was
eventually hired as a late-night host for ABC as an attempt to counterpro-
gram late-night talk shows such as *The Tonight Show* and *The Late Show with David
Letterman*. Maher's ABC show lasted for several seasons until he made unpopular remarks less than a week after the September 11 terrorist attacks, in
which he sought to counter a popular narrative about the hijackers who flew
planes into the World Trade Center, claiming that they had not been "cow-
ards." Although Maher was not defending the hijackers, his show, *Politically
Incorrect*, quickly became the target of boycotts by a number of influential
groups, resulting in the show getting cancelled. Notably, Maher was actually
responding to—and reinforcing—comments by conservative cultural critic
Dinesh D'Souza, while Arianna Huffington can also be seen in the background
agreeing with Maher's claims. The comments were incorrectly interpreted as
an attack on the bravery of U.S. soldiers, and Maher sought to clarify that
the "we" he was describing was, in fact, alluding to the U.S. military policy.
Maher eventually relaunched his show on HBO in 2003, renaming it *Real Time*

with *Bill Maher*. Appearing on HBO gave Maher additional freedom to present positions that were not necessarily popular in the political mainstream and provided HBO with a culturally relevant and engaging show.

Maher's HBO show also permitted Maher to become more recognized as a significant political observer, allowing him to bring on more prominent guests, including actors, musicians, authors, and politicians. *Real Time with Bill Maher* typically features three primary segments: an opening monologue that follows the format of late-night talk shows, a panel of four guests who discuss the week's news stories using a comedic lens, and a final segment known as "New Rules," in which Maher engages in a political rant, offering unofficial "rules" for political discourse. As Jeffrey P. Jones has noted, Maher's HBO show has given him "an uncensored political stage" where he can satirize the representatives of political authority.[13]

The central feature of all of Maher's shows has been the panel. Maher has typically sought to include a diversity of voices from both the worlds of politics and popular culture in order to generate humorous, but thoughtful political discussions about current issues. The panel often served as a device for making sense of Washington's political culture, of using dialogue to sort out explanations for why American voters seemed to vote in ways that were against their financial or personal interests. In this sense, the show serves as an important example of what Jones has called the use of a "common sense vernacular" to make sense of a wider political culture.[14] For example, immediately after the 2014 midterm elections, Maher bluntly sought to remind his viewers that elections have consequences. Focusing on the issue of climate change, Maher connected a scientific report that further emphasized the link between human activity and increasing carbon concentrations in the atmosphere and the related problem of rising sea levels. He went on to cite a range of quotations from climate change deniers who had been elected to Congress. For example, Iowa Senator Joni Ernst reinforced the idea that there was still scientific debate about the causes of climate change, stating, "I have not seen proven proof that it is entirely man-made . . . . I don't know the science behind climate change. I've heard arguments from both sides." Similarly, Alaska Senator Dan Sullivan claimed, "The jury is still out on climate change." While Maher initially reads this as an example of the stupidity of the American voters—and of the people who have been elected to represent them—Vermont Senator Bernie Sanders quickly challenges this frame, stating that the elected officials are not dumb. Instead, he notes that making statements against climate change are in the interests of politicians who receive large donations from individuals and organizations that benefit from lax environmental regulations: "They get huge sums of money from the Koch brothers and the fossil fuel industry and they are not going to stand up to the people who contribute to their campaigns." Thus, although Maher starts the discussion with one assumption about political behavior, other guests on the show could complicate the argument and add additional context.

Maher was also attentive to the harmful effects of certain forms of political discourse, especially when that language might be used to support policies that would limit personal freedoms and opportunities, especially for his youthful audience. This focus became explicit during the 2014 Congressional elections when Maher sponsored a contest to "Flip a District." In this contest, Maher invited fans of the show to nominate their representative to become the target of a weekly negative campaign on *Real Time*. Maher would also visit the district to campaign against the "winner" of the contest. Maher eventually created a bracket of 16 nominees, allowing his audience to help choose the district that would hopefully get flipped. The eventual target of Maher's campaign was Wisconsin Representative John Kline, who was largely chosen because of his position on the House Committee on Education and the Workforce.[15] Maher's contest was read by the political press primarily as an attempt to change the result of one district, presumably with the hope of making Congress more progressive or Democratic, with one *Politico* reporter gloating when Maher was unable to change the outcome of the race.[16] However, instead of reading Maher's playful meddling as an attempt to defeat an incumbent candidate, his actions should instead be understood as pedagogical, as an attempt to raise awareness about political issues—such as student loan debt and women's issues—that the host wished to address in a more public forum.

In fact, Maher repeatedly couched his participation in the "Flip a District" campaign in entirely oppositional terms, explaining that he would not be endorsing a candidate, and adding playfully, "our purpose—and our attitude—is completely negative." From one perspective, this statement might be read as just another example of a political comedian fostering more cynicism towards Washington politics. However, Maher's involvement in the "Flip a District" campaign was, in fact, much more complicated. First, endorsing a candidate via his late-night talk show would have put him at risk of violating campaign finance law for illegal coordination. But Maher also hoped to use his platform to bring awareness to important issues. The contest also helped to "nationalize" the issue of Congressional elections by illustrating that the policies and legislation supported by one locally elected official could have an effect nationwide.

Finally, rather than focus on someone who could be an easy punch line, Maher chose instead to emphasize a politician whose blandness made him even more dangerous and powerful and therefore a more harmful participant in a "dysfunctional" political system. The campaign against Kline highlighted his support for predatory for-profit colleges, which, Maher joked, have a dropout rate "worse than celebrity rehab."[17] The high dropout rate, combined with the incredibly high interest rates on many student loans, left many poor and non-traditional students with massive, crippling debt and little education to show for it. Thus, although the "Flip a District" contest was widely read by political pundits as a "failure" because the incumbent won, its larger pedagogical purpose was far more important because it helped to bring greater scrutiny to the for-profit diploma mills, a topic that Maher's HBO colleague John Oliver also addressed in one of his comedic investigative reports. While Maher couched the contest in purely negative terms, his actions showed a keen awareness of how the political system operates and how it can work against the interests of voters, in large part because it protects incumbents from facing competitive races. By further nationalizing a number of Congressional races, Maher was able to remind viewers of how candidates in other political races could still exercise influence on our daily lives.

POINTING OUT THE ARTIFICE: *THE DAILY SHOW WITH JON STEWART*

The most pivotal and influential fake news show has been *The Daily Show with Jon Stewart*. While *The Daily Show* was often blamed for exacerbating political cynicism, Stewart's position as a cultural critic was grounded in a sincere set of expectations about what the political media should be doing.

Instead of merely dismissing politics as a source of mockery, The Daily Show helped to illustrate how the political media could foster a more vibrant critique or examination of political institutions in order to ensure they would better serve the needs of the public. As Stewart explained during the final episode of his show, he saw the show's mission as helping viewers to detect the "bullshit" that is being used to manipulate or mislead the public. Explaining that "bullshit is everywhere," Stewart went on to discuss the ways in which political and corporate leaders could deceive people using a variety of rhetorical strategies, including complex language, false controversy, and other techniques. At the same time, The Daily Show's use of parody provided audiences with a series of critical reading strategies that served a larger pedagogical purpose. In much the same way that Bill Maher taught audiences to think about political discussion differently, Jon Stewart worked to undermine the discursive practices that propped up political authority. Like Michael Moore's shows, The Daily Show began as a parody of overblown news magazine shows that were associated with the derogatory label "infotainment," wedding that with the late-night talk show genre to create an irreverent, if somewhat apolitical commentary show. When Jon Stewart took over in 1999, the show became increasingly dedicated to politics, a focus that became even more explicit during the chaos of the 2000 election, in which the winner was not declared until several weeks after election day, an incident that made the show's "Indecision 2000" coverage seem all the more prescient. As a result, the show seemed to transition from a parody of news magazine shows into a satire of cable news programming.

Most episodes follow a deceptively simplistic structure that weds the tropes of nightly newscasts with the format of a late-night talk show to create a hybrid format that serves to parody the failures of political discourse, especially as politics is represented through cable news. In fact, the show's humor depends heavily on contextual references that serious fans of the show are much more likely to recognize. Because Stewart's show has been so widely analyzed, I will highlight a small number of tactics that Stewart used to promote his form of media criticism. First, Stewart used the gag "Chaos on Bullshit Mountain" as a device for repeatedly highlighting the ways in which Fox News perpetuated false narratives about national politics. Other long-running segments included Jon Stewart's incisive satire of the Bush administration's promotion of the wars in Iraq and Afghanistan, *Mess O'Potamia*. Finally, *The Daily Show* mocked the pretentions of cable news punditry through the use of artificially inflated titles, including senior black correspondent, usually played by Larry Wilmore, or senior women's correspondent, Samantha Bee, in order to parody the assumption that a single person can speak for an entire demographic group of people.

Many of the show's techniques for criticizing Fox News were exemplified in a series of segments in which Stewart referred to Fox News and the Republican spin machine as "Bullshit Mountain." The first mention of Bullshit Mountain took place on August 19, 2012, as Stewart responded to Fox News's attempts at damage control after a surreptitiously recorded video showed Mitt Romney describing 47 percent of the U.S. population as dependent on the government. Stewart frames the segment by describing Fox News as "Romney campaign headquarters" before outlining three strategies the network used to control the response. First, he uses a montage to show Fox News hosts tried to dismiss the video by pointing out that it was posted on a left-wing website and that the video had been discovered by a Democratic activist. Stewart characterizes this technique as "attacking the messenger," a move that allowed them to avoid engaging with the content of the video. Second, he uses another montage to illustrate how several

Figure 3.1 Jon Stewart attacks Fox News on *The Daily Show*

Fox hosts tried to re-interpret Romney's comments. Finally, he quotes several pundits who actually defended the 47 percent formulation, with Sean Hannity, among others, asserting that Romney was telling the truth.

Stewart then "drills deeper" into the "bullshit" Fox News promoted, quoting a segment from *Hannity*, which suggested that 49 percent of U.S. citizens lived in households that received what Hannity referred to as a "handout," adding that this was the percentage of the public that Obama was "enabling." By highlighting this language, Stewart shows how Hannity is engaging in the process of scapegoating and in the deceptive use of data, pointing out that the statistic included people on Social Security and Medicare. Stewart then reminds his audience that a number of corporations, including Exxon Mobil, AT&T, and General Electric, had received tax breaks and government subsidies totaling in the billions of dollars. Thus, in the course of a single segment, Stewart was able to depict multiple strategies that Fox News had used to try to spin Romney's unfiltered comments.

But even while Stewart mercilessly mocked Fox News's unapologetic partisanship, he reserved much of his outrage for CNN, in no small part because CNN arguably could have occupied the role of an objective and engaging news source. Instead, Stewart grew frustrated by CNN's practice of blowing dramatic stories out of proportion, while ignoring other, more pertinent concerns, as when he mocked CNN's non-stop coverage of the disappearance of Malaysian Airlines flight 370. During one segment, Stewart opened by playing a clip of CNN anchor Anderson Cooper soberly describing the flight's disappearance before showing a number of increasingly absurd clips of CNN anchors using unnecessary graphics to depict the airplane and the course it followed. From there, he showed clips of commentators offering increasingly absurd theories for why the plane had disappeared, many of them taken from social media, most notably Don Lemon, who asks at one point whether the plane might have been swallowed by a black hole, a version of the Bermuda Triangle, or even, most inexplicably, that the fantasy show *Lost* had somehow become real. These clips required little commentary, but Stewart also made a point to note that CNN's ratings actually doubled due to their coverage of the missing plane, an observation that showed how ratings were driving CNN's decisions about what stories to cover, whether they were relevant or not.

He also attacked the news network for substituting dramatic visuals—holograms of reporters, digital graphics of virtual Iowa voters, and splashy maps—for genuine reporting. Finally, Stewart also criticized individual hosts, such as Tucker Carlson, Rick Sanchez, or Don Lemon, whom he saw as deflating or dumbing down political news reporting. In particular, Stewart blasted Lemon for his tendency to sensationalize, as he did in a January 27, 2014 segment that showed a live report on a snowstorm in which Lemon drove around the streets of Manhattan from what he called the Blizzard Mobile, with Stewart retorting, "Settle down, Batman, it's a Ford Explorer." Although other cable networks sometimes relied on sensationalized news coverage, Stewart often singled out CNN for its desperate attempts to hype what amounted to a non-story with the result that Lemon himself became the story.

THE DAILY SHOW INTERVIEWS: DELIBERATION, ACCOUNTABILITY, CRITIQUE

The final segment of *The Daily Show* typically consisted of an interview with a guest. Like most late-night shows, Stewart often interviewed celebrities promoting a new movie or TV show; however, he also frequently provided a forum for journalists, politicians, and authors. Notably, *The Daily Show* also addressed the time constraints associated with the broadcast television schedule by taping extended interviews with certain guests that could then be posted to the show's website. In fact, these extended interviews often dive deep into policy details and political philosophy, even without any clear commercial purpose, by encouraging viewers to continue to engage with the show online.[18] For the most part, interview segments are often treated as a "natural" or transparent part of a late-night show; however, Geoffrey Baym argues that Stewart's interview style deserves special attention, in part because of Stewart's effort to use his interviews in order to "enact a more deliberative model of political exchange," one that is aligned with the values of civility and conversation, even when Stewart disagrees with his guest.[19] These values of civility are often grounded in Stewart's implicit desire that media and government institutions fulfill their responsibilities.

Stewart's interview with CNBC host Jim Cramer after the financial melt-down of 2008 is a powerful example of this form of institutional critique. Stewart saw the interview as a means of obtaining some form of account-ability from Cramer, who had made a number of investment recom-mendations of companies that were making risky investments. During the segment, Stewart openly criticized Cramer's profession, pointing out that it helped intensify false expectations about get-rich-quick stock market schemes. In defending himself, Cramer pointed to the audience for CNBC and explained that there was a market for shows that hyped stocks, to which Stewart angrily responded, "There's a market for cocaine and hookers, too." Although Stewart's comment was admittedly harsh, it also illustrated Stewart's belief in accountability and his concern that financial news shows could serve to exploit casual investors who couldn't afford to lose money in the marketplace.

Similarly, on April 29, 2015, Stewart interviewed disgraced *New York Times* journalist Judith Miller, who had been widely blamed for publishing articles that helped the Bush administration to make the case that Saddam Hussein had weapons of mass destruction, reporting that helped to justify the Iraq War. At the beginning of the interview, Stewart politely acknowledges that he blames Miller, in part, for enabling "the most devastating foreign policy mistake we've made in, like, 100 years." The colloquial tone mollifies the adversarial stance that Stewart takes towards Miller. Throughout the inter-view he goes on to counter many of her attempts to defend her reporting, particularly her assertion that many other reporters and politicians on both sides of the aisle had been fooled:

Miller: It took persuading, and they persuaded a lot of Democrats—Hillary Clinton, John Kerry. The intelligence was what it was.

Stewart: Turns out, idiocy is bipartisan, but that's not exculpatory that it captured Democrats and Republicans.

Miller: The intelligence was what it was. People like me didn't make it up.

Stewart: No but the intelligence was not what it was and not everyone got it wrong.

Although Stewart adopted an adversarial tone throughout much of the interview, he concluded with something closer to a somber acknowledgement that critics of the war likely would never get a satisfactory explanation for the factors that led to war: "These discussions always make me incredibly sad because they point to institutional failure at the highest levels and no one will take responsibility for them." Thus, in much the same way that Stewart used adversarial techniques to frame a critique of harmful economic reporting, he used similar methods to serve as an institutional critique of the news media's failures in reporting on the evidence used to justify the war in Iraq.

Although most media critics identify Stewart as progressive, he was also willing to confront Democrats whom he perceived to be responsible for failing in their responsibilities. One of Stewart's most focused adversarial interviews was with Kathleen Sebelius, the secretary of health and human services under Barack Obama, and the public figure most responsible for the rollout of the website for the Affordable Care Act (ACA), colloquially known as Obamacare. During the interview, Stewart demonstrates many of the website's glitches that initially made signing up for Obamacare unnecessarily difficult. He also repeatedly addressed a logical inconsistency within the legislation that allowed businesses to request a one-year delay in signing up, while individuals who requested a similar delay would have to pay a fine, a question that Sebelius persistently avoided. The interview with Sebelius, therefore, was consistent with similar interviews by Stewart of a wide range of public figures, whether politicians or media personalities, in which Stewart would seek accountability for the broader institutional failures that led to the Iraq War, economic collapse, and the glitchy rollout of the ACA. As a result, Stewart's interviews, like the rest of his show, could serve as an important device for questioning political authority.

THE COLBERT REPORT

Like *The Daily Show, The Colbert Report* used the fake news genre to offer an institutional critique of the abuses of political power. Debuting in October 2005, just a few months after George W. Bush had been re-elected president, the show featured Stephen Colbert as a pompous, and often poorly informed, conservative news anchor who satirized Fox News pundits such as Bill O'Reilly and Sean Hannity. Thus, the show explicitly functioned as a form of satire, one that requires at least some familiarity with the genre of political punditry. Like other fake news programs, *The Colbert Report* typically consisted of two segments that featured commentary on the day's headlines followed by an interview. Through his character, Colbert sought to personify the excesses of political punditry as a way of undermining it. As Colbert himself said in an interview for *Slate*, "I embody the bullshit."[20] That is, instead of simply calling attention to institutional, political, and media failures, Colbert used his character to satirize the excesses of the political media to their logical limits. Like most satire, Colbert's performances had a pedagogical purpose, most frequently by pointing to the ways in which the institutional, legal, and informational aspects of the political news media were serving us poorly.

"THE WØRD"

One of Colbert's most densely satirical segments was "The Wørd," which featured the host offering a commentary on a specific topic—built around a word or phrase—while satirical bullet points were projected on a screen. The segment was designed to parody Bill O'Reilly's nightly "Talking Points Memo" commentary, in which he would pontificate about an issue. These segments, especially in early seasons of the show, would serve as an ironic counterpoint to truth claims, especially when those claims are based on popular opinion or emotion rather than some larger truth. As a result, "The Wørd's" sidebar comments performed the work of undermining the authoritative tone taken by political pundits like Colbert by calling attention to how their truth claims are constructed. For example, during the July 31, 2006 episode of the show, Colbert introduced the concept of Wikiality, a mashup of the terms Wikipedia and reality. The term was built around the core principle of the online encyclopedia Wikipedia, which anyone can edit. The show's sly intertextuality and its commentary on the truth were established from the beginning. As the sequence opens, Colbert addresses the camera, stating, "I'm no fan of reality," while a graphic on the other side of the screen reads, "It has a liberal bias," a phrasing that echoes a popular remark from Colbert's 2006 speech at the White House Correspondents Dinner. Colbert then launches into a tongue-in-cheek attack on traditional encyclopedias that might contain uncomfortable truths about America's history, asking rhetorically, "Who is Britannica to say that George Washington had slaves? If I want to say he didn't, that's my right." Colbert deliberately blurs the distinction between free speech rights and concerns about the validity of truth claims, dramatizing the ways in which partisan cable news outlets have used free speech rights as a protection against criticism. From there, Colbert explains his (again ironic) admiration of Wikipedia, initially joking about its excessive attention to trivialities, by pointing out they had a longer entry on him than on Lutheranism, but more pertinently on the fact that "anyone" can edit a Wikipedia entry. Colbert then proposes the idea that he could work to convince the public that the African elephant population is increasing—a claim that is distinctly untrue—and if enough people support the idea, then it would become true and "would be a real blow to the environmentalists." This time, Colbert's comments are accompanied by the phrase "An Inconvenient Tusk," a pun on the recently released environmental documentary *An Inconvenient Truth*, featuring former Vice President Al Gore, which had been widely credited with revitalizing conversations about and activism around the issue of climate change but had also been attacked repeatedly in the conservative media. As his framing of "Wikiality" suggests, Colbert is not specifically criticizing Wikipedia's editorial policies as much as he is using the website as a metaphor for describing the ways in which an idea's popularity is a measure of its truthfulness and the politicization of knowledge, in which personal beliefs supplant existing scientific information.

This satirical critique of politicizing knowledge becomes even more forceful when Colbert "compliments" the Bush administration's information management for its ability to create confusion about whether Iraqi dictator Saddam Hussein had weapons of mass destruction (WMDs). Noting that the number of people who believed that Hussein had WMDs grew from 38 percent of the population in 2003 to over 50 percent in 2006, Colbert remarks that Bush has succeeded in "bringing democracy to knowledge," with the message in the sidebar dryly adding, again in an echo of a notorious Bush administration phrase, "definitions will greet us as liberators." Although Colbert's "Wikiality" treatise has received less attention than his similar neologism, "truthiness," it was equally crucial in helping to articulate both the Colbert character and the show's complex engagement

Figure 3.2 Stephen Colbert's "The Word" segment on *The Colbert Report*

with how truth is constructed. Subtle intertextual references, many of them displayed in sidebar messages, provide the political, social, and cultural contexts that give specificity to Colbert's broader claims about the use of popularity as a criterion for measuring the validity of a factual statement. Thus, in much the same way that Jon Stewart called attention to the failures of cable news in informing the public, Colbert calls attention to the media culture that allows that to happen.

COLBERT SUPER PAC

Although *The Colbert Report* is most frequently celebrated for its satire of political punditry, the show also served to inform audiences about political issues. One of the more powerful examples of this pedagogical function was Colbert's series of episodes on campaign financing, which featured Trevor Potter, a former chairman of the Federal Elections Committee and General Counsel for the 2008 John McCain presidential campaign. The series served to educate audiences on the ways in which the 2010 Supreme Court case,

Citizens United vs. the Federal Elections Commission, opened up the floodgates for unlimited corporate donations to political campaigns. The episodes familiarized viewers with the concepts of PACs (political action committees) and Super PACs, while also demonstrating how the lack of regulations governing campaign donations could ultimately poison the political process by allowing unfettered election spending. Colbert did this by creating his own Super PAC, Americans for a Better Tomorrow, Tomorrow (ABTT), and by interviewing Potter about what he could (and couldn't) do with it.

Colbert's satirical analysis of campaign financing began during an episode on March 30, 2011, during the Republican primaries for the 2012 Presidential election, when Colbert expresses a desire to get a PAC. Potter eagerly explains the benefits of starting a PAC, noting that individuals are limited in terms of how much they can donate directly to a campaign, but by creating a PAC, groups who have shared interests can pool their money to back a candidate. He adds that PACs cannot coordinate directly with the campaigns they support, so that "even if they don't want you to do ads, you can't ask them." Potter then helps Colbert to fill out the paperwork, which consists of just a couple of pages, a detail that illustrates how easy it is to form a PAC. Just a few weeks later, Colbert and Potter addressed concerns from lawyers for Comedy Central's parent company, Viacom, that worried they would be making what is called an in-kind contribution to Colbert's PAC by providing him with airtime for his show and by paying the staff that produces Colbert's show, news that prompts Colbert to pretend to shred his PAC forms. Potter then informs him that he can create a Super PAC—"a PAC that got eaten by a radioactive lobbyist," Colbert jokes—which would allow a corporation to spend unlimited money and resources. Colbert then refills the form and Potter explains that the FEC hasn't created a new Super PAC form, so he provides him with a standard, one-page cover letter. When he learns that there are no restrictions on how much he can raise, Colbert punctuates the point, saying, "Unlimited amounts? Oh, I like the sound of that." Throughout this process, Colbert was, in fact, receiving donations, although he made no clear statement on how the money would be used.

In September 2011, Colbert took his satirical lesson in campaign financing a step further when he created a shell corporation, which could funnel money into ABTT. By creating the shell corporation, donors who wished to remain anonymous could give money to the corporation, which would, in turn, donate the money to the Super PAC. When Colbert asks Potter how this process is different than money laundering, Potter cheerfully replies, "It's hard to say." Again, the segment reveals the lack of transparency produced by the Citizens United decision and illustrates the real challenges that voters might have when confronted by manipulative political advertisements produced by groups with no official connection to a candidate.

Finally, Colbert and Potter—with a little help from Comedy Central colleague Jon Stewart—helped to call attention to the fiction of non-coordination. In January 2012, just before the South Carolina Republican primary, Colbert announced his intentions to run for "President of the United States of South Carolina," which also happened to be Colbert's home state. When Colbert makes this announcement, Potter dutifully explains that Colbert cannot run for office and keep his Super PAC "because that would be coordinating with yourself," and that Colbert could instead get someone to run it for him. Jon Stewart steps in and agrees to run ABTT, and Potter again provides an official document for Colbert and Stewart to fill out, with Stewart wryly observing that the form is double-spaced, again suggesting the lack of serious regulation or oversight. Before completing the form, Stewart then jokes that he and Colbert may become business partners ("We're about to open that combination bagel place and travel agency, From Schmear to Eternity"), and Potter assures them that being business partners is not a concern, as long as they don't "coordinate." They ask if there are any concerns about Stewart running ads on Colbert's behalf, about whether Stewart may "accidentally" overhear Colbert's plans while watching his show, or about hiring Colbert's staff, and Potter assures him that none of these activities is a serious issue.

During this process, ABTT paid for and ran a negative advertisement against the Republican frontrunner, accusing him of being a serial killer by taking literally Romney's terse assertion that "corporations are people, my friend," and then pointing out that as CEO of Bain Capital, Romney had been responsible for shutting down dozens of companies. Because Colbert could not get on the South Carolina ballot, he also encouraged people there to select Herman Cain, who had suspended his political campaign, when voting, with the result that Cain actually finished fifth in the primary, garnering over 5,000 votes.[21]

In interviews, the "real" Colbert has disclosed that they began this series in part because of a genuine curiosity about how campaign finance worked, and once they began discovering what was permissible under political fundraising rules, it felt as if he and his writers had gone "down the rabbit hole and we couldn't believe the wonderland of possible corruption on the other side," adding later that he and his research team "never found a rule we couldn't circumvent."[22] Notably, Colbert's Super PAC series went beyond contributing to the wider conversation about campaign financing. During the Super PAC's existence, he managed to raise over a million dollars, and after expenditures on a small number of political ads, had over $700,000 left in ABTT, which he donated to a Hurricane Sandy relief fund, Habitat for Humanity, and two organizations focused on campaign finance reform, the Campaign Legal Center and the Center for Responsive Politics.

THE COLBERT BUMP: SATIRIZING PUBLIC AFFAIRS INTERVIEWS

If Colbert's satirical persona could be used to mock punditry, it presented an unusual challenge when it came to interviewing guests. Colbert's strategies for interviewing guests can be illustrated through his interactions with Democratic Senator Elizabeth Warren. The Warren interview is a textbook example of Colbert's skill at feigning disagreement with a guest, even while providing her with a platform to promote her political philosophy. At first, when Warren appears on the show, Colbert takes credit for the fact that she was recently elected to the Senate, an accomplishment that he attributes to the "Colbert bump," the positive attention a guest ostensibly receives from appearing on his show. From there, Colbert invites Warren to explain the thesis of her new book, which she does, at first, by describing her working-class background. At this point, Colbert cuts her off, in a contrived attack: "Don't try to out-humble me. My father was an Appalachian turd farmer." Warren then deftly uses this transition to explain that her success was due to the resources that the government invested in children, such as funding for education, before she goes on to point out that this focus began to change in the 1980s. Colbert again interrupts her, asking rhetorically, "You mean when [Ronald] Reagan came in, and it was 'morning in

America?'" Colbert's question subtly mocks conservative Reagan worship, while again allowing Warren to further unpack her thesis about the deregulation of Wall Street and the moral implications of the government bank bailout. Finally, as Warren begins to make the argument that Wall Street executives who violated the law should have gone to jail, Colbert again pretends to challenge her, asking her to "name one law they broke," a question that Warren easily answers. Thus, although the satirical Colbert character disagrees with Warren, the interview questions are clearly designed for her to be able to respond in such a way that she can articulate her message about progressive economic policy.

Similarly, Colbert could use his overconfident but ignorant persona to promote scientific literacy. In particular, one of Colbert's most frequent guests was *Cosmos* host and astrophysicist Neil deGrasse Tyson, with whom Colbert would feign a combative relationship, even while touting his impressive credentials as a researcher and educator. In one segment, Colbert initially invited Tyson to describe his experiences meeting Carl Sagan, which allowed the astrophysicist to describe how Sagan had been an early mentor for him. Colbert then turned to a discussion of the Big Bang, again affecting an oppositional tone to create a straw man argument that Tyson can easily deflect. As a result, Colbert could, by performing ignorance, actually serve as one of the most useful voices for promoting scientific literacy within popular culture.

JOHN OLIVER AND HUMOR AS POLITICAL ACTIVISM

The conclusion of *The Colbert Report* and Jon Stewart's departure from hosting *The Daily Show* have raised significant questions about the future of fake news. Both shows had a profound influence on the wider political culture and have frequently been praised for their role in providing audiences with tools for reading political news more critically. But the success of these shows helped to prove that there was a significant niche for this type of political humor, and while the late-night political comedy block was a significant component of Comedy Central's brand, other cable channels have embraced the genre as a means of attracting a younger, politically savvy audience. With that in mind, HBO hired former *Daily Show* Senior British Correspondent John Oliver. Oliver's show has departed somewhat from the fake news formula perfected by Stewart and Colbert that overtly mocks news genres. Instead, Oliver deploys what might be called a type of weekly comedic investigative report on an important social, cultural, economic, or political issue. Thus, rather than mocking that week's headlines, Oliver instead does extensive research that will allow him to unpack a complex idea.

Like a number of comedians and actors, *The Daily Show* also provided British comedian John Oliver with a platform for developing his wry commentary on the news. In fact, Oliver often uses his Britishness as a posture that allows him to denaturalize tropes of American identity, even while emphasizing his choice to become a United States citizen, a background that proved especially poignant when Oliver did a segment of his show on the fact that U.S. territories, the Virgin Islands, Puerto Rico, Guam, and the Northern Marianas Islands, do not have voting rights. Oliver then points out that over 98 percent of the residents of these territories are members of racial or ethnic minority groups and draws from a 2010 documentary, *The Insular Empire*, to show that denying statehood to these territories was a deliberate strategy rooted in racist and orientalist ideologies. *Last Week Tonight with John Oliver*, which launched in April 2014, cultivated a distinct approach to fake news, one that enables more in-depth analysis of specific issues that shape U.S. politics. Unlike its late-night comedy predecessors, *The Colbert Report* and *The Daily Show*, which broadcast four nights a week, *Last Week Tonight* airs only once a week on Sundays, allowing Oliver and his team of writers a full week to develop a detailed analysis about a pertinent social or political topic. However, unlike the Comedy Central fake news shows, which faced a rigid structure of three seven-minute segments divided by advertising breaks, John Oliver could take full advantage of HBO's position as a premium cable channel that was not reliant on advertising revenue or even a rigid programming schedule. Like Bill Maher, Oliver could produce segments that ran longer than those seen on a commercial television station, and many of Oliver's segments could easily run for fifteen or twenty minutes without interruption. More crucially, because HBO was less dependent on advertising revenue, Oliver did not have to worry about the risk of offending potential sponsors, whether for his own show or for other shows on the network. Of course, even with this lack of concern about advertisers, it is important to recall that HBO is owned by Time Warner and part of a massive media empire that is focused exclusively on maximizing profits, raising questions about the possible limitations of the fake news genre, even when it resided outside the more explicitly commercial world of ad-supported television.

Like Colbert and Stewart, Oliver used his show to inform audiences about the harmful effects of issues such as corporate personhood and unlimited campaign spending, calling attention to what he saw as undemocratic policies. On June 29, 2014, the night before the *Hobby Lobby* ruling, John Oliver's monologue on his HBO show, *Last Week Tonight*, directly addressed the ramifications of the verdict and the absurdity of extending the individual rights of speech and religion to corporations. As Oliver developed his argument, he joked about the "religions" of several prominent chain restaurants, joking that Einstein Bros. Bagels is "obviously" Jewish before acknowledging that the chain not only serves bacon but also is open on Saturdays. He joked that Ben and Jerry's must be Buddhist, but then added that "they're not too Buddhist" lest they start serving flavors like "cookies and nothingness." He then characterized Taco Bell as Hindu because "there is no beef in there." In each case, Oliver mocks the branding of fast food franchises using ethnic or

Figure 3.3 John Oliver's investigative comedy tackles net neutrality

cultural stereotypes, while his remarks about Taco Bell also call attention to a scandal, in which it was revealed that their taco meat, indeed, contained little actual beef. Oliver's argument doesn't end there, however. He goes on to deconstruct the complaint—whether this objection comes from liberals or conservatives—about seeing one's tax dollars used to support an activity they oppose. Through montage, he shows a peace activist complaining about her tax dollars going to support Israel's defense while another grumbles about paying for other people's birth control, the issue that was at stake in the Hobby Lobby case. He then quotes a Fox News commentator who takes this complaint to absurd extremes, arguing, "I'm sure that Pam in Kansas doesn't want her tax dollars being spent on certain things, especially Mexican prostitutes." By using montage to take this complaint to its logical extreme, Oliver is able to portray these anti-tax expressions as both illogical and part of a wider ideology that places partisan identifications over a sense of national unity. Later, he weaves back in his references to fast food franchises by again treating the Wendy's and Burger King brands to make a point about women's pay and the absurdity of treating corporations as people with the same rights of free expression and freedom of religion. Finally, the monologue culminates with an attack on GM, pointing out that a faulty safety feature in some of their cars has likely resulted in the deaths of 13 people and pointing out that in that circumstance, humans likely wouldn't "get away with just a fine" over a Photoshopped shot of GM's logo strapped to an electric chair. As a result, Oliver's segment about the Hobby Lobby verdict riffs from the specific Supreme Court case to a wider discussion about corporate "rights." He subtly mocks the practices of corporate branding that attempt to put a benign face on massive corporations. He also touches on the healthiness of fast food by dropping a reference to the scandal over the meat content in Taco Bell's menu.

Like the segments from Saturday Night Live, The Daily Show, and The Colbert Report, John Oliver's monologues often circulate well beyond their original broadcast on television. As a result, they can be mobilized to support a wide range of political causes or arguments. In fact, in one notable case, Oliver offered a detailed, but again deeply funny, explanation of the implications of the upcoming FCC hearing on net neutrality, the idea that Internet providers could not offer preferential access to content online. Oliver uses his monologue to describe the challenges of making communications policy less boring while also establishing the importance of preserving net neutrality. Notably, he finished the sketch by calling on his viewers to go to the FCC comments page on net neutrality, which he linked to from HBO's website and from the YouTube page where the video was stored, and to leave comments. The result was that literally thousands of viewers went to the FCC website, causing it to crash briefly. Thus, although Oliver did not explicitly satirize news discourse, his show has provided a vital, comedic force in shaping and commenting on political culture.

THE NIGHTLY SHOW

When Stephen Colbert left Comedy Central to go to CBS, it marked the end of a significant cultural and political moment. Stewart and Colbert had spent more than a decade mocking the discourses of cable news. Thus, replacing Colbert presented a significant challenge. Comedy Central ultimately tapped Larry Wilmore, the longtime Senior Black Correspondent on *The Daily Show*, who had also been a writer and producer for *The Bernie Mac Show* and *In Living Color*. Initially, the show was slated to be titled *Minority Report*, an explicit reference to Wilmore's African-American identity; however, the show was eventually retitled as *The Nightly Show*. Notably, while Wilmore has embraced many of the tropes associated with his fake news predecessors, the show followed more readily in the comedic news comedy tradition associated with Bill Maher's shows *Politically Incorrect* and *Real Time with Bill Maher*. In fact, like Maher, Wilmore has made the panel the centerpiece of his show, frequently characterizing the show as the televisual equivalent of a "barbershop," in which no subjects are considered off-limits, as long as guests on the show remain respectful, a position he reiterated frequently while promoting the show's debut in January 2015.[23] Wilmore also took over as the only active African-American host of a late-night talk show, a detail that *Village Voice* writer Inkoo Kang highlighted in his review of the show. As Kang pointed out, Wilmore's "laidback persona" belied his political authority on issues of racial violence.[24]

The Nightly Show initially began with a seven-minute monologue on a specific issue (the state of public protests, money in politics, the tensions surrounding black fatherhood, the anti-vaccine movement). After the opening monologue, Wilmore then orchestrates a conversation about that issue with three or four panelists, including activists, authors, politicians, and comedians, some of whom are regular contributors to his show. Like Bill Maher's *Politically Incorrect* panels, Wilmore typically includes panelists that represent diverse points of view, a strategy that reflects his framing of the show as a barbershop. Notably, *The Nightly Show*'s panel format placed less emphasis on what *Variety* referred to as "glamour booking," the practice of casting celebrity guests and instead focusing on guests that will contribute to the show's conversational vibe.[25] Wilmore, however, makes a deliberate effort to include a larger percentage of African-American panelists. Initially, the final major segment of *The Nightly Show* was meant to be the show's signature: the rapid-fire question-and-answer bit called "Keep it 100," in which Wilmore asks his guests a provocative question, challenging them to answer completely honestly. Guests who were judged to have answered authentically, by both Wilmore and his studio audience, are awarded with a "Keep it 100" sticker. Guests who didn't were barraged with tea bags for offering a "weak tea" response. The tone for this segment was established in the premiere episode when Wilmore directly asked Senator Cory Booker if he aspired to run for president. When Booker demurred, Wilmore showered him with tea bags. While this segment initially felt gimmicky, it could in some cases provoke some remarkably candid responses, such as campaign finance reform activist Zephyr Teachout's admission that she would not reject support from the Koch Brothers if she thought it would ensure that she would win a race for governor. However, in keeping with the expansive approach to fake news afforded by the web, *The Nightly Show* eventually began posting most "Keep it 100" segments online, in part as an enticement to draw viewers to their web content. Further, as the show has evolved, Wilmore has returned to the more classic structure in which he will usually do monologues for the first two segments, while cutting down the panel to one seven-minute section. The result has been a show with a somewhat more explicit editorial voice, one that could comment on important social and political issues, rather than a loosely structured panel show that relied on panelists who often seemed to struggle to come up with topical jokes on the spot.

In some cases, *The Nightly Show* panel format served the show well, allowing Wilmore to orchestrate a forum around important issues. In fact, in one of his most successful early episodes, Wilmore skipped the opening monologue, devoting an entire episode to the state of black fatherhood, with four African-American male guests including hip-hop artist Common and *New York Times* columnist Charles Blow, among others. The episode was, in part, a response to the ongoing crisis of police violence against African-American men that had begun to receive increasing attention on the news. During this panel, Wilmore and his guests turned over the remarkable statistic that 72 percent of African-American children are born out of wedlock. Blow, for example, pointed out that the statistic should be read in terms of the so-called War on Drugs and the related expansion of the prison industrial complex, while Common pointed out that the category of "unwed mothers" does not mean that the father is completely absent from the life of the child.[26]

One of Wilmore's most powerful monologues dealt with the mass murder of nine African Americans at the Emanuel African Methodist Episcopalian (AME) Church in Charleston, South Carolina, by white supremacist Dylann Storm Roof. After a brief clip montage, in which Wilmore introduced viewers to the news of the shooting—including an interview with a survivor who quoted Roof as saying that he'd come to the church to shoot black people—Wilmore pauses to acknowledge the limits of fake news in dealing with the aftermath of mass violence: "Now I have to tell you guys, we weren't going to talk much about this at all. I mean, seriously we're a comedy show, right?" From there, Wilmore begins to establish one of the major themes of his monologue: a critique of Fox News for pushing the argument that the shooter's motivations were unclear. Wilmore does this by stating what would appear to be the obvious conclusion: "I think we can all agree that this was a racially motivated attack . . . . It couldn't be clearer when it comes out of the killer's mouth, right? But even with all that evidence—and on a day like today—Fox News just makes my fucking head explode." Wilmore, drawing from the discourses of political exasperation, then presents a series of clips taken from Fox News in which their anchors present Roof's motives as unclear or as an attack on the Christian faith. Wilmore then offers an interpretation of how some of Fox News's strategies function as a means of creating uncertainty about the responsibility for the shooting. Specifically Wilmore points out that one Fox guest commentator, a black preacher, E.W. Jackson, repeats the news channel's talking points that the shooting could have been motivated by religion, rather than race. This assertion leads Wilmore to speculate that the use of a black preacher, whom he refers to as "the Fox brother," might be designed to "confuse" viewers about the motivations behind Roof's actions as a way of preserving a more comfortable narrative about race. Finally, Wilmore reminded viewers about the history of violence against blacks at places of worship, specifically evoking the bombing of a Birmingham, Alabama, church during the Civil Rights movement, as well as the history of the Emanuel AME Church in Charleston, where one of its pastors was killed in the 1800s because he planned a slave rebellion. Thus, Wilmore provided important contextual information about the shooting, about the history of violence against blacks in places of worship, and a quick lesson on Fox News's attempts to craft another possible narrative for why the shooting took place.

Many of these observations were reinforced during the panel, with panelists, including Joshua DuBois, thoughtfully explaining the ideological underpinnings that prevent Fox News from acknowledging that Roof was motivated by race. DuBois further emphasized the fact that the AME church, in particular, had a policy of welcoming guests into their congregation, making the violence even more appalling. Meanwhile, Christina Greer, an assistant professor of political science at Fordham University, powerfully insisted that media pundits use precise language when describing the shooting, pointing out that Roof's actions should not only be considered both a hate crime and an act of domestic terrorism but also a political assassination because one of the congregants who was killed had been a leader in the South Carolina legislature. The panel also rejected the common rationale of attributing a mass murderer's actions to mental illness. Wilmore neatly summarized this cognitive dissonance when he stated that "racism trumps nostalgia" when it came to South Carolina's use of the flag. The panel was also attentive to the fact that Roof had posted a photograph of himself wearing a jacket with patches depicting flags associated with Rhodesia, an unrecognized state in Southern Africa run by a predominantly white government, and Apartheid-era South Africa. Greer again provides context for the symbols and pushes the point that Roof's appropriation of these racist symbols were not significantly questioned by his friends and family. As a result, *The Nightly Show* managed to devote nearly 20 minutes of time to detailed analysis of a culture that contributed to the violence that took place in Charleston. Wilmore continued to pay attention to the cultural and institutional embrace of the Confederate flag in future episodes of the show, culminating in an interview with political activist Bree Newsome, who scaled a flagpole to remove the flag from the South Carolina state capitol grounds, a moment that provided an important symbolic achievement for many people. Although Wilmore's relaxed "barbershop" style may produce less heat than Jon Stewart or Steven Colbert, his analysis of the ongoing issue of racial violence served a valuable pedagogical role, especially given Wilmore's high-profile position as part of Comedy Central's late-night political comedy block.

CONCLUSION

Fake news has played a vital role in its tireless scrutiny of political discourse. With Stewart and Colbert concluding their long-running shows, however, the genre appears to be in a significant moment of transition. As Bill Carter lamented, Stewart's departure meant "losing the most focused, fiercest, and surely funniest media critic of the last two decades."[27] Although Stewart has sometimes been faulted for contributing to a political culture driven by outrage, much of Stewart's indignation has served an important purpose in challenging cable to provide more responsible political coverage. Meanwhile Colbert, by inhabiting the persona of the arrogant but ignorant pundit, helped to make primetime news commentary shows seem increasingly absurd, especially when those shows relied on "truthiness," rather than truth. To be sure, these satirical observations may have done little to change our political culture (despite the best hopes of some media critics). Just days before Stewart was wrapping up his show, he could still play a montage of Republican politicians stridently rejecting a treaty with Iran while admitting seconds later that they actually hadn't read the treaty. Both Stewart and Colbert proved indispensable during the early years of the Iraq War, often by deconstructing the faulty justifications used to promote it. However, these shows did far more than simply fact-check political discourse. They pointed out and, in the case of Colbert, embodied the rhetorical postures and unstated assumptions that upheld the Washington consensus.

Colbert's power as a critic of Washington's political culture was never more visible than during his 2006 address at the White House Correspondents Dinner, an annual event in which the city's political leadership and the White House press corps meet for a banquet, an event that has become known as "nerd prom." Although Colbert's comments about Bush received the most attention, his satirical "compliments" to the DC press are even more significant. Turning to some of the most powerful members of the press, praising them for their role in not questioning Bush's claims: "Over the last five years, you people were so good—over tax cuts, WMD intelligence, the effect of global warming. We Americans didn't want to know, and you had the courtesy not to try to find out." Colbert doubled down on this criticism, further pushing the idea that the press had, for the most part, served as stenographers for the Bush administration during the Iraq War: "But, listen, let's review the rules. Here's how it works. The President makes decisions. He's the Decider. The press secretary announces those decisions, and you people of the press type those decisions down. Make, announce, type. Just put them through a spell check and go home." Thus, Colbert, like Stewart, proved to be a powerful media critic, removing the curtain on the failures of the Washington press and on the politicians who manipulated it. During an era of mass deception, they provided not only a way of reading the media but also nurtured a community of viewers who shared their indignation about political media culture.

The current generation of news comedy—John Oliver and Larry Wilmore, in particular—seem less motivated by satirizing the press than by using the podium of news comedy to engage in forms of social and institutional critique. Wilmore, for example, has been attentive to the ways in which police brutality against black citizens has become a national concern. Oliver, by comparison, has used his model of institutional critique to get his viewers engaged on issues they might otherwise ignore or take for granted, such as the voting rights of U.S. citizens living in island territories or the use of taxpayer money to pay for sports arenas. Thus, by making politics accessible, fake news shows play a valuable role in encouraging political participation. Some of these activities may seem trivial, as when Stephen

Colbert invited his audience to edit Wikipedia pages, but in some cases, these actions can have political consequences, as when John Oliver prodded his viewers to contact the FCC. As Jeffrey P. Jones has argued, news comedy shows "have made politics pleasurable, but not just through laughter. Rather, those pleasures also occur through the deeper levels of identification and activity they provide for viewers as citizens."[28] Similarly, as Liesbet van Zoonen argues, citizenship involves more than being informed. Instead, it entails "everyday talk and actions, both in the public and private domain. Citizenship . . . is something that one has to do, something that requires performance."[29] News comedy shows have played a vital role in this process, not just by entertaining and informing but also by provoking viewers to become more involved in political conversation and activity. News comedy shows aren't making us cynical, as some would argue. They are exposing the underlying cynicism of the political process itself and imagining healthier and more beneficial alternatives.

NOTES

1 Katerina Eva Matsa and Jeffrey Gottfried, "Jon Stewart to Step Down from The Daily Show, Where He Pioneered News through Comedy," *Pew Research Center*, February 11, 2015, http://www.pewresearch.org/fact-tank/2015/02/11/jon-stewart-steps-down-from-the-daily-show-where-he-pioneered-news-through-comedy/.

2 "Journalism, Satire, or Just Laughs: 'The Daily Show with Jon Stewart,' Examined," *Pew Research Center*, May 8, 2008, http://www.journalism.org/2008/05/08/journalism-satire-or-just-laughs-the-daily-show-with-jon-stewart-examined/.

3 Jones, *Entertaining Politics*, 233.

4 Jonathan Gray, *Watching with The Simpsons: Television, Parody, and Intertextuality* (New York: Routledge, 2006), 37.

5 Gray, *Watching with The Simpsons*, 26. See also Mikhail Bakhtin, *Speech Genres and Other Late Essays*, trans. Vern W. McGee, eds. Caryl Emerson and Michael Holquist (Austin: University of Texas Press, 1986), 114.

6 For a discussion of the role of audiences in using intertextual strategies to make sense of political campaigns, see Richard L. Edwards and Chuck Tryon, "Political Video Mashups as Allegories of Citizen Empowerment," *First Monday*, 14.10 (October 2009), http://firstmonday.org/article/view/2617/2305.

7 Jody Baumgartner and Jonathan S. Morris, "The Daily Show Effect: Candidate Evaluations, Efficacy, and American Youth," *American Political Research* 34.3 (2006): 341.

8 Roderick P. Hart and E. Johanna Hartelius, "The Political Sins of Jon Stewart," *Critical Studies in Mass Communication* 24.3 (2007): 263.

9 Jones, *Entertaining Politics*, 249.

10 Amber Day, *Satire and Dissent: Interventions in Contemporary Political Debate* (Bloomington: Indiana University Press, 2011), 43.

11 Steve Almond, "The Joke's On You," *The Baffler* 20 (2012), http://www.the baffler.com/salvos/the-jokes-on-you.

12 Jeffrey P. Jones, *Entertaining Politics*, 72.

13 Jeffrey P. Jones, *Entertaining Politics*, 85.

14 Jeffrey P. Jones, *Entertaining Politics*, 109.

15 Eleanor Clift, "Bill Maher Wants You to Meet—and Beat—Republican John Kline," *The Daily Beast*, September 16, 2014, http://www.thedailybeast.com/articles/2014/09/16/bill-maher-wants-you-to-meet-and-beat-republican-jeff-kline.html.

16 Lucy McCalmont, "Bill Maher Does Not Flip a District," *Politico*, November 5, 2014, http://www.politico.com/story/2014/11/bill-maher-does-not-flip-a-district-112555.html.

17 Clift, "Bill Maher Wants You."

18 Geoffrey Baym, "Political Media as Discursive Modes," 14.

19 Geoffrey Baym, "Political Media as Discursive Modes," 15.

20 David Plotz, "The 'How Does Stephen Colbert Work?' Edition," *Slate*, October 16, 2014, http://www.slate.com/articles/podcasts/working/2014/10/stephen_colbert_on_his_improv_background_and_how_he_gets_in_character_for.html.

21 Padmananda Rama, "Herman Cain Gets a 'Colbert Bump' in South Carolina," NPR, January 21, 2012, http://www.npr.org/sections/itsallpolitics/2012/01/21/145583425/herman-cain-gets-a-colbert-bump-in-south-carolina.

22 "Stephen Colbert on 'Colbert's Super Pac,'" *The Peabody Awards*, 2012, http://www.peabodyawards.com/stories/story/stephen-colbert-talks-about-his-2nd-peabody-award.

23 Brian Steinberg, "Larry Wilmore's 'Nightly Show' Raises Laughs and Eyebrows in Comedy Central Debut," *Variety*, January 19, 2015, http://variety.com/2015/tv/news/larry-wilmores-nightly-show-raises-laughs-and-eyebrows-in-comedy-central-debut-1201409400/.

24 Inkoo Kang, "Gonna Miss Jon Stewart? Don't Worry, Larry Wilmore's Hitting His Stride," *Village Voice*, June 30, 2015, http://www.villagevoice.com/film/gonna-miss-jon-stewart-don-t-worry-larry-wilmore-s-hitting-his-stride-7316943.

25 Steinberg, "Larry Wilmore's 'Nightly Show.'"

26 Aisha Harris, "Last Night Was Larry Wilmore's Best Episode Yet," *Slate*, February 5, 2015, http://www.slate.com/blogs/browbeat/2015/02/05/the_nightly_show_black_fatherhood_common_charles_blow_and_others_join_larry.html.

27 Bill Carter, "How Jon Stewart Changed Media (and Made Megyn Kelly Cry)," *The Hollywood Reporter*, August 7, 2015 http://www.hollywoodreporter.com/features/bill-carter-how-jon-stewart-812269.

28 Jones, *Entertaining Politics*, 233.

29 Liesbet van Zoonen, *Entertaining the Citizen: When Politics and Popular Culture Converge* (Lanham, MD: Rowman & Littlefield, 2005), 123.

4

COMEDY AND THE
POLITICAL SPECTACLE

This chapter will focus on sketch comedy shows, such as *Saturday Night Live* (SNL), and comedy series, such as *Tanner '88*, *Parks and Recreation*, and *Veep*, and their role in commenting on political culture. And while the fake news genre used satire and parody to call attention to the failures of the political media and to imagine alternatives to it, scripted comedy shows combine narrative techniques with the strategies of intertextuality to comment on political culture. Like fake news, these comedies often make use of the techniques of critical intertextuality, parody, and satire to mock public figures or the political media in order to illustrate their limitations and failings. However, these comedies, especially within the genre of the serialized sitcom, can also use relatively complex storylines to depict more thoughtful and reflective political cultures by showing politicians, reporters, and even everyday citizens engaging with how political systems operate at both the local and national levels. This can entail the quandaries that a group of senators face on a show such as *Alpha House* as they balance personal conviction with the desire to get re-elected for office. Or it can involve the respectful dialogue between characters with vastly different political philosophies found on *Parks and Recreation*, where the liberal Leslie Knope and the libertarian Ron Swanson support each other emotionally, even when they disagree politically.

As a result, this chapter advocates for the remarkable flexibility of scripted comedy as a device for commenting on a broader political culture. It also raises questions about the ways in which genre categories and industrial practices can offer distinctive ways of engaging with politics. One of these is the issue of distribution timing, of the production and distribution schedules that exist for any given show. Sketch comedy shows, like news comedy shows, often have a faster production schedule, appearing live or nearly live, allowing them to provide timely political commentary as they respond to events that took place over the previous day or week. Further, SNL typically runs new episodes during the election season, allowing them to satirize the staged media events—debates, press conferences, convention speeches, and campaign announcements—that tend to attract attention from the news. The show's status as a flagship program for broadcast network NBC also positions it as a show with broad national appeal, meaning that its commentary will likely have a wider reach, one that is amplified by being replayed on cable news and on social media. In turn, although other sketch shows, such as *Key & Peele* and *Inside Amy Schumer*, may have a smaller niche audience, their sketches also have the potential to reach a wider audience if a clip resonates politically. Serialized sitcoms, by comparison, are often written weeks or months in advance. Thus, while their humor may be less topical, they can draw from familiar narratives in order to make broader observations about political culture. For the most part, scripted comedies are less commonly associated with overt forms of activism; however, in many cases, they have played a useful role in contributing to conversation by providing us not just with informational or entertainment content but also by sparking opportunities for deliberation, reflection, argument, and engagement.

SATURDAY NIGHT LIVE

The NBC sketch comedy series *Saturday Night Live* has long enjoyed a privileged perspective in shaping the use of comedy to comment on political events. Because SNL is, for the most part, performed live, the show's creators can be highly flexible in producing sketches that comment on or satirize news stories that took place over the previous week. Although

SNL enjoys a much greater visibility than other comedy shows due to its cultural centrality and its prominent place on NBC's broadcast schedule, its power to influence perceptions of Washington's political culture has been widely discussed. For the most part, SNL, as a branded network property, one that seeks to hold onto its status as a cultural institution, may be somewhat more reluctant to take what might be perceived as radical or even strongly partisan stances. Further, because the show had long been viewed as a central site for political comedy, as Jeffrey P. Jones argues, the show generally offers little substantive critique of political discourses or policies, instead choosing to find humor by exaggerating the personality traits of public figures.[1] These traits often have little connection to the figure's political stances and the impersonations typically function as a means for the performer to cultivate a star persona through their performance. In fact, as Amber Day and Ethan Thompson observe, SNL's desire to remain commercially viable for a mass audience often blunts any satirical edge the show might have.[2] However, this does not mean that the show's presidential impersonations have no effect on our political discourse. Even while SNL has sought to avoid overt political commentary, the show does participate in the process of defining the images of major political figures. For example, during the show's inaugural season, Chevy Chase played then-president Gerald Ford as a bumbling klutz, despite the fact that Ford had been a star athlete in college, after Ford tripped and fell on the steps of Air Force One. Chase's performance helped foster his reputation as a comedian associated with pratfalls and other forms of physical comedy while also unfairly aligning Ford with being clumsy physically and politically. By comparison, Dana Carvey's exaggerations of George H. W. Bush's hybridized cowboy-patrician speaking style were so innocuous that the president ended up embracing the caricature. Meanwhile Darrell Hammond's playful depictions of Bill Clinton's multiple voracious appetites for fast food and sex transformed the president into a "fun-loving and harmless character."[3] Finally, Will Ferrell's depiction of George W. Bush as an affable but unintelligent "Decider in Chief" likely had little effect on how Bush was perceived. More recently, however, Tina Fey's performance as vice presidential candidate Sarah Palin may have contributed to perceptions that she was not ready to lead the country. That being said, focusing solely on how SNL engages with perceptions of presidential candidates is not enough. Instead, by looking at these performances, we can also begin to identify a wider critique of the artificiality of the Washington political spectacle and the media culture that often works to uphold it. Through their political caricatures, SNL offers both a light-hearted parody of the candidates and a more pointed satire of the process that allows these candidates to get elected (or at least nominated) in the first place.

SNL's place in political comedy has evolved considerably over its 40-year run, even while the show has sought to retain its cultural centrality. SNL comments on political issues through two distinct techniques:

1. It comments on current events through impersonations of public figures and through re-enactments of important current events, such as debates or press conferences.
2. SNL also comments directly on the news media itself through its "Weekend Update" segments, in which cast members play the role of news anchors providing a comedic take on the previous week's events.

In both cases, the segments function primarily to enable cast members to develop characters and cultivate star personas that could increase their profile on the show or, in some cases, to create characters that could be spun off into television shows or feature films.[4] However, while SNL continues to have a relatively significant audience that watches the show "live," its status as a true water-cooler show derives from its genre as a sketch comedy, making it easier to post and share short clips on social media. This ability to share clips has expanded the show's ability to remain relevant. More crucially, as Jones reminds us, journalists and bloggers facilitate this process by "crafting articles and news stories that explicitly proclaim to readers how and why SNL still matters."[5] In some cases, as David Gurney argues, SNL's second act online can even help to foster more engaged forms of participation, as sketches inspire "tributes, adaptations, and remixes" by fans of the show.[6] For this chapter, I will focus primarily on the political sketches, rather than the "Weekend Update" segments, in part because they tend to offer a more overt depiction of Washington's political culture.

POLITICAL SKETCHES

SNL's critique of both political candidates and the process can be seen in a sketch from 1988 parodying the debate between George H. W. Bush (Dana Carvey) and the Democratic candidate, Michael Dukakis (Jon Lovitz). During the sketch, Bush, as played by Carvey, does little other than repeat political catchphrases—"stay the course" and "a thousand points of light"—that reveal nothing about his policies but show him to be inarticulate at best. As Bush repeats these clichés, Dukakis glances briefly at the camera, stating, "I can't believe I'm losing to this guy." However, rather than serving as just a critique of Bush himself, the political media and the voters are implicated in supporting someone who offers absolutely no substantial reason for why he is qualified to be president. Political sketches typically receive a place of prominence on SNL, especially during the increasingly protracted campaign season when such segments usually serve as the show's "cold open," the segment that precedes the opening credits. Title cards announce "a message from the president" or use the logos of CNN or C-SPAN in order to parody the official discourse of televised news and other forms of political spectacle, strategies that are also readily visible in the absurd graphics and the faked reports on shows such as *The Daily Show*, in which the "correspondent" is clearly standing in front of a green screen across the room from the host, rather than whatever distant location they claim to be visiting.[7]

In some cases, SNL used the political sketches' reality effect to reflect on wider issues connected to the politics of representation, including issues of race and gender. These questions re-emerged around SNL's decision to cast Fred Arminsen, who is of German, Japanese, and Venezuelan descent, as Barack Obama, in a move that many observers described as a form of blackface. Although Lorne Michaels sought to defend the move by claiming that Armisen had won the part after auditioning against several black cast members, including Keenan Thompson, many media critics and bloggers viewed the casting choice as inappropriate, while others regarded the complaints as a form of enforced "political correctness." In her analysis of this controversy, Mary Beltrán points out that viewers who criticized Armisen's "Fauxbama" portrayal often had little awareness of the history of blackface and minstrelsy.[8] But the more crucial concern is that the demographics of the show's cast had significant political implications beyond even the desire to provide opportunities for a more diverse grouping of actors. Instead, including a more diverse cast would "allow the show to include impersonations of a broader range of public figures in the U.S. and global landscape," choices that implicitly at least impact wider perceptions about what issues and what individuals are worthy of our attention.[9] Thus, SNL as an important site for defining what counts as news (and who counts as a newsmaker) was constrained by casting decisions that prevented them from depicting a wide range of public figures who play an important role in shaping contemporary political culture.

A few years later, when *Scandal* star Kerry Washington guest hosted the show on November 2, 2013, the show used the occasion to acknowledge *SNL's* lack of diversity in its cast. During the opening sketch, Michelle Obama, played by Washington, enters the Oval Office to greet the president (Jay Pharoah) before a state dinner. President Obama then tells his wife, "Michelle, this is such a treat. I feel like it has been years since I've seen you," followed by a dramatic pause that punctuates a point familiar to most *SNL* audience members: The "SNL Obama" hasn't seen his wife in years because there is no regular black female cast member who could play her,

Figure 4.1 Kerry Washington as Michelle Obama with Jay Pharoah as Barack Obama on *Saturday Night Live*

thus making it impossible for the show to include her (or any other black female public figure) as a significant part of their routine political sketches. Following their very brief reunion, they are notified that Oprah Winfrey was visiting the White House and wished to see the president. Washington (as Michelle Obama) gets up from the couch and steps out of the room, stating with a sly glance at the audience that she would leave and that "in a few minutes Oprah will be here." While Obama and his press secretary sit and wait for Oprah to arrive, a voice-over announces an "apology" to Kerry Washington for "the number of black women she would be required to play" and offering to correct the lack of cast diversity "unless of course we fall in love with another white guy first." A few seconds later, Washington bursts into the room, winded from the long journey from the fitting room. Washington then is forced to exit the stage again when Obama is informed that Beyoncé was also dropping in for a visit. The segment concludes by playfully undercutting any importance their sketch might have by inviting MSNBC pundit and political activist Al Sharpton to step onto the stage, playing himself, and asking, "What have we learned from this sketch? As usual, absolutely nothing." Sharpton's cameo was, at the very least, a joking reminder that the show needed to address its casting choices. As a result, the sketch focused less on depicting anything specific about Barack Obama, Michelle Obama, or Oprah Winfrey than it did on SNL's role in commenting on a wider political culture.

THE FEY EFFECT

During the 2008 presidential election, the power of *Saturday Night Live* to shape perceptions of a public figure reached new heights when the Republican nominee for president John McCain tapped a relatively unknown Alaska governor, Sarah Palin, for the role of vice president. Palin was played by Tina Fey, who bore an uncanny resemblance to the Alaska governor and, more memorably, managed to perfectly capture Palin's regional accent. More crucially, Fey brought a sense of indignation that Palin was being taken seriously as a politician when she was so clearly unprepared for office. Fey's impression of Palin was especially powerful because SNL was not constrained by the professional standard of objectivity that requires journalists to cover both sides of a story. As a result, Bruce A. Williams and Michael X. Delli Caprini have argued that Fey's impression "thoroughly disrupted the emerging journalistic narrative of Sarah Palin."[10] What made Fey's performance more powerful was the fact that she was often directly repeating Palin's public statements, often with a slight inflection to make them seem even more ridiculous. When Fey did exaggerate Palin's statements, they still captured an essential truth not just about Palin but about the Republican party's cynical efforts to appeal to female voters, who they believed might be disaffected after Barack Obama defeated Hillary Clinton for the Democratic nomination. SNL frequently highlighted the idea that Palin was a political lightweight by having Fey play off of Amy Poehler's Hillary Clinton, who was portrayed as a hyper-competent and ambitious politician, to more clearly show the contrast between the two.[11]

During a September 13, 2008 sketch, Fey and Clinton took the stage together in a "joint address" to denounce the place of sexism in the media. The sketch begins with them explaining their divergent political views, with Clinton stating that "I believe that diplomacy should be the cornerstone of any foreign policy," followed by Palin quickly adding, "and I can see Russia from my house." Although the real Palin never claimed that she could see Russia from her house, the segment referred to an interview with Charlie Gibson from the previous week in which Palin claimed foreign policy experience because "you can actually see Russia from land here in Alaska."[12] While Palin's impersonation slightly embellishes Palin's actual explanation, the absurdity of claiming foreign policy experience because of a shared border helped to further entrench a view of her as unprepared to handle the difficult task of managing U.S. foreign policy. Later in the sketch, Clinton describes her disappointment at losing the nomination despite decades of public service while Palin flirts with the audience and camera, as if she is a candidate for a beauty pageant. The contrast between the two politicians was made remarkably clear, and as Amber Day explains, Fey's depiction of Palin left the indelible impression of her as "an uninformed but dangerous beauty queen."[13] In this sense, Fey's performance seemed perfectly calibrated to damage Palin's reputation by depicting it in this light. However, like other presidential parodies, Fey's Palin impression was also driven by a wider critique of the cynical political culture that allowed her to become a vice presidential candidate and, in many cases, propped up her qualifications even while recognizing her limitations.

Fey's performance played a crucial role in shaping expectations for many of Palin's other media appearances. After Fey's depiction began to inflict political damage, Palin participated in an extended interview with CBS's Katie Couric that appeared over the course of two nights, an appearance that was considered a significant disaster when Palin failed to name a single news publication that she read or when she was unable to answer standard policy questions about the economy. In the September 27, 2008 cold open, SNL parodied the interview between Couric (played by Amy Poehler) and Palin. During the SNL segment, Palin makes a series of mis-statements, in which she referred to Bono as "the King of Ireland" and remarks on the large number of foreigners working at the United Nations. Couric then asked Palin to describe how she would fix the economy, with Palin offering a rambling, long-winded, often contradictory response, in which Palin eventually suggests, "also having a dollar menu at restaurants, that's gonna help." When a frustrated Couric pushes Palin to name "one specific thing" she would do, Palin stammers before declaring in a reference to the TV game show, Who Wants to be a Millionaire, "Katie, I'd like to use one of my lifelines, I'd like to phone a friend." The segment mocked Palin as a political lightweight who didn't have any answers for pressing political questions, as well as someone who was getting by on her camera-ready charm.

The political damage to Palin's reputation was so extensive that the vice presidential candidate was forced to appear on the show as herself in order to perform some damage control. Notably, Palin's appearance reportedly generated the show's largest audience in well over a decade, 17 million viewers, suggesting that Fey's depiction of Palin was having a significant cultural impact upon conversations about the race. During the cold open, Palin gamely plays along in a backstage sketch with the show's producer, Lorne Michaels, in which they watch a TV set featuring Fey playing Palin at a press conference, in a scene that subtly functions to reinforce SNL's brand image as a cultural institution that plays an important role in shaping the practices of topical comedy.[14] Later in the sketch, Alec Baldwin, pretending to mistake Palin for Fey, coaxes Palin into repeating her "Caribou Barbie" nickname. Palin's appearance in a "Weekend Update" sketch in which she sat by—and eventually danced along with—a "gangsta rap" performance by Amy Poehler with lyrics such as "all the mavericks put your hands up!," and images such as Poehler shooting and killing a man dressed in a moose costume, did little to repair Palin's damaged image. Thus, even while Palin quietly endured being the target of SNL's jabs, the show clearly had an effect on perceptions of her as a candidate. Although SNL typically focuses on parodying the personalities of public figures, these comedy sketches, at their sharpest, could help to contribute to a wider political conversation. While it would be tempting to focus solely on how Fey's impersonation affected Palin, however, it's also worthwhile to point out that these sketches offered an implicit commentary on the cynicism of political operatives who sought to pander to women voters and on the news media itself for being too lazy or cautious to pose serious questions that could reach a broad, politically literate audience.

NEWS PARODY

In addition to its satire of politicians, SNL also parodied the political media itself, pointing to the ways in which partisan media shows offer simplistic narratives to support their preferred political ideology. The most vivid example of this form of critical intertextuality involves its sketches that parody the morning news magazine show Fox & Friends. For example, in "Fox & Friends: Obamacare and Climate Change," the hosts Steve Doocey (Taran Killam), Elisabeth Hasselbeck (Kate McKinnon), and Brian Kilmeade (Bobby Moynihan) smugly boast that the newly launched Obamacare would not be reaching its enrollment goals, but they do this by using a misleading bar graph that uses bars that are not to scale. In fact, the actual numbers show that Obamacare did meet its goals, but by using a misleading graphic, Fox News viewers (and its blithely ignorant hosts) could be affirmed in their beliefs that Democrats and Obama, in particular, were not succeeding. They then interview an "average" American who was unable to keep her doctor, but it turns out the doctor has a restraining order against her. Later in the same sketch, the hosts interview scientist Neil de Grasse Tyson, (played by Keenan Thompson) who attempts to explain climate science while the hosts offer increasingly absurd examples, culminating in Kilmeade's claim that the animated film Frozen is a documentary to counter Tyson's scientific evidence. All of the *Fox and Friends* segments end with a long scrolling list of satirical factual corrections, many of them having some political importance, but many others focusing on trivial, but utterly silly, mistakes that the hosts have ostensibly made. Like other SNL parodies, the sketch's humor relies, in part, on the audience's familiarity with the original text, but it also serves as a harsh critique of the role of casual morning news magazine shows in promoting misinformation, often by presenting truth as being grounded in belief, rather than fact. In this sense, these sketches reinforce Colbert's argument about Fox News's use of "truthiness" rather than presenting information that might be of value to a voting public.

Notably, SNL's satire of political news has been relatively bipartisan. Although the *Fox & Friends* parody became a recurrent sketch, SNL also criticized the excesses on MSNBC's liberal political branding. In a segment that was broadcast on October 7, 2012, after the first debate between Barack Obama and republican nominee Mitt Romney, which Obama was widely perceived to have lost badly, SNL mocked MSNBC's desperate post-debate analysis. Like the *Fox & Friends* hosts, the MSNBC pundits—Rachel Maddow, Chis Matthews, and Al Sharpton—desperately grasp for rationalizations for why their chosen candidate could have done so poorly. Matthews, for example, appears drunk and completely adrift. Sharpton initially reasoned that Obama might have been suffering from "altitude poisoning" because the debate took place in the mountain city of Denver. Matthews then repeatedly asserts that Obama should "stop being a pussy," a direct commentary on that host's embrace of hardball political tactics. Sharpton then adds another theory, speculating wildly that Obama and Romney must have inadvertently switched bodies. Thus, like the *Fox & Friends* sketches, the MSNBC parody may also rely to some extent on our familiarity with the original text for this humor to work fully. However, even without that background, it is almost impossible to deny the limitations of our media in offering rational, thoughtful analyses of our political culture.

SKETCH COMEDY IN THE ON-DEMAND ERA

The sketch comedy show *Key & Peele*, featuring comedians Keegan-Michael Key and Jordan Peele, drew from the playbook of SNL through its use of presidential impersonations. However, instead of a straightforward impression, Key and Peele tweaked this format to include a secondary character, Luther (played by Key), Obama's "anger translator." In the sketches, Obama would speak calmly, while Luther would offer an uncensored and unfiltered interpretation of what the president really *wanted* to say. In this regard, Luther could openly confront the hostile accusations against the president, such as the claim that he was not born in the U.S. or the belief that he is a Muslim, in a way that Obama himself could not. The tone for these sketches was established in "Meet Luther," a segment that circulated on YouTube before the show premiered in 2012. Like many other promotional videos that accompany the launch of a new show, this segment helped to prepare audiences not only for what to expect from the show but also function as a device for establishing preferred interpretations of the show. As Jonathan Gray explains, promotional videos like this one activate "the process of creating textual meaning, serving as the first outpost of interpretation."[15]

"Meet Luther" initially appears to open like any other *SNL* presidential impersonation sketch. A title card promises "a message from the president" before cutting to a close-up of Peele playing Obama as he addresses the public. Obama begins by repeating a popular myth about the president: the perception that he rarely expresses anger. As the camera tracks back, we see

Figure 4.2 Jordan Peele as Barack Obama with "Luther", his Anger Translator on *Key & Peele*

Key standing above Obama, who introduces him to viewers before transitioning into what sounds like a relatively standard policy speech. Initially, Obama addresses countries in the Middle East, telling them in a neutral tone to stop fighting, at which point, Luther interrupts him, flexing his muscles and showing the bravado of a professional wrestler, to say, "All y'all dictators around there, keep messing around and see what happens." This initial translation sets the tone for the entire series. Obama then speaks to his political opponents at home, specifically the so-called Tea Party, a group of conservative Republicans who consistently cast Obama as a socialist and frequently questioned his citizenship in an attempt to delegitimize his presidency: "To my domestic critics, I hear your voices and I'm aware of your concerns," which Luther, becoming increasingly agitated, expands by saying, "so maybe you could chill the hell out for like a second so I could focus on some shit." Eventually, Luther becomes so exasperated that he paces off screen, returning with a megaphone, into which he begins shouting, "I am not a Muslim!" The anger translator served, in part, to mock stereotypical assumptions about Obama, but as Ethan Thompson notes, it also functioned as a form of "catharsis" that allowed viewers (and reportedly Obama himself) to relish some form of pushback against conservative hostility towards the president.[16]

Luther proved to be such a popular character that Obama himself performed a sketch with him at the White House Correspondents Dinner, allowing Obama to land some pointed jokes at some of his political opponents and some of his harshest critics in the media. Notably, Key and Peele have adapted the concept of the "anger translator" to other politicians and other public figures, including Michelle Obama and Hillary Clinton. In *Key & Peele's* season five premiere, Obama and Luther seemed to pass the torch to Hillary Clinton (Kate Burton) and her anger translator, Savannah (Stephanie Weir). While the two politicians engage in pleasantries, the two anger translators face off, exchanging all of the resentments and frustrations that seemed to simmer beneath the surface during their primary battle in 2008 and their uneasy working relationship during Obama's first term. Weir plays Savannah as an embittered Southern matriarch, full of anger at the lost opportunity when Obama won the election, leaving her to "eat all that shit" and stand "there smiling next to my pussy-hound husband," while taking the lesser job of secretary of state. She becomes increasingly agitated as she angrily complains, "I'm gonna win this fucking election and I am gonna bury you and every goddamn man who ever stood in my way!" While it would have been easy to depict Hillary as a victim, the sketch seems to offer a reasonable "translation" of Clinton's legitimate frustrations at the perceptions of her that have developed over the course of her political career. As a result, the anger translator proves to be a highly flexible form, one that is capable of expressing the uncensored frustrations with a political system that encourages personal attacks rather than on the actual goals of governing the nation.

Like *Key & Peele*, *Inside Amy Schumer* used sketch comedy for satirical purposes. In Schumer's case, a number of her sketches have addressed issues of gender inequality and harmful beauty standards within the media. One of her more overtly political sketches was "Ask if Birth Control is Right for You." In the sketch, Schumer appears in what initially appears to be a straightforward parody of prescription drug advertisements. The segment opens with a shot of Schumer in a kitchen frantically getting ready for work, dressing, eating, texting, and reading a computer simultaneously, while a cheerful female voice-over explains that "you lead a busy life. The last thing you want to worry about is your birth control." The Pill is described as having few side effects—unlike many other drugs, where the list of side effects

Figure 4.3 Amy Schumer consults her doctor for a birth control prescription on *Inside Amy Schumer*

is often longer than the list of benefits. We then see a shot of Schumer talking to her doctor as the voice-over tells us, "Ask your doctor if birth control is right for you." Then, in a match cut, we see Schumer talking to her boss, with the voice-over adding, "Then ask your boss if birth control is right for you. Ask your boss to ask his priest." As the voice-over continues, we see an exasperated Schumer continuing to seek permission from other unlikely authority figures: "Find a Boy Scout and see what he thinks. Tap a mailman on the shoulder. Put it online and see how many likes it gets. Ask your mom's new boyfriend. Then ask the Supreme Court." Then, after the pharmacist finally hands her the prescription, the voice-over narrative concludes, "Finally, ask yourself why you insist on having sex for fun." As a final punch line, the mock commercial shows a young boy walking up to the pharmacy counter and asking for a gun. The pharmacist readily tosses him a small handgun, spinning it across the counter while adding, "Remember, that's your right!" The segment is rich in intertextual detail, not only in its parody of cheerful prescription drug ads but also in its implied references to the legal and institutional barriers that women face when obtaining birth control. Although it is not directly mentioned, Schumer's sketch is referring to *Burwell vs. Hobby Lobby Stores, Inc.*, a 2014 Supreme Court case that allowed "closely-held" corporations to be exempt from a law if its owners object to it on religious grounds. In this case, Hobby Lobby, a nation craft store chain, refused to provide insurance for its employees that covered birth control prescriptions. Notably, all of the "experts" that Schumer is forced to consult about her reproductive rights—the mailman, Boy Scout, and boyfriend included—are all male. Again, the humor of the sketch relies heavily on the viewers' knowledge not only of the forms of pharmaceutical advertising but also of the politics of religion and medicine that inform women's rights. As these segments illustrate, the sketch comedy format can be remarkably flexible, allowing comedic performers to engage in timely commentary about important political issues.

POLITICS AND SITUATION COMEDY

This chapter now turns to the serialized comedy genre. Although serialized comedies frequently make use of parody and satire, they can also craft narratives that engage with questions about a wider political culture. In some cases, these comedies use genre or style as a device for commenting political issues. For example, *Parks and Recreation* weds the long-running genre of the workplace comedy with the single-camera mockumentary format in order to tell a larger story about the role of local politics in our daily lives. By comparison, Amazon's *Alpha House* tweaks the formula of the domestic sitcom by portraying four unlikely roommates—a group of Republican senators with vastly different backgrounds and personality quirks in order to approach broader questions about Washington's political culture. Thus, once again, audience familiarity with genre can help to categorize a show and structure our expectations of how the characters will interact.

TANNER '88:

Tanner '88 was a mockumentary focusing on the efforts of liberal Democratic Representative Jack Tanner to secure the nomination to be the Democratic candidate for president in 1988. The series was produced for HBO by filmmaker Robert Altman and political cartoonist Garry Trudeau, and it offered a compelling mix of scripted satirical comedy and a verité-style documentary, in which actors and scenes blended with actual politicians and public figures, creating what amounted to a hybrid genre that could powerfully comment on the political spectacle, and, in particular, the role of consultants and campaign advisors in constructing it. This style was expressed through techniques common to Robert Altman's film work, such as overlapping dialogue and off-screen sound, to satirize the excesses of political campaigns. Notably, Altman and Trudeau took advantage of the backdrop of the 1988 Democratic primaries, filming on location as the actual candidates and the media were conducting their campaigns. The result was what Craig Hight referred to as a "guerilla satire" approach.[17]

Like many other forms of political entertainment, the show featured a mockumentary style that was made to appear even more realistic through its improvisational style and through cameos by prominent Democratic and Republican candidates for president, including Bob Dole, Gary Hart, Jesse Jackson, and Pat Robertson. During the first episode, for example, Tanner is seen schmoozing with Republican Senator and candidate Bob Dole, telling him that he expects that the two of them will face each other in the general election, while televangelist Pat Robertson cheerfully warns Tanner than his campaign is "playing for keeps." These cameos and the genre features of the mockumentary turned the lens away from the political stage to the processes of political spectacle, including the ways in which political candidates are performing a version of themselves, responding to the camera in scenes that involved a deft mixture of scripted and improvised scenes. As *The New York Times* TV critic John Corry pointed out, *Tanner '88*'s essential observation is that "a Presidential campaign, apparently, is performance art."[18] For those of us living in the age of social media, we are acutely aware of the ways in which we perform our identity on a daily basis. However, *Tanner '88* offered a prescient critical lens that attacked the constructedness of this political spectacle, expertly mocking many of the conventions of both political campaigns and the news media that cover them.

The attempt to satirize conventions of political media is evident from the first episode of the series. The first episode of *Tanner '88* establishes the show's critique of political media by focusing on the control room for a news show called "Close Up" covering the New Hampshire primary, a reminder of the state's significant role in defining the political process. It focuses on an interview with Jack Tanner, who is running for the Democratic nomination for president. When asked where he is from, Tanner says he is from eight different states, a claim that might seem like a form of political pandering in order to claim multiple "home" states, but quickly adds that he is an "Air Force dependent," an explanation that also positions him as someone associated with the military. The episode then takes us backstage to a hotel room where the campaign staffers are working, doing things like producing a biographical film for Tanner. Like other biographical films produced by political candidates, Tanner's biographical film serves to create a narrative about the candidate, one that will hopefully both turn him into a relatable human being and someone who is uniquely equipped for the challenges of the presidency. Tanner's film features a montage of ringing phones from people calling on him to run for president, a detail that mocks the cheesy tropes found in political advertising and other promotional media.

The show also mocks many of the conventions associated with the early primary campaigns, exposing the romance of so-called "retail politics" as a comforting fiction. Instead of voters who hope to learn about a candidate's positions, the people Tanner visits are more focused on the pleasures of meeting someone "famous." In one case, Tanner visits an elderly New Hampshire family. The husband comes to the door and tells Tanner and his daughter that he has sent the television crew away because Tanner had shown up late—he also complains that the TV crews tore up his lawn. Later, the wife takes a Polaroid of Tanner posing with her husband and then proudly showing her collection of Presidential Polaroids to Tanner's daughter. She happily reports that she hopes to trade a couple of "Doles" with her friend who has a good collection of "Kemps." When asked if she wants a Tanner button, she turns it down flatly, stating, "I don't collect those." Meanwhile the husband tells Tanner that he is probably voting for "Dudakis," mangling the name of Massachusetts governor, Michael Dukakis, to which Tanner replies that he shouldn't vote for someone if he can't pronounce his name.

But one of the most pivotal moments in the series involves what was originally depicted as a private moment between Tanner and his campaign staff that is initially only captured by the documentary filmmakers who happen to be in the room. Tanner delivers an impassioned, impromptu, and informal speech in a college dorm room, one that mocks the other candidates because they were unable to tell reporters who was their favorite Beatle. He suggests that this shows the candidates to be out of touch and goes on to describe the fact that America is the envy of the world, not because it is perfect but because Americans are armed with the knowledge that "we have insisted that we could do better. We've always been willing to reinvent ourselves for the common good. And in our darkest hour, leaders, real leaders, have always stepped forward to hold the American people to the responsibility of citizenship," adding in conclusion that "the correct answer" to the Beatles question is John—the political visionary. Notably, the entire speech is filmed, apparently secretly, from underneath a glass coffee table, with the glass of the table both distancing us from Tanner and turning his image into a series of reflections, imagery that subtly calls attention to the impossibility of seeing the authentic Jack Tanner.[19]

During a later episode, Jack is shown a photo of himself carrying his own suit bag in a local newspaper as he arrives in his home state of Michigan—one of his campaign advisors tells him that it sends the wrong message ("the wrong symbol for the wrong time"), that it shows that "he can't or won't delegate." He's told that he should be "more comfortable with power." Responding to this bit of advice, Tanner offers what is in some sense the "thesis" for *Tanner '88*, telling his advisor that the incident was "what Daniel Boorstin alluded to in his book as a human pseudo-event; invitation to self-deception, to hide reality from ourselves."[20] In this sense, the series presents Jack as "authentic candidate," one who challenges the conventions of political campaigns. In fact, Jack's "authenticity" as a candidate—the fact that he was a fictional character who could perform the role of an honest political candidate—allowed the show to comment directly about political issues in ways that might have challenged political norms. During one campaign stop, Tanner advocates for a "comprehensive boycott of South Africa" because of apartheid, the policy of racial segregation that was enforced through legislation by the ruling National party. More notably, during a political debate, Tanner argued for the legalization of marijuana, a stance that would have still very much been on the margins of mainstream politics: "America is tired of being dragged into wars it can't win, and the War on Drugs is a loser. Any law that makes 25 million Americans into criminals is a loser." Even while the show mocked political discourse, it could also use the character of a fictional Presidential candidate to express views that might otherwise have gone ignored or neglected during the election, as when Jack engages in an unscripted, but passionate, debate over inner-city decline. Thus, although *Tanner '88* was a relatively short-lived series, it offers a fascinating glimpse at the political spectacle, as it was understood at that time.

PARKS AND RECREATION

The NBC sitcom *Parks and Recreation* serves as an antidote to political cynicism by offering an affirmative depiction of an office of government employees working in the office of the Pawnee, Indiana, parks and recreation department. In general, as Heather Hendershot argued, the show espoused the basic thesis that "government is a positive force that provides necessary, basic services."[21] The show used the tropes of the workplace sitcom mixed with the single-camera, mockumentary style made popular by *The Office* in order to develop storylines that help to show that most government employees have good intentions, a theme that is vividly expressed through the character of Leslie Knope (Amy Poehler) and later, in a more modest way, through the competent and well-intentioned Ben Wyatt (Adam Scott), who consistently supports Leslie in her efforts to improve the community. The show's mockumentary style was expressed in part through the single-camera cinematography that emulated the style of an observational documentary, a storytelling mode that allowed characters to offer reflections about their lives, confiding in the unseen filmmakers. The show also used a loose serial structure that allowed storylines to develop over multiple episodes while other narrative threads could be wrapped up in the course of a single episode.

Many of the show's episodes avoided explicit partisan politics, and the show offers a calculated balancing act between Leslie Knope's liberal efforts to use government to enact positive change and Ron Swanson's libertarian opposition to all forms of government intervention. Ron's libertarian philosophy is humorously explained in season 3, episode 14, "The Road Trip," in which he finds himself assisting a nine-year-old girl who was writing a report on why government matters. Sensing an opportunity to share his values, Ron immediately begins demonstrating his anti-government and anti-tax philosophy. As he dumps her lunch on the table in front of them, he asks rhetorically, "You should be able to do whatever you want with this right?" He then plays the role of the tax collector, taking and eating 40 percent of her lunch, and then for good measure, taking more to collect a capital gains tax (one that would likely only affect a small minority of Americans). Although Swanson's anti-tax sermon proves seductive for his young disciple, we also see Leslie using her role as a government service to engage in actions that will improve her community, such as working to host a statewide baseball tournament. As a result, the episode carefully balances an image of the value of local government with Swanson's narrative of self-sufficiency. However, rather than treat Swanson and Knope as antagonists, the show makes a deliberate effort to depict their relationship as one characterized by mutual respect and even admiration. In fact, Swanson will occasionally violate his libertarian principles out of loyalty to Knope. In this sense, the show serves to depict a political culture that featured characters with positive intentions for the community, even if their philosophies of government were vastly different.

In addition to depicting a complex portrait of small-town life, the show's format also allowed it to satirize national and global issues in a creative and engaging way. In one early episode, Leslie performs a wedding at the zoo between what turns out to be two male penguins, opening up local debates about gay marriage that were being addressed on a more serious level in the state legislatures, federal courts, and ballot initiatives. Furthermore, the season-long cycle of episodes depicts Leslie's decision to run for city council, her political campaign against Bobby Newport (Paul Rudd), and the eventual recall election after she is elected. Episode 4.3, "Born and Raised," for example, gently satirizes some of the excesses of American political paranoia, even while offering a celebration of community. During the episode, Leslie is promoting a book she has published on the greatness of Pawnee, and she hopes to get an endorsement—depicted as a giant sticker that would obscure the entire cover of the book—from a local TV host, Joan Callamezzo (Mo Collins), in a parody of the role that Oprah Winfrey's book club played in launching dozens of bestsellers. However, when Leslie appears on the show, Joan traps her with a "gotcha" question about her place of birth, which Leslie incorrectly believes to be Pawnee. Later at a public book signing, local residents challenge her to provide her "long-form" birth certificate in an explicit satire of right-wing paranoia about Barack Obama's citizenship. Eventually, Leslie learns that she was born in the neighboring town of Eagleton, a hated rival for all Pawnee residents, but realizes that Pawnee is her true hometown.

Once she is elected, however, Leslie finds that her efforts to improve Pawnee aren't always appreciated. One of her first acts as a councilwoman is to propose and pass legislation that would impose a tax on 64, 128, and 512 ounce sodas (approximately 2–15 liters), a plot that simultaneously mocked Michael Bloomberg's highly unpopular soda tax and raised questions about the government's role in curbing the consumption of sugary sodas that contribute to a wide variety of health problems, including obesity and diabetes. Knope's actions prove so unpopular that members of the community begin a recall campaign against her, one that evoked the relatively recent event when Wisconsin citizens attempted to recall their governor, Scott Walker. To some extent, these topical references seemed designed to comment lightly on the absurdities of national politics, but more importantly, they functioned as a good-natured civics lesson, one that embraced a life of public service. This belief in the power of government to improve people's lives was vividly expressed in the final episode of the series. During the final season, *Parks and Recreation* used an innovative flash-forward narrative to show how the characters' lives would evolve. Although much of the show's final season takes place in 2017, the final episode flashes forward even further into the future, initially to the year 2025, as we learn that Leslie has been approached by the Democratic party leadership to run for governor of Indiana. When Leslie makes this announcement to the parks and recreation staff, she tells them, in what becomes a perfect summation of the series: "We fought, scratched, and clawed to make people's lives better. That's what public service is all about, small incremental change every day." Later, the episode flashes even further forward to the year 2035, with Knope delivering the commencement address at Indiana University after two successful terms as governor, where she delivers more or less the same message, but adding humorously, "Not to say that public service isn't sexy, because it definitely is, but that's not why we do it," before imploring the graduates to devote themselves to public service work they will find meaningful and rewarding.

VEEP

The HBO show *Veep*, starring Julia Louis-Dreyfus as Vice President Selina Meyer, by comparison, uses the workplace comedy genre to depict political leaders and staffers as essentially incompetent and self-absorbed. *Veep* was created by Armando Iannucci, the creator of the BBC series *The Thick of It* and the writer and director of the feature film *In the Loop*, both of which satirize British politics, and Frank Rich, a longtime *New York Times* political columnist, whose observations about Washington were often peppered with pop culture references. Like many other political TV shows, *Veep* mocks the political spectacle that promotes an idealized image of democracy. However, the show is also attentive to the ways in which that spectacle permeates into the everyday lives of the characters as they work to uphold it. In fact, *Veep*'s political consultants don't just sustain the spectacle; instead they inhabit it, as characters jockey for leadership positions within Selina's staff and devote endless energy to tracking who has access to power at any given time. This attention to the political spectacle, the show suggests, also drives legislation, as well, with characters making decisions about what policies to promote based on how popular they might be with the public.

As *Veep* begins, Selina already holds the position of vice president, and the show traces her journey as she attempts initially to exercise her political power, and later, as president, a position she assumes when the current president, who never appears on screen, resigns when the First Lady develops mental health issues. *Veep* offers a much more cynical perspective on American politics through its biting satire of scheming, incompetent, political operatives who typically operate inside a bubble that isolates them from the general public (the so-called "normals" as Meyer condescendingly refers to them when she is forced to interact with voters on the campaign trail). In fact, during one episode where Selina catches a nasty virus on the campaign trail, she blames her illness on "meeting people."

Where Leslie Knope genuinely values deliberative democracy, holding public forums where Pawnee residents can have their voices heard, Meyer and her campaign staff often seem disinterested in the citizens who have elected her into office. The show's cynicism is on display in one early episode when, during one early episode, Selina is caught napping in the Senate while waiting to vote on a crucial bill. Reacting to this news, Selina's assistant, Amy (Anna Chlumsky), remarks, in a comment that seems to reflect the spirit of the show, that "democracy is fantastic, but it's fucking dull." Where *Parks and Recreation* offers a belief in the value of government services, *Veep* focuses instead on the machinations of those people who profit from our belief in democracy and who will do almost anything to remain in power or to obtain a coveted position in a political campaign. In many ways, *Veep* tells us "what we already know" about politics: that the people involved are vapid and self-serving, that little gets done by design, and that politicians know nothing about the people they ostensibly serve.[22] That being said, Amy and Selina, in particular, occasionally show glimpses of genuine belief in the value of government, although for the most part, they struggle to balance public perception with their desire to make a difference.

When we are first introduced to Selina, she is depicted as essentially powerless and isolated from the Oval Office. Her one connection to the president—who is never seen and whose name isn't revealed until the end of season three—is a self-promoting, but utterly oblivious, liaison Jonah (Timothy Simons). The show carefully avoids identifying Meyer's political party, a tacit affirmation of the belief that both parties are essentially the same. Her one major political goal seems to be to push through a Clean Jobs Initiative that has as its centerpiece a plan to have the White House use cutlery made of cornstarch rather than plastic, a goal that viewers immediately recognize as a trivial gesture in the face of the real challenges associated with climate change. Once Selina takes over as president, her first initiative is to pass a Families First bill that, again, uses an innocuous title that suggests the public relations of appearing to do something positive for "families" means more than any specific policies. And, in fact, as Selina's campaign goes on, Families First becomes so unpopular that she and her staff conclude their only solution is to have the bill fail. As a result, Selina sends her staffers and other allies to quietly lobby against the bill even while she continues to pretend to support it publicly.

Veep's engagement with the political spectacle becomes central during Selina's run for the presidency. Selina campaigns against a group of stereotypical candidates, including Danny Chung, an Asian-American war hero, and Joe Thornhill, a Southerner and former baseball manager, who speaks in nothing but sports clichés, along with George Maddox, an African-American military leader. In each case, the candidates' images seem to be more of a concern than any policy positions or qualifications they might have. More crucially, the show satirizes how political campaigns can hinge upon superficial factors, such as the ability to appear presidential during canned moments such as debates, where candidates seek to deliver memorized responses to questions that are usually anticipated well in advance. In fact, during her primary debate, Selina initially appears to stumble badly, forgetting the third item in a list of immigration policies (all of which begin with the letter "R"), a gaffe that clearly evoked Texas Governor Rick Perry's similar mental lapse during a debate in 2012. However, unlike Perry, Selina is able to improvise, pulling the word "repel" out of thin air and structuring a response around that. Although a prominent supporter initially worries that her response makes her appear to be a "Nazi," her staff quickly points out that Selina becomes more popular every time she says the word "repel"; and despite her failure to present a coherent stance on immigration, the gaffe seems to revitalize her campaign.

Like *Parks and Recreation*, *Veep* also addresses some of the challenges that women face when running for political office. In season three, episode two, "The Choice," Selina, who still has not declared as a candidate, is pressured to take a position on the hot-button issue of abortion. Once again, Selina and her staff demonstrate almost complete disregard for the public they represent and instead focus on how best to craft a message and an image that will make that public wish to support them. Even if her actual views on abortion are undeniably clear—at one point she asks rhetorically, "Why can't I just say, 'get the government out of my fucking snatch?'"—Selina is reluctant to take a clear position or make a strong statement on the issue. "The Choice" is, perhaps, most notable for Selina's initial refusal to ground her political position in her identity as a woman. When Mike (Matt Walsh), Selina's press secretary, suggests that she preface her remarks about abortion by saying "As a woman," she immediately recoils by saying, "No, no, no, I can't identify myself as a woman. People can't know that." Later in the episode, she again reiterates her refusal to qualify her response within her experience as a woman: "as a woman, I am not going to say 'as a woman.' I am not going to go putting all my eggs in that basket." But once she is before the cameras, Selina chooses to use the language she has rejected in her speech, in a scene that powerfully reflects what is permissible on the political stage when it comes to talking about abortion. Later, as Selina makes a series of bad decisions as president, Amy resigns dramatically in a monologue where she eviscerates Selina for her failures as the first female president: "You have achieved nothing apart from one thing: The fact that you are a woman means we will have no more women presidents because we tried one and she fucking sucked." Amy's comments take on additional power given the background of a political context, in which Hillary Clinton was the clear favorite to win the Democratic nomination for president, a challenge that Clinton herself explicitly evoked when she described the "hardest, highest glass ceiling" facing women—the possibility of the first female president.[23] Although Clinton's comments were embedded within a narrative of progress, one that evoked female abolitionists who fought against slavery, the suffragists who fought for the right to vote, and other forms of personal success, the remarks also served as a powerful reminder of the pressure that the Clinton campaign faced.

ALPHA HOUSE

Like *Veep*, *Alpha House* satirizes the behaviors of elected officials, in this case a group of Republican senators who share a Capitol Hill house. *Alpha House* is notable, in part, because it was one of the first shows produced by Amazon Studios as part of Amazon's strategy to supplement their deep catalogs of movies and TV shows with original content as a way of competing with Netflix, which had also begun to produce original programming with its politically themed show *House of Cards*. Amazon made the pilot for *Alpha House* available on its website along with the pilot episodes for several other shows and invited viewers to vote on which show they would like to see turned into a series, a move that allowed Amazon to collect vast amounts of data about its users' interests and tastes.[24]

Alpha House is a serial half-hour comedy show loosely based on a house owned by Democratic Representative George Miller who shared his home with a number of Democratic senators including Dick Durbin and Chuck Schumer.[25] But the show's creators, Garry Trudeau, the Doonesbury cartoonist, and Jonathan Alter, a political journalist, chose to focus the show on a group of Republican senators, in part because they felt that Republicans faced bigger challenges in retaining the support of their political base. The show's lead character, Gil John Biggs (John Goodman), is a former University of North Carolina basketball coach turned politician with a hearty appetite for Carolina barbecue, while Robert Bettencourt (Clark Johnson) is a moderate black Republican from Pennsylvania. Louis Laffer, Jr. (Matt Malloy), meanwhile, is a hawkish Nevada senator who is portrayed as a closeted gay man. Finally, Florida Senator Andy Guzman (Mark Consuelos) is a recently divorced Latino sex addict who has presidential ambitions and moves into the house after their previous housemate—also a senator—is hauled off to prison on corruption charges. Like *Veep*, *Alpha House* treats its subjects sympathetically, even while using humor to satirize aspects of Washington's political culture, including the detrimental effects of money in politics and the rising influence of the Tea Party as a political force.

Louis, loosely modeled on South Carolina Senator Lindsey Graham, demonstrates a blithe unawareness of how the contemporary political process works, making appearances on *The Colbert Report* (where Colbert's satirical pundit eviscerates him), embarrasses himself in an attempt to prove that he is the funniest politician in Washington, and later stumbles badly when he tries to "evolve" on the issue of gay marriage when one of his staffers reveals that she is a lesbian. Similarly, Gil John, whose status as a former UNC basketball coach makes him a statewide hero, faces a Tea Party challenge from the current Duke basketball coach: bringing basketball and political rivalries to the surface. However, Gil John also stumbles badly when several viral videos of him making verbal gaffes begin circulating online, a plotline that evoked a number of similar incidents where political careers were destroyed by mis-statements that happened to be captured and shared. Finally, Andy, due to his charm and his Latino identity, is depicted as a potential Presidential candidate; however, his performances on the national stage—including a poorly executed response to a State of the Union address, modeled on a similar performance by Florida Senator Marco Rubio—show him to be unprepared. In all cases, the politicians also bend over backwards in their desperate attempts to gain support—in campaign donations—from the Watt Brothers, a pair of secretive, but incredibly wealthy, billionaires who are clearly modeled on the Koch brothers, a plot device that calls attention to the overwhelming influence of money in politics.

CONCLUSION

By looking at a broad range of comedies, we can begin to trace out how these shows work to map out a portrait of aspects of Washington's political culture, especially regarding the role of campaign consultants in upholding the political spectacle and, to some extent, in charting how that spectacle has changed over time. First, by looking back to HBO's *Tanner '88*, we can begin to see the increasing awareness of the role of consultants, pollsters, and other political professionals who may have little interest in the process of governing but may instead be more concerned with creating an image. While Jack Tanner could still cite Daniel Boorstin in order to condemn the "pseudo-events" that drive presidential campaigns—whether debates and speeches or even the retail politics of meeting everyday citizens—the politicians in *Veep* and *Alpha House* are essentially incapable of stepping outside of it. Even in *Parks and Recreation*, which offers a more romanticized picture of the role of government in everyday life, political consultants are most likely to be held up for scrutiny, as when Leslie runs for city council in a race that becomes dominated by poll-tested TV ads and other staged events. In all cases, serialized and sketch comedies attempt to make sense of a political process that, to a significant extent, seems to be failing the public that it ostensibly serves and represents. Although many of the politicians and their staffers may have good intentions, they are confronted by a political culture in which personal ambition outweighs the public good and fictions about what voters want overshadow more authentic forms of addressing the public. Thus, although much of the material in these shows may appear to simply function as topical references to recent events that happened to grab headlines, scripted comedies can, in some cases at least, offer a powerful critique of the political spectacle in all its various forms.

NOTES

1 Jeffrey P. Jones, "With All Due Respect: Satirizing Presidents from *Saturday Night Live* to *Lil'Bush*." in *Satire TV: Politics and Comedy in the Post-Network Era*, ed. Jonathan Gray, Jeffrey P. Jones, and Ethan Thompson (New York: NYU Press, 2009): 37–63.

2 Amber Day and Ethan Thompson, "Live from New York, It's the Fake News! *Saturday Night Live* and the (Non)Politics of Parody," *Popular Communication* 10.1–2 (2012), 170–171.

3 Jeffrey P. Jones, "Politics and the Brand: *Saturday Night Live's* Campaign Season Humor." in Saturday Night Live & *American TV*, ed. Nick Marx, Matt Sienkiewicz and Ron Becker (Bloomington: Indiana University Press, 2013), 83.

4 As of this writing, 11 feature films, including two sequels, have been spun off from SNL sketches, including *The Blues Brothers, Wayne's World, Wayne's World II, Coneheads, It's Pat, Stuart Saves his Family, A Night at the Roxbury, Superstar, Blues Brothers 2000, The Ladies Man*, and *MacGruber*. Dozens of other SNL alumni have, of course, moved on to successful film and TV careers.

5 Jones, "Politics and the Brand," 78.

6 David Gurney, "Sketches Gone Viral: From Watercooler Talk to Participatory Comedy." in Saturday Night Live & American TV, ed. Nick Marx, Matt Sienkiewicz and Ron Becker (Bloomington: Indiana University Press, 2013), 256.

7 Jones, "Politics and the Brand," 87.

8 Mary Beltrán, "SNL's 'Fauxbama' Debate: Facing Off Over Millenial (Mixed-) Race Impersonation," in Saturday Night Live & American TV, ed. Nick Marx, Matt Sienkiewicz and Ron Becker (Bloomington: Indiana University Press, 2013), 197.

9 Beltrán, "SNL's 'Fauxbama' Debate," 205.

10 Bruce A. Williams and Michael X. Della Carpini, After Broadcast News: Media Regimes, Democracy, and the New Information Environment (Cambridge: Cambridge University Press, 2011), 4.

11 John Lopez, "And Now, Ladies and Gentlemen, a Message From the 'Saturday Night Live' President of the United States," Grantland, August 25, 2014, http://grantland. com/hollywood-prospectus/saturday-night-live-president-impressions/.

12 "House Call," Snopes.com, February 13, 2015, http://www.snopes.com/ politics/palin/russia.asp.

13 Amber Day, Satire and Dissent: Interventions in Contemporary Political Debate (Bloomington: Indiana University Press, 2011).

14 For a discussion of SNL's use of Lorne Michaels's backstage appearances as a form of brand management, see Evan Elkins, "Michael O'Donoghue, Experimental Television Comedy, and Saturday Night Live's Authorship," in Saturday Night Live & American TV, ed. Nick Marx, Matt Sienkiewicz and Ron Becker (Bloomington: Indiana University Press, 2013), 57–62.

15 Jonathan Gray, Show Sold Separately: Promos, Spoilers, and Other Media Paratexts (New York: New York University Press, 2010), 48.

16 Ethan Thompson, "Key and Peele: Identity, Shockingly Translated", Antenna: Responses to Media & Culture, February 7, 2012, http://blog.comments.wisc. edu/2012/02/07/key-and-peele-identity-shockingly-translated/

17 Craig Hight, Television Mockumentary: Reflexivity, Satire, and a Call to Play (Manchester: Manchester University Press, 2010), 148.

18 John Corry, "TV Review: 'Tanner '88,' A Satire on Presidential Campaigns," The New York Times, February 15, 1988 http://www.nytimes.com/1988/02/15/ arts/tv-review-tanner-88-a-satire-on-presidential-campaigns.html.

19 For a thoughtful discussion of this scene, see Dana Stevens, "Primary Colors: Robert Altman's *Tanner '88* Exposes the Fiction of Democracy," *Slate*, February 4, 2004, http://www.slate.com/articles/arts/television/2004/02/primary_colors.html.

20 See Daniel J. Boorstin, *The Image: A Guide to Pseudo-Events in America* (New York: Atheneum, 1987).

21 Heather Hendershot, "*Parks and Recreation*: The Cultural Forum," in *How to Watch Television*, ed. Ethan Thompson and Jason Mittell (New York: New York University Press, 2013), 206.

22 For a discussion of the show's cynicism, see Maureen Ryan, "'Veep' HBO Review: Political Comedy Misses the Mark," *The Huffington Post*, April 19, 2012, http://www.huffingtonpost.com/maureen-ryan/veep-hbo-review-political_b_1437554.html.

23 Kyle Anderson, "'Convention:' Amy Loses It—Like Really Loses It" *Entertainment Weekly*, May 10, 2015, http://www.ew.com/recap/veep-season-4-episode-5.

24 Todd Spangler, "Step Aside Netflix: Amazon's Entering the Original Series Race," *Variety*, October 22, 2013, http://variety.com/2013/biz/news/step-aside-netflix-amazons-entering-the-original-series-race-1200749146/.

25 Norm Ornstein, "In *Alpha House*, Politicians are People, Too," *The Atlantic*, November 13, 2014, http://www.theatlantic.com/politics/archive/2014/11/in-alpha-house-politicians-are-people-too/382717/.

5

POLITICAL PROCESS MELODRAMAS AND SERIAL NARRATIVE

While comedy and satirical news have provided important venues for allowing audiences to engage with politics, melodrama has also played a vital role in shaping perceptions of Washington's political culture. To address the role of political melodrama, I have divided it into two major categories, those that depict aspects of the political process and those that focus almost exclusively on issues of national security. In the case of melodramas of political process, plotlines depict characters attempting to navigate or manage the legislative process, election campaigns, and other forms of political activity. This mode of serial melodrama focuses its attention to questions of morality. Although melodrama is often associated with emotional excess, Linda Williams has more recently made the case that it functions as a means of developing questions around the "moral legibility" of competing values or beliefs through the use of serialized narrative.[1] These shows seek to make sense of how that process works and, again, one of the chief villains seems to be the political culture itself, one that is dominated by corruption and a focus on political spectacle, rather than on the needs of governing. Perhaps the most influential example of political process melodrama is NBC's *The West Wing*, which did offer a romantic or idealized version of the workers who inhabit the Oval Office; however, against this backdrop, we still encounter political operatives who are willing to sacrifice political principle in order to win an election. Other shows, such as *Scandal*, seem to offer a much more cynical portrait of American political culture, suggesting that Washington's elite power system is built almost entirely on the foundation of scandalous behavior that is carefully hidden from the public. As a result, these shows provide viewers with a venue for articulating their own values and beliefs about the political process, an activity that often takes place in the social media chatter associated with live-tweeting or producing episode recaps that attend to the political implications of controversial storylines.

THE WEST WING

One of the most influential political dramas in American television history was The West Wing. The show explicitly sought to reverse what has frequently been diagnosed as the pervasive cynicism surrounding American political life, offering instead an exploration of the conflicts that emerge among the dedicated and competent public servants who generally act in the interest of the people they represent. In fact, many of the president's staff members seem motivated not by personal ambition but by a genuine desire to contribute to the public good, even if there is often significant disagreement among the staffers about what this means. By providing this "backstage" perspective, The West Wing helps to provide context for political news stories and procedures that might otherwise be difficult for viewers to understand. As Donnalyn Pompper explains, The West Wing provides "simple explanations for complex issues so that audiences may understand policies."[2] Thus, the show performs an explicitly pedagogical function, one in which the traditions and practices associated with the presidency are explored. In turn, the show tackles a range of controversial issues, showing how the president's staff works to negotiate policy issues that emerge during the presidency and during two elections. In the case of The West Wing, the show combined "cumulative" storylines that took place over several episodes and often remained unresolved for months with shorter storylines that could achieve closure within a single episode.[3] Thus, short-term storylines about political decision-making, such as Matt Santos's (Jimmy Smits) initial refusal to use negative campaign advertising, could resonate with the more extended narrative of his overall run for the presidency.

The major storylines of *The West Wing* were structured around the White House's senior staff. The most prominent staff members included Bartlet's chief of staff Leo McGarry (John Spencer), the deputy communications director Sam Seaborn (Rob Lowe), press secretary C. J. Cregg (Allison Janney), the White House communications director Toby Ziegler (Richard Schiff), and the deputy chief of staff (Bradley Whitford). They are joined by Bartlet's "body man," or personal assistant, Charlie Young (Dulé Hill), and Josh's assistant, Donna Moss (Janel Moloney). Later seasons would focus on the conclusion of Bartlet's second term as president and a closely contested election between a young, charismatic Latino Democrat, Matt Santos (Jimmy Smits), and a moderate, pro-choice Republican, Arnold Vinnick (Alan Alda), who provided a useful foil for the less experienced Santos, creating an idealized Presidential campaign that was ostensibly based not on spectacle but on a genuine debate about political philosophies. *The West Wing's* narrative strategies carefully balanced ongoing, serial narratives with weekly storylines that typically served to provide what McCabe calls "a vibrant civics lesson on a broad range of issues."[4] These civics lessons also helped to teach the audience to believe in certain political values, but they are typically grounded in the audience's emotional attachment to the characters and the dramatic scenarios they must negotiate.

THE WEST WING AS WEEKLY CIVICS LESSON

The West Wing deftly navigated a wide range of political topics. Although it addressed a wide range of concerns, *The West Wing* was often at its strongest when it engaged with questions about the role of the news media in serving to inform the public about political affairs. Although the press was, to some extent, treated ambivalently by the Oval Office staffers who saw the White House press corps as a threat that needed to be managed, several of the show's episodes placed emphasis on the importance of a vibrant political media. For example, Episode 1.21, "Lies, Damn Lies, and Statistics" (May 10, 2000), focuses on the issue of how political campaigns are financed. Invoking the debate over campaign finance reform, the episode depicts Bartlet's efforts to close a 1978 regulation that enabled so-called "soft money" donations, contributions that are given directly to a political party rather than a specific candidate, a discussion that anticipated the current era of unlimited political funding. In the episode, Bartlet collaborates with a Republican Congressman who shares his concerns about campaign financing to nominate people to the Federal Elections Commission (FEC) who will vote to change the rule. Although there is little discussion of the effects of soft money, one FEC commissioner is quoted as saying that "money isn't speech," a slogan that had been used by advocates of reform.

Likewise, Episode 2.3, "Midterms" (October 18, 2000), featured a subplot in which President Bartlet meets with a group of radio broadcasters. Although Bartlet initially sees the event as an opportunity to charm a few members of the press, he quickly spots Dr. Jenna Jacobs (Claire Yarlett), a conservative radio host who provides psychological advice to guests who call in to her show and who had frequently vilified gays and lesbians. Rather than continuing to schmooze his guests, Bartlet singles Jacobs out and begins by questioning her credentials, getting her to admit that her doctorate was in English literature, rather than in a medical or social science field. He then challenges her on her theological justifications for condemning homosexuality as an "abomination," mostly by quoting other verses from the Bible that warranted the death penalty for activities we now regard as completely benign (planting two different crops next to each other, for example). Viewers watching the show when it originally aired in 2000 likely would have recognized Jacobs as a thinly veiled stand-in for Laura Schlessinger, a popular conservative radio host who had made similar statements.

These questions about the role of the media industries in shaping political culture were also addressed in "The Black Vera Wang" (May 8, 2002), an episode from season three, which focused one of its subplots on the role of the broadcast networks in covering political conventions. After being told that the major broadcast networks only intend to devote one hour of their primetime schedule to each convention, Toby reminds the network representatives that their broadcast license from the FCC entails a requirement that they provide programming that is in the public's interest. While Toby lectures the network executives, he reminds them—and the viewers—that the American public "owns" the airwaves and that the broadcast networks are required to devote at least some of their schedule to shows that will serve the public interest, although the episode ignores, to some extent, the ways in which these "public interest" requirements were largely put to the side beginning with the rise of cable. While the concept of the "public interest" is only implicitly defined, Toby asserts that it should include convention speeches, one of the few times in which "our leaders" are speaking directly to the voters.

"20 HOURS IN AMERICA"

Despite its efforts to depict a diverse political landscape, The West Wing often reinforced stereotypical and romanticized notions of American identity, one where "real" citizens struggled to navigate an increasingly inaccessible political system. Although the show frequently made reference to electoral politics and to democratic principles, it rarely ventured outside the Beltway, the interstate highway that circles the nation's capital. One significant exception to this was the two-part episode, "20 Hours in America," in which Josh, Toby, and Donna are left behind at a Presidential campaign stop in Indiana after Bartlet has given a stump speech. While attempting to return to Washington in what amounts to a mock journey narrative, the three go through a variety of comic mishaps: a truck that runs on biodiesel fuel breaks down leaving them stranded, and later they miss a flight because of confusion about Indiana's policy of not observing daylight savings time. As Trevor Parry-Giles and Shawn Parry-Giles point out, their travels through this version of the "real" America leads them to encounter people who are almost exclusively white and rural, offering a limited portrait of the country.[5] Throughout the episode, Josh and Toby complain about the rural culture around them. Josh calls Indiana's seemingly arbitrary time zones a "schmuck-ass system." And Toby later complains when the diner where they stop doesn't claim to offer a "local delicacy" and doesn't have CNN. These scenes mock Josh and Toby's lack of awareness about the behavior of "real" Americans who are—in this scenario at least—rural, agrarian, and for the most part, oblivious about the political messaging they obsess over.

Resigned to the fact that they are stuck in Indiana, Josh and Toby strike up a conversation with a middle-aged man who is on a college visit with his daughter. Their discussion turns the humor of the previous scenes on its head, bringing out a moment of emotional connection. Josh asks the man whether he's invested in the stock market, which had experienced a dramatic decline, and after responding that he has a mutual fund that's supposed to cover his daughter's college costs, goes on to reflect:

> I never imagined, at $55,000 a year, I'd have trouble making ends meet. And my wife brings in another 25. My son's in public school. It's no good. I mean, there's 37 kids in the class, no art and music, no advanced placement classes. Other kids, their mother has to make them practice the piano. You can't pull my son away from the piano. He needs teachers. I spend half the day thinking about what happens if I slip and fall down on my own front porch, you know? It should be hard. I like that it's hard. Putting your daughter through college, that's a man's job. A man's accomplishment. But it should be a little easier. Just a little easier.

The speech taps into genuine political concerns that many *West Wing* viewers might share: the rising costs of college education, the lack of funding for public schools that has gutted arts and music programs, and the precariousness of income in a labor force where one injury could destroy a family's financial security or where one downturn in the stock market could eat up their savings. Parry-Giles and Parry-Giles ultimately fault the episode for depicting "true Americans" as "agrarian, white, economically struggling, and members of households headed by males," a complaint that might have some validity.[6] However, such complaints overlook the—admittedly nostalgic—recollection of a functioning democracy that takes care of its citizens when they fulfill their end of the political bargain by working hard and contributing to the workforce. Although this vision of America may be somewhat idealized, it functions as an implicit critique of the conservative tendency to provide tax breaks for wealthy donors even while cutting vital social programs that support hard-working middle-class families.

HOPE AND CHANGE ON *THE WEST WING*

The West Wing also sought to provide storylines that challenged cynical perceptions about elections, a major focus of the show during its last two seasons, which featured a closely fought contest between two likeable candidates, Matt Santos, a young charismatic Latino politician who sought to build coalitions across party lines. Notably, Santos was based loosely on Barack Obama, who was then a junior senator from Illinois best known for his speech at the 2004 Democratic Convention, in which he sought to articulate a vision of national unity.[7] Competing against Santos was the Republican Arnold Vinick, a fiscal conservative and a social moderate from California. By making Vinick moderately pro-choice, Sorkin, Laurence O'Donnell, and the show's other writers, sought to create an election in which the Religious Right did not play a defining role. In that sense, the *West Wing* race served as an implicit fictional critique of the 2004 election between George W. Bush and John Kerry, in which issues such as abortion and gay marriage were frequently seen to overshadow topics such as the economy and global terrorism.

The *West Wing* election narrative also sought to place emphasis on the candidates' mutual respect, a quality that seemed notably absent from the 2004 election in which John Kerry's military service was frequently and derisively mocked by conservative political action committees to the point that many delegates at the Republican National Convention were spotted wearing Band-Aids with purple hearts on them to dismiss Kerry's military record. Both Vinick and Santos are depicted as being reluctant to use negative advertising, choosing instead to hold an election that was about competing political beliefs. This desire for genuine dialogue was expressed most explicitly in "The Debate," an episode from season seven. The episode, which was a stunt timed to attract a larger audience and higher ratings, is notable for a number of reasons: unlike most other scripted programs, it was filmed live, emulating the format of an actual political debate. Second, the episode used several strategies to create a more realistic appearance. It featured CBS news anchor Forrest Sawyer as the moderator, lending the show an added degree of verisimilitude. In addition, the episode was only loosely scripted, allowing the candidates to improvise, a scripting strategy that made the dialogue feel more conversational in tone. However, what was most notable about "The Debate" was its willingness to alter the traditional format of political debates by dispensing with rules that often limit answers to political questions to soundbites. As a result, Santos and Vinick were able to have a substantive debate about contrasting political philosophies and how their viewpoints might affect the types of policy debates they—or politicians who share their values—might make. As *New York Magazine's* John Leonard observed in his review of the episode, the show was unusual in its willingness to spend several minutes of primetime television focusing on topics ranging from debt relief in Africa to drug company profiteering, among other issues.[8]

The logic of "The Debate" is established early in the episode when Vinick complains to his campaign manager Bruno (Ron Silver) that the short time allotted for each candidate to respond to a question will make it impossible to address serious political questions. Once Vinick is on stage, he interrupts the moderator to propose that he and Santos ditch the rules that their campaign staffs have carefully negotiated:

> When the greatest hero of my party, Abraham Lincoln debated, he didn't need any rules. He wasn't afraid of a real debate. Now I could do a 2-minute version of my Sensible Solution stump speech and I'm sure Congressman Santos has a memorized opening statement ready to go. And then we could go on with this ritual and let the rules decide how much you're going to learn about the next President of the United States, or we could have a debate Lincoln would have been proud of.

Figure 5.1 Candidates step from behind the podiums to have a "real" debate on *The West Wing*

Vinick's framing helps to define "real debate" as something associated not only with a heroic politician but also against the presumably artificial rituals that debates have become.

Following the opening credits, the episode almost immediately launches into a back-and-forth dialogue between Vinick and Santos about the issues of border security and illegal immigration, particularly from Mexico, while in turn linking those issues to the question of free trade agreements. Vinick proposes that his administration would double the budget for border security, a strategy that Santos immediately portrays as futile. However, both candidates acknowledge the basic assumption that illegal immigration is driven in part by economic factors. As Santos succinctly puts it, "This is not a law enforcement problem. This is an economic problem." As a result, the candidates quickly shift the discussion to a debate about the Central American Free Trade Agreement (CAFTA), a free trade agreement that was ratified in June 2005, just a few months before "The Debate" aired in November of that year. Thus, although debate about CAFTA was several months old, The West Wing could frame the issue in a way that its viewers might understand the history of free trade agreements and the potential implications of them for both workers and consumers.

But in all cases, Vinick and Santos attribute their disagreements to contrasting beliefs about the role of government in people's lives. Santos, for example, makes the case for universal health coverage, which he characterizes as "Medicare for everyone." By comparison, Vinick argues for free market policies, arguing, for example, that price controls over prescription drugs limit innovation. The distinctions between the two candidates' governing philosophies were spelled out in Vinick's closing remarks. Although there was some friction during the debate, Vinick adopts a conciliatory tone in which he admits that he believes both candidates have the best interests of the country at heart but that their policies grow out of a broader set of values regarding the role of government. Rather than simply describing a series of seemingly disconnected policy ideas, Vinick and Santos grounded their views in a political philosophy, making the episode into a compelling, open-ended dialogue, one that seemed to offer a genuine clash of ideas.

As an example of "stunt television" timed to attract audiences to a fading TV series, "The Debate" was a masterful event, one that simultaneously evoked scripted television's relationship with liveness and its role in promoting political spectacle through the production of media events. It was also consistent with the spirit of TV show that sought to revive meaningful political debate over a system dominated by corruption and conflict. In this context, the "space of innocence" depicted on *The West Wing* turns out to come from its imagined White House staffers who all work for the good of the country while generally upholding the liberal principles that motivated them to seek a career in government in the first place.

SCANDAL

By comparison, Shonda Rhimes's ABC drama *Scandal* seems to portray a political culture in which the utopian aspects of Washington are increasingly attenuated, if not absent altogether, submerged under personal ambition. The show depicts the work of "fixer," Olivia Pope (Kerry Washington), as she and her employees work to handle various public relations crises faced by Washington's most influential people. Pope is consistent with female characters in other recent political melodramas, including *The Good Wife* and *Homeland*, which feature women who are "consummate problem solvers" in the (political) workplace while struggling to manage their personal lives.[9] In Pope's case, she displays a remarkable acumen for protecting the interests of the powerful: it is her job to ensure that countless scandals never go public. Although *Scandal* has frequently been associated with melodrama in the entertainment press, this connection is usually treated negatively, with reviewers defining the show as "soapy." The show's serial narrative invites protracted feelings of suspense as the show's major characters face moments of physical or professional danger, ranging from the political scandals that could potentially sink the presidency, and with it the reputation of the nation itself, to Olivia's kidnapping by her father. In turn, these suspense plots fit within larger goals of attaining some form of "moral legibility" within what seems to be a hopelessly corrupt political system, a search that is linked to a larger desire to locate goodness. In the case of *Scandal*, this search seems linked to the emotional and physical suffering that many of the show's characters have endured, often in the context of serving the country, such as Huck's emotional trauma after serving the country in a top-secret military organization. Finally, *Scandal* fits more commonplace definitions of melodrama, with its emphasis on emotional and stylistic excesses. Although melodrama is often faulted for its excessiveness, these stylistic flourishes help to make many of the show's moral and ethical questions more legible. Thus, in essence, *Scandal*'s overarching narrative is not simply about how the Washington elite preserve and consolidate power. It consistently illustrates the psychic costs involved in preserving an illusion of national innocence. But these melodramatic aspects have invited many popular critics to dismiss the show. Alyssa Rosenberg, in an early assessment of the show, remarks that "*Scandal* is a deeply silly show without much to say about the way that Washington actually works," even if she appreciates some of the political stances taken in select episodes.[10] Such complaints about *Scandal*'s fidelity to actual Washington miss the larger purpose of the show's calculated use of melodramatic storytelling in order to make sense of how power functions within political culture.

Notably, Pope also has a long-simmering relationship with the Republican president, Fitzgerald Grant (Tony Goldwyn), which began when Pope worked on his campaign. As a result, the show has often been criticized for its portrayal of a professional African-American woman who still is lovesick over an even more powerful white, married man. The show fleetingly addresses this issue in one early episode, in which Pope explains her concern, telling Grant "I'm feeling a little Sally Hemings-Thomas Jefferson about all this," a shorthand way of referring to the power imbalance between the two of them. In addition, the show depicted the complicity of several people who worked on the Grant campaign in tampering with voting machines in Defiance, Ohio, actions that likely turned the election over to him. Thus, at the very heart of the show is the realization that Grant's presidency is, in many ways, an illegitimate one.

In the show's first two seasons, *Scandal* tends to focus on how Pope engages with her wealthy clients. In the second episode of the first season, Pope helps to protect a DC-based madam, Sharon Marquette (Mimi Kennedy), with several high-profile clients. As Rosenberg notes, the episode offers a sympathetic pop culture retelling of the story of Deborah Jean Palfrey, who committed suicide before going to trial, although Pope works to protect her DC madam, in part, by contacting Sharon's clients and threatening them.

Later, the series begins to focus more explicitly on Olivia's relationship with her father, Eli Pope (Joe Morton), who runs a secretive governmental organization known as B-613. During one particular scene, Eli lectures his daughter on her continued affair with the president, reminding her that she is placing herself in a vulnerable position. Although Pope defends the president, suggesting that he would not do anything to destroy her career, Eli asserts that the office of the presidency is more powerful than any one individual: "Whose victory do you think they will fight for? Whose body do you think they will bury? That is the presidency versus you . . . . You and I both know that he is not in charge. He is never in charge. Power is in charge. Power got him elected." Later, in one of the more iconic lines of the series, Olivia's father compels her to repeat that as an African-American woman she would have to be "twice as good as them to get half of what they have."[11] Eli's presence on the show helped bring to the surface some of the complicated issues of political power associated with Olivia's role in upholding a corrupt system that tended to reinforce the interests of wealthy and powerful individuals who control political institutions even while providing us with the illusion of democratic control.

"THE LAWN CHAIR"

Many of these moral and ethical questions about Pope's role in preserving the political status quo were turned on their head when the show addressed questions about police violence against African Americans. Written in the wake of several incidents of police violence against African-American males, an episode of Scandal titled "The Lawn Chair" was broadcast on March 5, 2015, just one day after a grand jury ruled that Ferguson, Missouri, police officer Darren Wilson would not be charged with civil rights violations in the death of unarmed black teenager, Michael Brown. More crucially, the Department of Justice had also released a report documenting systemic abuses by the Ferguson Police Department. Although the exact timing of the episode was something of a coincidence, it also functioned as a site for using narrative television to address real social and political concerns in a powerful way. The episode was widely seen as a departure from Scandal's usual focus on the political corruption associated with Washington, DC. However, rather than seeing the episode as a standalone storyline, the conflict in "The Lawn Chair" bears the weight of the entire series, including Pope's conflicted relationships with two major authority figures, President Grant and her father. In fact, its adoption of a ripped-from-the-headlines procedural drama format allowed the show to participate in what Yvonne Tasker referred to, in a different context, as "crime drama's ongoing engagement with the ethics of policing and the politics of race in the United States."[12]

The episode's opening sequence features Olivia Pope driving to a crime scene in which a 17-year-old African-American teenager was killed during a confrontation with the police. We are told by the police chief that the teen was waving a knife and that the officers were "well within their rights" to shoot. Pope, spotting the myriad cell phone cameras held up by protestors, worries that the situation could escalate into a riot and promises the police chief that she will work to get the federal government involved. Moments later, the boy's father, Clarence Parker (Courtney B. Vance), walks into the crime scene, fires a shotgun into the air, and demands to see the officer who killed his son. At this point, Pope is unable to convince the attorney general (Joshua Malina) to get involved, and the boy's father is joined by a local activist, Marcus (Cornelius Smith, Jr.), who brings him a lawn chair so that

Figure 5.2 Kerry Washington as Olivia Pope on the "Lawn Chair" episode of *Scandal*

he will not have to stand. Olivia again asks the two men to leave so that the situation can be "defused," but both men refuse, even as Olivia reasserts her access to the attorney general. Marcus, suspecting that she is working for the police, admonishes Clarence to stay. Olivia defends herself saying, "I'm not the enemy." Marcus responds by asking, "Are you sure?" This confrontation places emphasis on Pope's complicity with political institutions that have not addressed the interests of African Americans like those in Marcus and Clarence's community.

Later, Olivia's "Gladiators" go through computer records to find background information on Marcus, Clarence, and his son. Marcus is an honors graduate from Georgetown with a podcast on Civil Rights issues. Clarence is a steady employee, and his son is set to graduate high school, and is represented via photos showing him smiling in a football uniform. Marcus leads a chant of "Stand up . . . fight back . . . no more black men under attack." While the protests are taking place, Olivia questions the officer who shot the teen. The officer appears sympathetic, stating that he feared for his life and that he felt for the boy's parents, again echoing the circumstances in which Missouri teenager Michael Brown was killed. Marcus continues to question Olivia's credibility, calling attention to her Prada handbag and questioning whether she has ever experienced the poverty and racism of his neighborhood, while also adding that he knows she has worked to get a white Republican president elected twice.

Later in the episode, after talking with Clarence about how he tried to protect his son from police brutality—requiring him to say to his father where he was going, putting a university bumper sticker on the back of his car—Olivia becomes increasingly disapproving of her role in managing the "optics" of the protests for the police. This is particularly the case after President Grant makes the decision to vet a vice president, deflecting attention away from the situation, prompting Olivia to join the chanting protestors and pushing the police chief to delay bringing out riot gear designed to disperse the crowd. Olivia also learns that the police have a video recording of the shooting but have been suppressing it because, we are told, it shows the shooting did not take place as the officer described it. Once again, Olivia confronts David, the attorney general, begging him to open an investigation and admitting that her powers as a political fixer cannot address the legacies of institutional racism that have created the situation: "I can't fix this, David! It's too much."

After describing the experience of living in a state of constant fear that many black people face, Olivia convinces David to subpoena the footage of the shooting, which reveals that the officer had arrested another suspect for the shoplifting crime and shot Brandon for no apparent reason and planted the knife on him. Once Olivia reveals this information, the officer is shown to be racist, arguing that he risks his life daily to deal with people who show no respect to him: "Brandon Parker is dead because he didn't show respect." The episode culminates with David reporting that the officer is being arrested for altering evidence, perjury, and filing a false report and that his office would be conducting an independent investigation. Olivia tells Clarence that Brandon was reaching for a receipt for the cell phone he was suspected of stealing. As the episode concludes, it reaches something of a false utopia with Olivia leading Clarence past the famous portrait of John F. Kennedy, his arms folded in front of him, to meet President Grant in the White House. This meeting is crosscut with David's press conference announcing the federal investigation.

The episode provoked both effusive praise and harsh criticism for how it addressed the issues related to the issue of police violence. Lauren McEwen of *The Baltimore Sun* argued that the show's departure from its normal campy, soapy mode marked the episode as "brave and powerful and necessary" in its attempt to tackle racial privilege.[13] *The A.V. Club's* Joshua Alston, by comparison, complained that the show "comes across as condescending wish fulfillment," in which video evidence is taken seriously by well-meaning public officials who then pursue justice against the actions of a clear-cut example of abuse of power.[14] Meanwhile, *Slate's* Aisha Harris is more ambivalent, pointing out that the episode was one of the first times that *Scandal* requires Olivia "to fully grapple with her complicated role as a black woman serving the mostly white federal government."[15] However, Harris was also attentive to the fact that the episode left little to no room for any complexity: Brandon is essentially a good kid who gets framed by an undeniably racist cop. Brandon's death is captured on camera, and the video is treated as indisputable evidence that the officer acted illegally, which was not the case with other high-profile cases, including the death of Eric Garner. Reactions to the episode were so divided that Shonda Rimes, the showrunner for *Scandal*, felt compelled to explain on Twitter that the resolution had been the subject of significant debate as the episode was being produced: "We had a great deal of debate about this ending. Whether to be hopeful or not. It was really hard. In the end we went with what fulfilling the dream SHOULD mean. The idea of possibility. And the despair we feel now."[16] I mention this discussion, in part, because it helps to illustrate how political TV, using "ripped-from-the-headlines" narratives, can introduce and work through topics that are often politically polarizing. More crucially, prominent TV critics helped to frame the interpretations of the episode, placing it within current debates about police violence.

HOUSE OF CARDS

Like *Scandal*, *House of Cards* also uses melodrama to explore the multifaceted relationships among the power-hungry political players in Washington, DC's political and media cultures. Notably, *House of Cards* offers little hope that a truly democratic politics can ever be restored. Politicians on *House of Cards* either cynically manipulate the system to serve personal gain or, when they have good intentions, they are essentially powerless, often because of their sincere desire to advocate for justice or transparency. The show focuses on Frank Underwood, who begins the series as a South Carolina Congressman who embarks on a ruthless pursuit of power after he is snubbed by the president for the position of secretary of state, setting in motion an ongoing narrative in which Underwood manipulates his way from the House of Representatives to the vice presidency and eventually the White House. Frank's defiant attitude toward his political opponents is even expressed in the initials engraved on his signet ring: "F. U." *House of Cards* is, perhaps, best known for being the first original series picked up by the subscription video service, Netflix. The show was based on a 1990 BBC series, one that offered an overtly partisan commentary on the failures of the Conservative party rather than a more general expression of cynicism about electoral politics.[17] But unlike the British version, the Netflix version is less interested in a partisan political critique than in dramatizing a more generalized disdain for the ease with which the political process can be manipulated by power.

Frank's relentless pursuit of power is established during the first season when Underwood makes a pact with an ambitious young journalist, Zoe Barnes (Kate Mara), with whom Underwood has an affair while also feeding her scoops about his political rivals. Zoe initially works on the margins of the DC media bubble on the metropolitan beat for the *Washington Herald*, a newspaper loosely based on *The Washington Post*. Through their collaboration, Underwood is able to manipulate his way into the vice presidency. He also coerces a younger colleague, Peter Russo (Cory Stoll), into running for the governorship of Pennsylvania before turning on him and driving him into drug addiction and self-destruction, then murdering him and making it appear to be a suicide. Later, during the second season, Frank begins to realize that Zoe now represents a threat to his goals of gaining power because she knows information that could destroy his reputation. As a result, Frank arranges to meet her in a Washington subway station, where he pushes her in front of an oncoming train, again with the result that her death appears to be a suicide.

By the third season, Underwood has manipulated his way to the presidency; however, he also faces the challenge of getting re-elected in a hostile political environment. Frank's signature piece of legislation is a massive jobs program called America Works, in which he promises to achieve full employment. The jobs program evokes both the New Deal programs passed by Franklin Roosevelt and more contemporary calls for jobs stimulus packages. However, when Congress fails to pass Underwood's America Works bill into law, Frank defiantly works around the legislative system, using an obscure law to declare the city of Washington, DC, a "state of emergency" because of mass unemployment, allowing him to use money set aside for natural disasters through FEMA, the Federal Emergency Management Agency, to create jobs for DC residents, in order to demonstrate the value of his program so that he can sell it on a national level. Frank's gambit partially fails when a hurricane hits, forcing him to divert the money for his jobs program back to its intended purpose of aiding communities that have been hit by natural disasters. Although Frank's cynicism makes it impossible to view America Works as a sincere attempt to alleviate the problems of mass unemployment, his legislation does evoke some aspects of the American Dream, the idea that everyone should be able to succeed if they are willing to engage in a little hard work. However, rather than creating work that is meaningful and rewarding, Underwood creates jobs that serve no real purpose other than to provide work for the inner-city (read: black) unemployed, an approach that reinforces Frank's paternalistic attitude toward the public he serves.

During his election campaign, Underwood faces two major challengers: Heather Dunbar, a grassroots politician who has campaigned against income inequality, and Jackie Sharp, his protégé in political manipulation in the House of Representatives. By episode 3.11, Sharp, recognizing that she is unlikely to get the nomination, begins playing both candidates against each other, seeking out what both candidates are willing to offer her in exchange for her endorsement. Thus, House of Cards almost entirely lacks the "utopian" impulses evident in other shows. Although Frank's political success may be hollow, there is little sense that the show can imagine anything resembling hope for a more democratic and just political system.

MELODRAMA AND FEMALE POLITICAL CAMPAIGNS

Although this chapter so far has focused on questions about general perceptions of Washington's political culture, a number of melodramas of political process have also focused more narrowly on the issue of how female candidates negotiate the political process. One of the pioneering shows to address this issue was the short-lived ABC series, Commander in Chief, which starred Geena Davis as Mackenzie Allen, a female vice president who takes over the Oval Office when the Republican president who nominated her suffers a brain aneurism. Appearing just a few years after the terrorist attacks of September 11 and during the height of the Iraq War, the show, as its title suggests, focused primarily on Allen's capacity to direct the masculine domain of the military, that is to serve as the country's commander in chief. In fact, this concern about her ability to lead is so pronounced that the dying president actually advises her to step down for the good of the country, allowing someone else to lead. Like many female political leaders—including Teá Leoni's Elizabeth McCord on the CBS series Secretary of State—Allen is depicted as a political outsider, someone who might not be prepared to lead the country and to navigate the masculine world of Washington's political culture. However, Allen is able to consolidate power during her first public speech when she appeals to the historic significance of the presidency. Later in the speech—which she ad-libs once her Teleprompter breaks, allowing her to speak honestly, rather than through a canned political speech—Allen takes a militaristic posture, promising to "defend our Constitution" and name-dropping Harry Truman as a model for her concept of power. Although *Commander in Chief* had only a brief run on ABC, it offers a useful framework for thinking about how female lawmakers have been depicted on political TV.

More recently, a number of shows have continued to address the possibility of a female presidency, many of them responding to the experiences of Democratic Senator and Secretary of State Hillary Clinton, who competed in a closely contested Democratic primary against Barack Obama in 2008 and announced that she would be running again in 2016. The USA Network mini series *Political Animals* featured Sigourney Weaver as Elaine Barish, the estranged wife of Bud Hammond (Ciarán Hinds), a popular former president and Southern governor who had a past history of being a womanizer and having a voracious appetite for fast food. Barish has been appointed secretary of state by her political rival after losing a closely contested Democratic primary to a more charismatic candidate, Paul Garcetti (Adrian Pasdar), a character transparently modeled on Barack Obama, Clinton's rival for the Democratic nomination in 2008. The show's creator, Greg Berlanti, adds some details not directly associated with the Clintons: Barish has three children, one of whom is a gay, suicidal drug addict. The show was an explicit bid by the USA Network to attract the "quality" drama audience through its explicit appeals to cosmopolitan taste cultures via its engagement with timely political content and innovative storytelling.[18] In addition to appealing to fans of political entertainment, the show's depiction of powerful women seemed designed to appeal to a largely female audience, as well, a continuation of a trend in U.S. television programming since the late 1990s.[19] Although *Political Animals* was not picked up by the USA Network as a regular series, the show offers what Emily Nussbaum aptly described as a "meditation on the toxic nature of the spotlight."[20] In this sense, *Political Animals* examines the personal toll of a life in politics, especially for women who face gendered expectations about women and power.

Political Animals, through its dramatic retelling of the Clinton/Obama rivalry, offers an engaging reflection on how the political media played a crucial role in shaping perceptions of powerful women as they seek high political office. During the opening episode, Barish has a frank conversation with her husband, a popular former president, honestly evaluating her popularity among American voters: "It's me they have mixed feelings about. And don't give me that crap about 'They'd love me if they knew me.' It's been twenty years. They know me." Barish's comments explicitly echo the evaluations of the 2008 Democratic primaries, in which many pundits asserted that Clinton lost because she was less "likeable" than Obama—an assertion that was often informed by gendered assumptions about women in power. In fact, during a debate prior to the 2008 New Hampshire primary, one debate moderator directly asked her how she would appeal to voters who liked her résumé but were supposedly struggling with the "likeability factor."[21] By inviting us to sympathize with Barish, the show was, in essence, using a melodramatic storyline to invite viewers to evaluate Clinton differently by showing the additional challenges she faced as a prominent female politician. The show also created a foil for Barish, a hardened, Pulitzer Prize-winning reporter, Susan Berg (Carla Gugino), a frequent critic of Barish and who was reportedly modeled on *New York Times* columnist Maureen Dowd, who was known as a vociferous critic of the Clintons.[22]

These questions about perceptions of female presidents were also addressed in HBO's docudrama *Game Change*, which depicted Sarah Palin's unsuccessful run for the vice presidency during the 2008 election. *Game Change* engages in a variety of aesthetic techniques that ground the film as a kind of intertextual docudrama, with its deft mix of archival interviews from CNN, MSNBC, and *Saturday Night Live* and actors portraying key players in the McCain–Palin campaign. In this sense, *Game Change* evokes past HBO political dramas, including *Tanner '88* and *K Street*, which each used a mixture of scripted drama and archival footage in order to develop a storyline around the concept of the political spectacle. This use of archival footage also helps to track media reactions to and depictions of Palin, showing their responsibility for defining her as a public figure as the 2008 presidential election continued to unfold. Like other HBO programs, *Game Change* was promoted within the discourses of quality television, but because it was a singular event, HBO also promoted it as what John Thornton Caldwell describes as "event-status programming," a political narrative that was original and distinct from other attempts to narrate the 2008 election.[23] As a result, *Game Change* is notable because it functioned as one of the more visible analyses of that election and the new visibility of the political operatives who sought to shape it. Thus, unlike the serialized narratives of television news that try to make sense of a campaign while it is happening, one of the strengths of a singular film or miniseries is the ability to make sense of a significant political event such as an election or political scandal.

More than anything, the movie functions as a critique of the role of political operatives in shaping election decision-making. The film opens with a post-election CNN interview with Steve Schmidt (Woody Harrelson) hosted by Anderson Cooper. Intercutting archival footage of Cooper with shots of Harrelson (as Schmidt) reflecting on the campaign, we see that Schmidt struggles to answer whether he has any regrets about the lost election. The film then flashes back to the pivotal moment when Schmidt recommended Palin (Julianne Moore) in part to counter Barack Obama's status as a celebrity, feeling that she could achieve a similar level of stardom based on a series of YouTube videos that convince him that Palin "is a star." However, Schmidt and other members of his campaign staff rush the vetting process that is routinely used to evaluate candidates, and they quickly discover Palin's significant flaws. From there, Schmidt works with Nicolle Wallace (Sarah Paulson) on shaping Palin into a viable vice-presidential candidate, a challenge that *Game Change* portrays as insurmountable given Palin's lack of knowledge about national and international politics.

While the movie is grounded in historic events, it is also a narrative reconstruction of those events, one that, in this case, collapsed a ten-week political campaign into a two-hour narrative. As a result, *Game Change* helped to reinforce a specific narrative about the place of Palin in the 2008 election. Notably, Palin is portrayed somewhat sympathetically as a naïve but sincere politician who was unprepared for the glare of the national spotlight. We first see Palin at an amusement park with her daughters wearing a loose-fitting sweatshirt that differs significantly from the stylish, perfectly tailored suits and skirts that she typically wore during the campaign. These scenes help to reinforce an image of Palin as an overwhelmed "hockey mom" who balances her domestic duties of caring for a small child and a family of teenagers with the rigors of running for political office. Invariably during phone calls, she is seen holding and sometimes feeding her toddler Trig. In addition to Palin's hockey mom persona, Game Change depicts her as mercurial and generally incurious about politics, unaware of what the Federal Reserve does and oblivious to the fact that the Queen is not the political head of state in Great Britain. She lashes out at Schmidt, Wallace, and the rest of the campaign staff for trying to turn her into a "puppet," even while she works to memorize sound-bite answers for political events such as debates and interviews. Eventually, the film implicitly blames her for fanning the populist attacks on Obama that reinforced perceptions of him as a Muslim or Socialist who was not born in the United States. Ultimately, Game Change depicts Palin not as an active agent who vigorously campaigned for office than as a product of the campaign itself, someone whose authenticity was destroyed by a political campaign's desperate attempts to create a narrative about her. At the same time, Game Change seems to have some sympathy for the overmatched political operatives Steve Schmidt and Nicolle Wallace, as they were confronted with the challenge of building a campaign around someone who clearly wasn't ready for a national political campaign.

LOCAL POLITICS AND *THE GOOD WIFE*

The legal drama The Good Wife also focuses on many of the concerns associated with women in politics. When the series begins, Alicia Florrick is a homemaker raising two children while her husband, Peter, works as a prominent attorney in Chicago. When it is revealed that Peter is having an affair, Alicia leaves him and also restarts her career as a lawyer. The series uses a complex, serialized narrative not only to track Alicia's growing prominence as a lawyer but also the implications for her personal life, as she makes choices about her relationship with her estranged husband, while also working to parent two children. In addition, the show also uses procedural narratives associated with courtroom dramas, many of which are resolved after a single episode, to address the complexities of the legal system and its role in interpreting the law. Notably, the show has been one of the most effective political dramas to address the relationship between technology and the law.[24] For example, in one season five episode, Alicia and her colleagues face the challenge of prosecuting a case in which a gun printed using 3D technologies goes off and accidentally kills an innocent bystander. Although the initial impulse is to pursue litigation against the designer of the gun, the issue becomes more complex when modifications to the original model, the environment in which the gun was printed, and the printer being used all become extenuating factors that might have contributed to why the gun misfired. In other cases, the show addresses the complex legal and moral issues at stake in prominent court cases, as when a gay couple sued a bakery because it refused to make a cake for their wedding. During the episode, Diane Lockhart agrees to a mock trial in which she and a rival lawyer map out the free speech and religious grounds that would define such a case if it were to go to court.

At the same time, the show also addressed some of the challenges that politicians, and women in particular, face when running for political office. Like many other melodramas of political process, The Good Wife offers a relatively cynical depiction of American politics, one in which elections often force candidates, even those who are highly principled like Alicia, to make ethical and political compromises. Similarly, even while an election to a local office like the state's attorney may seem like it has relatively minor stakes, the potential for corruption still very much exists. During at least one episode, in fact, Alicia and her opponent, Frank Prady, seek out donations from some of the exact same people, making promises that will satisfy the contributors' interests. However, even while Alicia and Frank become subsumed within a political machine that seems to swallow them up, they do make some effort to run a principled campaign. For example, Alicia, despite the non-coordination rules associated with political action committees, makes it known that she wants a robo-call alleging that Frank is gay to be stopped.

Perhaps the most notable example of Alicia and Frank's respectful rivalry comes in season 6, episode 12, "The Debate," in which the two candidates meet for a debate that, improbably enough, is being hosted by MSNBC's Chris Matthews, a detail that intentionally overstates the spectacular aspects of the event. The debate plot intersects with another storyline, in which two police officers are on trial for the death of an unarmed black man, a story that loosely invokes similar incidents in Ferguson, Missouri, and Staten Island, New York. The debate sequences powerfully satirize the ways in which actual

Figure 5.3 Alicia Florrick debates with her opponent in a kitchen on *The Good Wife*

debates tend to result in sound-bite responses that are short on details. In fact, at one point Matthews, with the trial verdict looming in the background, asks Alicia to "talk about race relations in Chicago," adding that she has 45 seconds to answer. When the not-guilty verdict is announced, it sets off a further change of events: peaceful marches, in which protestors chant "black lives matter," and in what appears to be a private moment between the two of them, a conversation between Alicia and Frank in a kitchen, which ultimately turns into an impromptu debate, where the absence of rules allows the two of them to have a productive conversation about their political philosophies. Meanwhile, a crowd of workers and staff members fill the kitchen, and they join the lively conversation, one that is shaped by the events unfolding outside the auditorium where the debate is taking place. Alicia and Frank reach some consensus on how to reduce conflict between the police and black Chicago residents, agreeing, for example, that the city should stop prosecuting minor drug offenses. Although the episode offers no full solution to the problem of police violence against blacks, it offers a more complex mapping out of the issue, recognizing that there are no simple solutions.

Ultimately, Alicia's campaign is undermined by a scandal, in which someone who was described as a supporter reportedly tampered with some voting machines in a small number of districts. Although it was revealed later that the dirty tricks involved were more complex, the Democratic party in Illinois pressures her to resign for the good of the party because they fear that a recount would trigger recounts in other races and as a result, they might lose their supermajority in the Illinois state house. As a result, Alicia, despite her good intentions in running for office, finds herself confronted by political and corporate powers that are larger than her, leading her, as season six concludes, to return to practicing law. As her husband, now the governor of Illinois told her, "Winning an election in Chicago is difficult. But winning an election in Chicago while keeping your integrity is a miracle." Although Alicia's miracle is ultimately tarnished, *The Good Wife* highlights how serialized political melodrama can engage with vital questions about our political process. Instead of clear heroes and villains, Alicia, in her career as a lawyer and politician, is forced to navigate complex questions of justice and morality, as they play out within the legal and electoral system. In this regard, the show, perhaps more powerfully than other political melodramas, offers a provocative exploration of the complexities of American political culture at both the local and the national levels.

CONCLUSION

Melodramas of political process invite audiences to sort through complex moral questions about the role of government in everyday life. These questions encompass everything from the processes of legislating and the backstage negotiations that shape passing laws to the practices of campaigning for office and even the role of the legal system in interpreting complex laws. *The West Wing*, as I have argued, cultivated melodramatic narratives that evaluated complex political questions through both episodic narratives and serialized storylines that could run for full seasons, as when Bartlet ran for re-election or when Matt Santos began his political campaign. In this sense, the show offered a utopian narrative that produced an imagined Washington political culture shaped less by the influence of money in politics than by the principled politicians and public servants who sought to use their power to make positive change in society.

By comparison, many contemporary serialized narratives, including *Scandal* and *House of Cards*, portray a political culture that seems hopelessly corrupt and unable to serve the interests of its citizens. In *Scandal*, Olivia Pope's work seems geared not to preserve democracy but to preserve the illusion of it, and many of the show's pleasures seem grounded in Pope's proficiency in holding this political system together, despite the fact that it is corrupt. In *House of Cards*, for example, Frank Underwood ascends to the highest office in the land without receiving a single vote in a national election, a narrative that seems to imply that a corrupt public official could manipulate the rules of the constitution to work around the will of the people. However, this narrative of political corruption, for the most part, ignores many of the real sources of power, including the role of campaign financing. Thus, Frank, in many ways, is part of a longer tradition of serial antiheroes—such as Tony Soprano or *Breaking Bad*'s Walter White—where viewers can find enjoyment not in a character's actions but in how that character operates, how he manipulates the system in which he operates, whether that entails the Mafia or the halls of political power. Thus, *House of Cards* embraces what Jason Mittell has called an "operational allegiance," in which we become invested in how the character's story is told.[25] Frank's audacious manipulation of the levers of power, his Shakespearean asides filled with contempt not just for his political rivals but even the general public, and his ongoing alliance with his wife all contribute to our fascination with him. In this sense, *House of Cards*, while utterly cynical about corruption, is also attentive to the ways in which political institutions, including the non-governmental organization for which Frank's wife works, can be manipulated for personal, rather than public gain.

Many of these questions about political power have been revisited in complex ways in the serial legal melodrama *The Good Wife*, which combines an episodic treatment of complex legal issues with a serial narrative following Alicia Florrick's rise from a homemaker to a lowly associate lawyer through a run for the office of state's attorney, producing what Mittell calls a "cumulative, multi-institutional serialized storyworld," in which Florrick constantly negotiates the halls of legal, corporate, and media power in the corrupt world of Illinois politics. Florrick's experience in running for the state's attorney office illustrates the real toll of running for even a statewide office. In fact, after Eli reports to Florrick that electronic ballots may have been hacked in order to ensure that she would win the election, Alicia says, in resignation, "It doesn't end, does it? You think it's over. It's never over."

As *The Good Wife* powerfully illustrates, running for political office increasingly entails both personal and professional scrutiny, leading to increasingly difficult moral choices. At the same time, Alicia and her colleagues consistently face conflicts about complex legal issues regarding free speech, and freedom of religion, especially as those issues are inflected by new communication technologies. In this sense, the show offers a powerful example of how the melodrama of political process can be used to engage with complex issues that affect both legal and legislative institutions.

NOTES

1 Linda Williams, "Mega-Melodrama!" 526. See also Mittell, *Complex TV*, 244.

2 Donnalyn Pompper, "*The West Wing*: White House Narratives that Journalism Cannot Tell," in *The West Wing: The American Presidency as Television Drama*, ed. Peter C. Rollins and John E. O'Connor (Syracuse: Syracuse University Press, 2003), 19.

3 The concept of "cumulative" narrative is taken from Horace Newcomb, *TV: The Most Popular Art* (New York: Anchor, 1974).

4 McCabe, *The West Wing*, (Detroit: Wayne State University Press 2012), 5.

5 Trevor Parry-Giles and Shawn Parry-Giles, *The Prime-Time Presidency: The West Wing and U.S. Nationalism* (Urbana: University of Illinois Press, 2006), 102.

6 Parry-Giles ad Parry-Giles, *The Prime-Time Presidency*, 103.

7 Jonathan Feedland, "From *The West Wing* to the Real Thing," *The Guardian*, February 21, 2008, http://www.theguardian.com/world/2008/feb/21/barackobama.uselections2008.

8 John Leonard, "They've Got Issues," *New York Magazine*, November 7, 2005, http://nymag.com/nymetro/arts/tv/reviews/15031/.

9 Diane Negra and Jorie Lagerwey, "Analyzing *Homeland*: An Introduction," *Cinema Journal* 54.4 (Summer 2015), 128.

10 Alyssa Rosenberg, "'Scandal:' Olivia Pope, Sally Hemings, and the Dangers of Race Neutrality," *Think Progress*, April 20, 2012, http://thinkprogress.org/alyssa/2012/04/20/467938/scandal-olivia-pope-sally-hemings/.

11 Alyssa Rosenberg, "Black Power, Black Responsibility and the Big Question for Olivia Pope from 'Scandal,'" *Washington Post*, April 18, 2014, http://www.washingtonpost.com/news/act-four/wp/2014/04/18/black-power-black-responsibility-and-the-big-question-for-olivia-pope-from-scandal/.

12 Yvonne Tasker, "Television Crime Drama and Homeland Security: From *Law & Order* to 'Terror TV,'" *Cinema Journal* 51.4 (Summer 2012): 46.

13 Lauren McEwen, "*Scandal* Recap, 'The Lawn Chair,'" *The Baltimore Sun*, March 6, 2015 http://www.baltimoresun.com/entertainment/bthesite/tv-lust/bal-scandal-recap-the-lawn-chair-20150306-story.html#page=1.

14 Joshua Alston, "*Scandal*, 'The Lawn Chair:' Cheap Shots Fired," *A.V. Club*, March 6, 2015 http://www.avclub.com/tvclub/scandal-lawn-chair-215985.

15 Aisha Harris, "Why *Scandal's* Ferguson-Themed Episode was so Frustrating," *Slate*, March 6, 2015, http://www.slate.com/blogs/browbeat/2015/03/06/scandal_police_brutality_episode_the_lawn_chair_tackles_michael_brown_video.html.

16 Quoted in Kat Ward, "'The Lawn Chair:' Ferguson Comes to Olivia Pope's Washington," *Entertainment Weekly*, March 5, 2015, http://www.ew.com/recap/scandal-season-4-episode-14.

17 Steve Erickson, "It's All in the Game," *The American Prospect* 24.2 (March–April 2013), 75–78.

18 For a discussion of the quality TV audience, see Mittell, *Complex TV*, 211.

19 See Amanda D. Lotz, *Redesigning Women: Television after the Network Era* (Urbana: University of Illinois Press, 2006).

20 Emily Nussbaum, "'Political Animals:' A Hillary Clinton Fever Dream," *The New Yorker*, July 12, 2012, http://www.newyorker.com/culture/culture-desk/political-animals-a-hillary-clinton-fever-dream.

21 "The Democratic Debate in New Hampshire," *The New York Times*, January 5, 2008, http://www.nytimes.com/2008/01/05/us/politics/05text-ddebate.html?pagewanted=all&_r=0.

22 Alyssa Rosenberg, "'Political Animals:' Finally a Show that Loves Powerful Women," *The Atlantic*, July 13, 2012, http://www.theatlantic.com/entertainment/archive/2012/07/political-animals-finally-a-show-that-loves-powerful-women/259752/.

23 John Thornton Caldwell, *Televisuality*, 163.

24 Clive Thompson, "From Anonymous to Bitcoin, The Good Wife is the Most Tech-Savvy Show on TV," *Wired*, September 27, 2013, http://www.wired.com/2013/09/screen-smarts/.

25 Jason Mittell, *Complex TV*, 163.

6

SURVEILLANCE CULTURE: MELODRAMAS OF NATIONAL SECURITY

While political process melodramas have sought to depict the complexities of political institutions, melodramas of national security address the question of the ethics of America's counterterrorism efforts. These questions unquestionably intensified significantly after the terrorist attacks on September 11, 2001, and have continued to evolve in the light of ongoing tensions associated with the threat of terrorist activity. Because of this enduring conflict, narratives about the role of the national security state in engaging with terrorism have continued to remain relevant—and, in some sense, urgent—as we attempt to grapple with the effectiveness of the response to terrorism and the larger moral questions about the practices associated with combatting terrorism, such as data mining and surveillance programs, racial profiling, and even the use of torture to obtain intelligence. With these concerns in mind, this chapter focuses on the genre conventions and narrative devices that national security melodramas have used to engage with these questions.

Like the melodramas of political process, national security melodramas fall within a number of textual and industrial models, ranging from what might be called political procedurals that use a case-of-the-week narrative to engage with a variety of security threats to complex serialized narratives that can weave storylines over the course of a single TV season (even if that season depicts events that take place over a single day) or even multiple seasons. This move from process to national security also entails a shift from the politics of spectacle to the politics of surveillance, to tweak Michel Foucault's famous formulation. Melodramas of political process frequently attend to the spectacular events—debates, conventions, speeches, press conference, and all other media events—that define campaign discourse. They call attention to the staging of politics, even when those performances are orchestrated in the proverbial smoke-filled backrooms, and power often seems to derive from the ability to craft a more compelling narrative than political rivals. National security melodramas, by comparison, engage with the processes and practices of surveillance by government intelligence agencies such as the FBI and CIA, or, in some cases, fictional agencies that are ostensibly even more secretive, hidden from the public and the accountability that would entail.

This chapter argues that national security melodramas have become a vital site for engaging with the morality and legality of spying and counterterrorism. Although a number of national security melodramas have been blamed for endorsing the use of torture or for offering stereotypical depictions of Arabs or Muslims as terrorists, I contend that many of these shows actually engage with the complexity of the moral choices made in the name of national defense. Of course, many of these shows do contain narrative elements or characters that reinforce stereotypes or intensify fears of terrorist attacks; however, most melodramas of national security often include content that is politically ambivalent. Thus, instead of a coherent position on American national security policies, these shows instead illustrate the ways in which characters' positions, values, and behaviors may evolve over the course of time.

This narrative complexity is the product not only of a cultural desire to engage with the moral nuances of national security but also an industrial logic driven by a quickly evolving television industry marked by new models of distribution. As Jennifer Gillan has demonstrated, the Fox show 24 emerged in an industrial culture in which the network television model of advertising-supported broadcasting was increasingly threatened by both time-shifting tools such as the DVR and by mounting competition from quality cable dramas on HBO and other channels. In order to keep viewers engaged with the show, Fox devised a number of innovative distribution strategies that would make the experience of the show more cohesive. Notably, Fox's parent company News Corp. dramatically shortened the show's distribution window, running marathons of 24 on their cable channel FX before the season was complete, in order to allow audiences to catch up on what they'd missed or to consume full seasons as one cohesive unit, rather than spreading the experience out over weeks or months. By the fourth season, Fox was experimenting with broadcasting double "blocks" of the show over consecutive nights, a strategy that served to turn the new season of 24 into an entertainment event, even while serving to hook fans of the show into its suspenseful real-time narrative. Finally, 24 and other serialized dramas could exploit tools such as DVRs, DVDs, and eventually streaming VOD services such as Netflix and Hulu, to court attentive viewing practices.[1] As these distribution strategies have become increasingly standardized, they have also normalized the activity of close engagement with a dramatic storyline, in some sense turning viewers into participants in the narrative.

This chapter will engage with three major national security melodramas, Fox's 24, Showtime's Homeland, and FX's The Americans. While all three shows belong to the category of serialized melodrama, they also present a range of industrial conflicts and dramatic storylines that illustrate how national security can be addressed. 24 is a network show that became an unexpected cultural touchstone after the September 11 terrorist attacks made questions of counterterrorism and national security more urgent, and although the show has been dismissed for what appears to be its narrative endorsement of using torture to obtain information from suspected terrorists, it offers a much more complex portrait of where and how terrorism originates. Meanwhile, Homeland appeared nearly a decade later on the premium cable channel, Showtime, and functioned more explicitly as a politically ambivalent engagement with the emotional trauma of intelligence work, even while reinforcing stereotypes of terrorists as being Muslims. Finally, the FX show The Americans flips many of the tropes of the national security melodrama on their head by focusing on relatively low-level Russian spies living in Washington, DC, during the Cold War, who are, for the most part, caught up within an espionage system that is beyond their control. Unlike other surveillance melodramas, The Americans invites viewers to identify with agents working on both sides, treating both the Russians and the Americans with equal sympathy. In fact, the show features several FBI agents who, like their Russian counterparts, are simply doing their job, even if that involves actions that may be dehumanizing and destructive. In all cases, the national security melodramas introduce complex legal and ethical questions about counterterrorism efforts, even while demonstrating the psychological and emotional scars that protecting the homeland entails.

24

Perhaps more than any other show, 24 has become the most recognizable example of a melodrama of national security. The show focuses on Jack Bauer (Kiefer Sutherland), who works at the Counter-Terrorism Unit, or CTU. Bauer is tasked with protecting the nation against a wide variety of terrorist threats, assassination plots, and other dangers, often using means that are of questionable legal and moral status. The most notable—and widely theorized—aspect of the show is its use of real-time narration, in which the action unfolds over the course of twenty-four hour-long episodes, with each season composing a full 24-hour day, a narrative structure that "privileges action over deliberation," as Jennifer Gillan has argued.[2] The real-time narration serves as a constant reminder that quite literally every second counts in the fight against terrorism. Because each of the show's seasons take place over the course of a single 24-hour period, seasons are often colloquially referred to as "days," so that season 2, for example, is "Day 2." The real-time effect is reinforced in part through the frequent use of a digital clock that serves as a bumper between commercial breaks and that inexorably counts down the minutes and seconds, often creating ticking time-bomb scenarios. The show also makes extensive use of split-screens in order to convey the idea of simultaneity in an aesthetic effect that recalls the visual style of cable news broadcasts, especially during times of crisis.[3] Although split-screens can be used to create powerful montage effects where two images serve to comment on each other, 24 realistically presents two or more actions that are both contributing to the crisis that Jack must resolve. As Daniel Herbert explains, "rather than causing significant narrative or aesthetic disruptions, the deft use of split-screens makes these elements all the more coherent," allowing the show to depict "the chronological simultaneity of its multiple narrative threads."⁴ Thus, 24's real-time aesthetic contributes to a profound feeling of suspense, one that is inseparable from the post-9/11 anxieties about national security. But 24 is also engaged with time in other ways, as well. The "days" typically occur weeks or months, if not years, apart, allowing the passage of time to impinge upon the experiences of the characters.

Although the first season of 24 began production well before the 9/11 attacks, the show quickly became an important site for negotiating questions about America's response to terrorism, and in some ways the show provided a reassuring narrative that courageous security agents were working endlessly to protect the country, often to the point of sacrificing their personal safety and well-being in the service of the nation. Of course, 24's impact extended well beyond addressing questions about national security. Notably, some critics have suggested that the show was instrumental in preparing American voters for the possibility of electing a black president because of the show's depiction of the smart and charismatic President David Palmer (Dennis Haysbert), even suggesting that the so-called "Palmer Effect" helped to pave the way for the real-life election of President Obama.⁵ Such arguments are complicated by the fact that opponents of Obama have sought to cast him as un-American, even to the point of claiming that his birth certificate was forged, as an attempt to delegitimize his presidency. In fact, 24's unstable presidency, in which most of the people who hold the office are either corrupt or incompetent—there were by some counts nine different presidents over the course of eight years—might have had an even greater influence on perceptions of political power and its abuses.

In part due to its innovative storytelling technique, 24 also functioned less as a standalone TV series and more as a media franchise that included online webisodes, soundtracks, books, comics and videogames, all of which served to supplement the narrative world of the show. Thus, rather than treating the show in isolation, it is crucial to read it via what Tony Bennett and Janet Woollacott refer to as "reading formations," the intertextual and historical contexts that open up possible interpretations of the text.⁶ While Bennett and Wollacott were specifically interested in how audiences negotiated the complex story world of James Bond, an intertextual reading of 24 would take into account a wide range of textual materials, including the sanctioned paratexts that served to promote the show, as well as the unofficial texts—public lectures, political debates, and newspaper editorials—that framed interpretations of the show around questions of Jack Bauer's morality.

Many critics of 24 have accused the show of providing narrative justification for the use of terror to extract information from suspected terrorists, as Bauer's harsh interrogation techniques—justified in part by the ticking time-bomb that threatens massive destruction—often bring out desirable results. And there were legitimate concerns that 24's seductive narratives about the efficacy of torture served as a justification for using harsh interrogation techniques during the war on terrorism. In fact, U.S. Army leadership requested that producers for 24 reduce the violence because soldiers were reportedly emulating the show during their interrogations of suspected terrorists.[7] Notably, one of the high-profile producers for the show, Joel Surnow, disputed the army's claims about the effectiveness of torture, claiming that it could work to obtain information about an imminent threat.[8] Perhaps even more famously, Colorado Congressman Tom Tancredo, when prompted to answer a question about the use of torture, stated: "You say that nuclear devices have gone off in the United States, more are planned, and we're wondering whether waterboarding would be a bad thing to do? I'm looking for Jack Bauer at that time." Tancredo's comments riffed off of the ways in which the show had become a cultural touchstone for debates about the effectiveness and morality of torture and in some ways served as a way for Tancredo to align himself with a popular conservative brand as he pursued the Republican nomination for president. Similarly, Supreme Court Justice Antonin Scalia told an audience that 24's use of torture was justified: "Jack Bauer saved Los Angeles . . . . He saved hundreds of thousands of lives. Are you going to convict Jack Bauer? Is any jury going to convict Jack Bauer? I don't think so."[9] The show's justification for torture becomes even more explicit when we consider the show as part of a larger media franchise that includes 24: The Video Game, in which the player, operating as Jack Bauer, is actually unable to proceed in the game unless they use torture to extract information from a suspected terrorist. Such a narrative makes use of what Mark Sample calls a kind of "procedural rhetoric," in which games teach players how something works, in this case modeling the idea that torture can be effective.[10] As these arguments show, 24 circulated within a set of historical and textual formations that positioned many people, whether they watched and enjoyed 24 or not, within debates about national security.

However, while these examples illustrate the historical context in which 24 was discussed or evaluated, they may also diminish the complexity of 24's melodramatic engagement with the morality of the national security state and its relationship to a corporate oligarchy, in which military contractors, oil companies, and other multinational corporations hold enormous power over America's national security policies. I argue that the show serves as a complex national security melodrama, one that is, in many ways, morally ambivalent about aspects of America's national security apparatus and that offers at least some complications of the idea that all terrorists are Muslims from the Middle East. As James Castonguay acknowledges, although 24 generally formulates its depictions of Arabs and Muslims through the context of national security thriller, the show does offer a somewhat broader range of Arab characters. More crucially, 24's threats to national security come from a variety of backgrounds, including internal threats at the highest levels of power.[11] Like other forms of melodrama, 24 powerfully uses serial narrative to create a sense of suspense, one in which Bauer applies a utilitarian approach to counterterrorism. However, even while Bauer's actions may have been interpreted as a partial justification for the Bush administration's use of "enhanced interrogation techniques," the show also engaged with other concerns including the role of multinational oil companies and military contractors in profiting from geopolitical instability.

In this context, the second season of the show offers a complicated engagement with the politics of national security. Like other seasons, the second season (Day 2) takes place over the course of 24 hours, and in this case, focuses literally on a ticking time-bomb scenario: a nuclear bomb is slated to detonate in downtown Los Angeles. The first 16 hours of the day entail Jack's efforts to locate the bomb and to find a way to defuse it before it explodes. However, Jack learns that the timer on the bomb cannot be stopped, and in order to protect the millions of inhabitants in the city of Los Angeles, Jack opts to fly the bomb to a remote section of the Mojave Desert in Nevada, where casualties would be minimal and where the fallout could best be contained. The remainder of Day 2 focuses on Jack's efforts to identify who planted the bomb and to uncover a conspiracy led by a CEO for an oil company and supported by the vice president to remove President David Palmer from power and to start an unnecessary war against three Middle Eastern nations.

Initial evidence suggests that a Middle Eastern terrorist cell is responsible for planting the bomb. An audio recording that becomes known as "the Cyprus recording," of Syed Ali and officials from three Middle Eastern countries seems to suggest that they are plotting against the United States, creating a scenario that would justify a retaliatory attack. President Palmer is reluctant to attack, in part because Jack, unlike others in the intelligence community who take the recording at face value, is skeptical about the recording's authenticity. In addition, Palmer actively works to contain civil unrest generated by the nuclear explosion, particularly as they have been spearheaded by militia groups in Marietta, Georgia, a suburb of Atlanta, announcing to the public, "We will not put up with racism and xenophobia. If this is where it's going to start, this is where it's going to stop." By episode 2.20 (20 hours into Day 2), there is mounting pressure to attack (as one government official acknowledges, "We're about to bomb the Middle East into next Wednesday"); however, Palmer continues to worry about going to war under false pretenses, leading to a scenario in which his vice president leads a political upheaval against him, manipulating the text of the 25th Amendment to the U.S. Constitution to justify removing Palmer from office on the grounds that he had displayed a "pattern of erratic and irrational behavior" that would make him mentally incompetent to hold office. Although the coup is only temporarily successful, the sequence does offer a brief lesson in constitutional history, even while establishing one of 24's most overstated tropes, its depiction of an unstable presidency, in which the president—both as an individual and as a symbol of the nation—is constantly under attack. Thus, even while 24 seems dedicated to depicting Palmer as an evenhanded political leader, he is frequently in danger from threats both at home and abroad.

During the final episode of Day 2, the president's wife Sherry, who had participated in the conspiracy against her husband, attempts to deflect Jack's heroic impulses by claiming that the world is more complex than his "simple" narrative of good and evil. However, Jack defuses this complexity argument, not by denying moral ambiguity but by asserting that his primary purpose is to resolve the conspiracy against the president and its link to the vice president's efforts to launch an unnecessary war. Eventually, Bauer convinces Sherry Palmer to wear a wire to get a recording that will implicate oil businessman Peter Kingsley as being complicit with the Second Wave terrorist group in detonating the bomb in order to justify a war. Notably, this fictional storyline was unfolding in the weeks and months leading up to the beginning of the Iraq War, a war that was itself largely justified on the basis of faulty evidence that asserted that Saddam Hussein had (or would have) access to weapons of mass destruction, a threat that was often characterized by Bush administration officials as a potential "smoking gun in the shape of a mushroom cloud." During the final episode, Palmer lectures his vice president and Cabinet that "we came dangerously close to war today." And in a message that could serve as a direct critique of the Bush administration case for war in Iraq, Palmer counseled that political leadership should involve the judicious use of force only when evidence supports it: "leaders are required to have patience beyond human limits. The kind of action we nearly took should only be exercised after all other avenues have been exhausted, after the strictest standard of proof has been met." Thus, although subsequent seasons of 24 may offer more hawkish narratives that often justify torture and other harsh interrogation techniques, Day 2 also features a melodramatic narrative in which the season's central villain is a wealthy oil executive who exploited cultural anxieties about Middle Eastern terrorism in order to create a pretext for a war that would serve his financial interests, while the two heroes worked to dismantle faulty evidence that implicated three innocent Middle Eastern countries. While this conspiracy narrative might offer what appears to be an overly simplistic storyline in which an individual villain presents a threat to America's safety, the season also traced out a compelling critique of the ways in which intelligence was manipulated to justify an unnecessary war against a country that had not attacked the United States. This is not meant as an endorsement of the show's explicit politics, which offer a narrative defense of the use of torture, but as an acknowledgement that its use of the techniques of the national security melodrama are far more complex than might initially appear.

The show's political ideologies are also tied up into wider questions about its depiction of family. If Jack's heroism derives in part from his role in protecting the country from attack, Jack's responsibility for protecting (or failing to protect) his family receives almost equal billing. During season one, Jack's attempts to prevent the assassination of presidential candidate David Palmer (Dennis Haysbert) are wrapped up in his inability to protect his wife and daughter, who are kidnapped as part of the assassination plot. In fact, Jack's wife is killed, an event that eventually leaves Jack estranged from his daughter during the show's second season, when she initially does not trust his repeated warnings to leave Los Angeles when the city faces the threat of a nuclear explosion. In fact, during Episode 2.14, Jack calls his daughter Kim, knowing that he is likely to be killed protecting Los Angeles from a nuclear blast by sacrificing himself, again reconciles with his estranged daughter, assuring her that their separation was "never your fault." Subsequent episodes in the season show him continuing to protect Kim, even directing her to shoot a kidnapper over the phone, while trying to prevent a nuclear weapon from destroying Los Angeles; exposing evidence of a conspiracy to overthrow President Palmer by his vice president; and stopping an "unnecessary war" against three Middle Eastern nations that had been framed for launching the nuclear weapon. Thus, although 24 includes plot devices that offer justification for the use of torture, it is also attentive to the genuine emotional and psychological tolls that counterterrorism work can have on family life. In turn, several of the show's seasons also present narratives that challenged simplistic depictions of terrorism and national security.

Notably, the most recent season, Day 9, also known as 24: *Live Another Day*, addressed the politics of government surveillance through a narrative in which Jack's trusted colleague, Chloe, becomes involved in a shadowy hacker collective that supports full government transparency, an issue that tapped into current debates about the former NSA employee, Edward Snowden, who leaked thousands of classified documents to reveal the extent to which the NSA was spying on American citizens. For the most part, 24: *Live Another Day* upholds the conservative political consensus on Snowden, who had been widely vilified for revealing details that were portrayed as putting national security at risk. The hacking organization Chloe joins proves to have nefarious intentions with some members hoping to foment a war between the United States and China. However, while 24's stance on surveillance remains primarily in line with an aggressive approach to counterterrorist intelligence, the show's depiction of the use of drones is more complex. In fact, much of the conflict of season nine revolves around Jack and Chloe's efforts to regain control over a drone stolen by a terrorist group. In one case, a drone is used to kill 26 innocent civilians, and in another, a drone strikes a hospital where an informant is hiding. Although these actions might be understood as the behavior of a terrorist, the specter of innocent civilians being killed by an unmanned device could also raise questions about their validity as weapons of war. However, despite these moments of critique, for the most part, 24 remains firmly in support of Bauer's relentless focus on protecting the homeland, regardless of the legal and moral boundaries he might cross to get there.

HOMELAND

When it initially appeared on the premium cable Showtime, many critics, including *The New Yorker*'s Emily Nussbaum, regarded *Homeland* as an "antidote" for the perceived excesses of 24.[12] Although both shows featured protagonists who were obsessed with the threat of global terrorism, *Homeland* was positioned as an artier, more thoughtful engagement with the moral implications of America's national security state. Instead of the procedural aesthetic of 24, *Homeland* seemed to offer an alternative narrative, one in which the practices of government surveillance are treated with some degree of ambivalence. More crucially, *Homeland* wedded the narrative complexity of the espionage thriller with the psychological complexity of agents who must confront the consequences of the actions they do in the name of national security.[13] Central to this narrative of national security is the character of Carrie Matheson, a bipolar and emotionally distressed CIA agent, whose mental illness seems directly linked to her ability to make improbable logical leaps that other agents have previously missed. And, to some extent, unlike 24, *Homeland* seems critical of aspects of the war. Like 24, *Homeland* uses season-long story arcs to trace out narratives involving threats to national security. The series opens with Carrie being reassigned to the

CIA's Counterintelligence Center in Langley, Virginia, outside Washington, DC, because she had conducted an unauthorized action in Iraq. While in Iraq, she is informed that an American prisoner of war had been "flipped" and comes to believe that it is Nicholas Brody, who had been held captive for years by Al Qaeda but is now being treated as a war hero. In fact, Brody embodies what Steenberg and Tasker refer to as the "trope of the sleeper," a white Marine who converts to Islam after developing an admiration for Issa, the son of a prominent terrorist, Abu Nazir.[14] Brody's role as a sleeper receives further emphasis when a video resurfaces that depicts Brody in full Marine uniform explaining his decision to conduct a suicide attack.

Season two opens with the news that Israel has bombed factories in Iran that are believed to house materials where nuclear weapons could be produced, actions that are at least implicitly criticized by the show itself as an unreasonable attack that resulted in the death of innocent civilians. In this sense, the show seems to offer at least a cautious critique of the use of drone warfare. And in the same episode, Brody's daughter, Dana, defiantly challenges her classmates' stereotypical depiction of Muslims, even correcting one student who erroneously refers to Iranians as "Arabs," and adding that Israel's attack is a "mass murder." Eventually, Carrie's hunch proves correct when Brody assassinates the vice president and three other people but stops short of engaging in a more destructive suicide bombing. The violence enacted in the name of national security faces further scrutiny when Abu Nazir challenges Carrie as she interrogates him, describing the drone attacks that have hit his country and asking, "Who is the terrorist?" However, as James Castonguay notes, although scenes like this "may open up possibilities for alternative and subversive meanings," they are ultimately reframed by the depiction of Muslims as terrorists.[15] Thus, even if *Homeland* displays some precision in differentiating between ethnic and religious identities, the show is less careful in its depiction of all terrorists on the show as Muslim. During the final episode of season two, the vice president has been assassinated, and during a memorial service at the CIA, a car bomb planted in the back of Brody's car explodes killing over 200 people, including the secretary of defense and the secretary of homeland security.

Season three deals with the aftermath of the Langley bombing and Carrie's attempts to defend herself against charges that she was in some way responsible for the bombing. In fact, the first episode of season three opens with Carrie testifying before a Senate committee, where she defends herself after the committee discovers a CIA memo offering Brody immunity for his help in killing Nazir, and he is briefly allowed to escape. Over the course of season three, Brody again flips back to his support of the United States and, in part out of love for Carrie, becomes a CIA asset. During their reunion, Carrie becomes pregnant with Brody's child, and the show focuses on her decision about whether or not she will keep the child. Brody eventually sacrifices himself in order to protect the U.S. against Iran when he engages in the assassination of the head of the Iranian National Guard. Soon after, Brody is captured, and within minutes he is hanged in the streets of Tehran, with hundreds of vengeful Iranians chanting "Allahu Akbar." Later, Javadi, an Iranian intelligence officer now working with the CIA, tells Carrie that Iranian citizens were placing pressure on him to capture the murderer and that Brody's death allowed him to maintain power in Tehran. Ultimately, with Javadi involved, Iran agrees to nuclear inspections if economic sanctions are lifted. In many ways, of course, this resolution illustrates the difficult politics of counterterrorism. On the one hand, it still, for the most part, depicts Iranians as vengeful and supportive of terrorism. At the same time, however, it holds out some hope that reasonable people on both sides can collaborate toward a peaceful solution. And even while Carrie continues to be associated with her bipolar disorder, season three also begins to imagine the possibility that she might be able to take on the adult responsibilities of caring for herself and her unborn child.

THE AMERICANS

The Americans, through its depiction of a pair of Soviet spies, presents viewers with a morally ambivalent melodrama of national security, one that focuses less on national security interests and more on the implications of spying on people caught up in the culture of international espionage. Unlike most shows addressing issues of national security, The Americans is set in the past—in the early 1980s, soon after Ronald Reagan has been elected to office—and it encourages viewers to identify with a group of spies working for the Soviet Union who have the goal of overthrowing the United States.

The show focuses primarily on the efforts of Philip (Matthew Rhys) and Elizabeth Jennings (Keri Russell), two KGB spies living in an arranged marriage in Falls Church, Virginia, a suburb of Washington, DC. The Jennings have two children, Paige and Henry, who are initially unaware of their parents' identities as Soviet spies. However, the older child, Paige, gradually learns their secret and begins to be drawn into the culture of espionage as a teenager. In many ways, Philip and Elizabeth work to conform to the appearance of a typical nuclear family, living in a modest suburban home and buying consumer products such as cars, electronics, and stonewashed blue jeans, even while they perceive U.S. consumer culture as an ideology, one that offers seductive, but seemingly false, pleasures. Watching the show in the light of more contemporary melodramas of national security, it's easy to forget the degree to which the Cold War—with its threat of nuclear annihilation—was a source of extreme anxiety. The series opens with the Soviets learning that Ronald Reagan has been elected president, news that provokes the KGB to take a more aggressive approach to uncover the president's new plans. Actions include Philip and Elizabeth trying to cultivate a friendship with the defense secretary's maid so that they can plant a listening device in his living room and, during season two, efforts to "bug" the Defense Department's newly developed ARPANET, the predecessor to the Internet.

Much of the show focuses on the ways in which the culture of spying upsets traditional notions of identity, as Philip and Elizabeth are constantly forced to assume alternate identities as they interact with other characters on the show. Many of the questions about identity and performance are addressed in a storyline that runs through seasons one and two, in which Philip and Elizabeth seek to balance their desires to provide their children with a "normal" American experience with their actual beliefs. During the second season, Paige becomes increasingly attracted to what appears to be a typical evangelical Christian church youth group. Fearing that their daughter will embrace what they regard as a false belief system, they initially forbid her to attend before backing down out of fear that their actions will only make the church even more attractive. Eventually, they allow her to attend a weekend trip with the youth group, where the church's charismatic youth pastor is arrested after chaining himself to a nuclear facility during a protest. Later, it is revealed that the Center, the agency that oversees the Soviet spies, has been working to recruit Paige. By the beginning of season three, Elizabeth joins Paige at the church, folding anti-war fliers while monitoring the Center's recruitment of Paige. In attempting to manage the recruiting process, Elizabeth tells one of her superiors that Paige is "ideologically open to the right ideas" and that she supports the causes of Apartheid and South American liberation but that they are worried about how the revelation that they are spies might shatter Paige's existence. This awakening is further suggested in episode 3.2, "Baggage," in which Paige reacts to a newspaper article reporting that the government was cutting support to universities with the hope that the private sector would make up the difference in costs.

Their conflicts about consumer culture and about American ideology emerge in Episode 3.4, "Dimebag," in a powerful scene in which Peter and Elizabeth discuss his decision to buy Paige a rock album without consulting her, resulting in a discussion about their conflicting identities and ideologies, with Philip acknowledging what sounds like a distinctly American set of aspirations for his daughter: "You know what most parents want? Good college, good marriage, good job." Philip's comments about what he wants for his daughter evoke questions about the ideal future for their child. Later in the same episode, Elizabeth continues to argue for revealing their identities as Soviet spies: "At least she'll know who she is." Notably, Philip and Elizabeth are having this argument while Paige plans to undergo the ritual of baptism, which she describes as an opportunity to start a new life, an ambition that simultaneously evokes the American characteristic of self-reinvention and the eventual political transformation Paige will face when she learns her parents' true identities. These questions culminated in a series of episodes at the end of the third season, beginning in 3.10, "Stingers," when Philip and Elizabeth decided to reveal their identities to their daughter. Although Paige initially struggles to absorb this information, remarking at one point that "everything is a lie," she quickly becomes curious, asking a number of questions including her parents' real names, and by episode 12, she is willing to travel with Elizabeth to meet her grandmother, an experience that leads her to betray her parents to Pastor Tim, confiding in him that "they are liars." In this sense, the show is attentive to the consequences of a life of secrecy on family and friends, even if the pastor, in some ways, is acting irresponsibly by creating further division between Paige and her parents, who are for the most part, caught up within a system that is beyond their individual control.

Throughout the series, *The Americans* raises questions about the moral implications of spying. On several occasions, Philip and Elizabeth are faced with the decision to kill "innocent" characters, people who are not actively involved in spying but who could endanger their safety. During the season two episode, "Arpanet," Philip is forced to shoot a computer engineer when the worker inadvertently catches him trying to bug the ARPANET. And, more disturbingly, Emmett and Leanne, two other KGB agents who are posing as U.S. citizens, were killed by their teenage son, who had also been recruited to the CIA. In addition, the Jennings must constantly perform alternate identities, with the effect of manipulating innocent people. For example, Philip, posing as an auditor named Clark, cultivates an ongoing relationship with Martha, a conscientious but naïve secretary working for the FBI. Philip, posing as Clark, even consents to marry Martha, despite the fact that he rarely spends the night at her house and even uses his influence to get her to bug her boss's office. He also continuously rebuffs her requests to have children, and even after she confronts him, he maintains the fiction both of his identity as Clark and of his affection for her. These questions about performance re-emerge at the end of episode 3.5, "Salang Pass," in which Philip and Elizabeth are again talking in their bedroom, one of the few places where they can reveal their genuine selves. Philip reflects back on his training—one of the few times we encounter a flashback to his adolescence in the USSR—and recalls a series of training sessions in which he was forced to have sex with a series of partners in preparation for the characters he might have to play, with Philip recalling that "they kept telling us, we have to make it real for ourselves." Notably Philip's reflections take place moments after he has seduced the 15-year-old daughter of a diplomat in order to place a surveillance device in her parents' home. Although Philip stops short of having sex with her, he is clearly mindful of the moral implications of his actions. In a rare moment of sympathy between the two of them, Elizabeth admits that she hadn't considered how hard the spy training might have been for men, before reflecting on the implications of Philip's comments, asking him nervously, "Do you have to make it real with me?" After a brief pause, Philip admits before gently kissing her, "Sometimes. Not now." Thus, even while Philip and Elizabeth have been placed in an arranged marriage, there are moments of genuine connection between them.

Adding to the intrigue, the Jennings' next-door neighbor, Stan Beeman (Noah Emmerich), is an FBI agent, a wrinkle that demands that the viewer experience the Cold War from both the Soviet and the American perspective. Like many of the Soviet characters, Beeman is presented as morally compromised. He is a workaholic whose lack of attention to his marriage results in his wife divorcing him during the second season. More crucially, he becomes involved with the Russian spy Nina Krilova (Annet Mahendru), who, at one point, is essentially acting as a triple agent. Meanwhile, Beeman is oblivious to the fact that his neighbors are also Russian spies, as well. Despite Beeman's limitations, he is still played sympathetically as someone who has good intentions of doing his job well but also as someone who is morally compromised. Thus, instead of treating either the Russians or the Americans as villains, the show seems to imply that the real villains, in the melodramatic tradition described by Linda Williams, are the bureaucratic institutions and the Cold War ideologies that drive them. More notably, The Americans complicates any simplistic notion of what Williams calls the "good home," where the Soviet characters could return to a utopian ideal.[16] Although Elizabeth, in particular, expresses allegiance to the causes of Communism, we see only fleeting glimpses of their lives in the Soviet Union, and many of those images—such as the cruel training sessions endured by Philip—often have negative associations. In season 3, episode 11, Elizabeth tells Paige that she and her mother shared a small apartment with three other families, and the access to consumer goods and the plenitude associated with American culture make life in the Soviet Union seem dreary by comparison.

Season three also provides historical context for America's ongoing participation in international conflict, including its involvement in wars in the Middle East. During one early episode, Soviet spies watch a grainy videotape of a pair of Afghani fighters beheading a Soviet soldier in a piece of video propaganda that will no doubt remind viewers of similar videos recorded more recently. But rather than treat the video as a means of generalizing about Muslim terrorists, the Soviets discuss the fact that these fighters are actually receiving covert support from the United States government. In fact, after witnessing the tape, one of the Soviet spies concludes in a moment of candor, "if we want to stop receiving these tapes, we need to get out of Afghanistan." Later in the same episode, Gabriel (Frank Langella), a former KGB supervisor for the Jennings admits that the United States is trying to turn their Afghanistan war into "our Vietnam," which he recognizes would have devastating consequences for their fragile empire. Afghanistan's status as a site for a proxy war between the U.S. and the Soviet Union re-emerges in season 3, episode 12, when Philip and Elizabeth, posing as CIA agents, talk secretly with a representative from the mujahedeen, who asks rhetorically why there are no wars in America and expressing a willingness to "cut the throats" of his Soviet enemies.

In the season three finale, intertextual references to the Cold War converge with the show's melodramatic narrative about good and evil during a breathtaking scene, which intercuts between Philip and Elizabeth watching Ronald Reagan's notorious "Evil Empire" speech, Henry and Stan playing a football board game, and Paige confiding in her pastor that her parents are spies. The scene dramatizes the complex morality that Reagan's notorious anti-Communist speech explicitly forecloses. Where Reagan warns against the "aggressive impulses of an evil empire" and pitches the conflict between the United States and the USSR as a "struggle between right and wrong and good and evil," The Americans depicts the Jennings family as being both sincerely concerned with broader questions of justice (unlike Reagan, they are explicitly opposed to the racist Apartheid regime in South Africa) and deeply concerned about the safety and welfare of their daughter as she navigates the news about her parents' true identities. And where Reagan warns that the USSR "is the focus of evil in the modern world," we see institutions that are marked by moral ambiguity and individual desires that may not conform to the interests of the State. Thus, unlike Reagan's unequivocal commitment to moral clarity, The Americans serves as a powerful reminder that simplistic narratives about good and evil cannot be sustained. Instead, we are presented with a nuanced world filled with human actors with complex—and even contradictory—motivations.

CONCLUSION

National security melodramas provide audiences with narrative material that allows us to engage with what Negra and Lagerwey have called the "ongoing debates about the securitization of American life."[17] Although these shows address issues such as torture, spying, and drone attacks, they also illustrate the intersections between the national security workplace and domestic life. In national security melodramas, your work inevitably follows you home, meaning that protecting the homeland becomes inseparable from protecting the family. These shows emphatically remind audiences about the emotional impact of the culture of spying and counterterrorism on the nuclear family. Jack Bauer must deal with the fact that his work endangers the life of his wife, daughter, and even others he comes to love. Carrie, Saul, and Brody from *Homeland* all face traumatic experiences that damage family relationships. Meanwhile, the arranged marriage in *The Americans* does contain moments of profound connection and identification, even while the duties associated with spying test their relationship. At the same time, the show's FBI agent, Stan, proves vulnerable to being seduced by the double (and eventually triple) agent, Nina, suggesting that our defenses against national security threats are often easily compromised. By focusing on these personal implications, national security melodramas can offer an expansive exploration of a surveillance culture, speaking to important questions that continue to inform our politics.

NOTES

1 Jennifer Gillan, *Television and New Media: Must-Click TV* (New York: Routledge, 2011), 78–82. See also Derek Kompare, "Publishing Flow: DVD Box Sets and the Reconception of Television," *Television and New Media* 7.4 (November 2006), 335–360.

2 Jennifer Gillan, *Television and New Media*, 79.

3 For a discussion of this aesthetic, see Ina Rae Hark, "'Today is the Longest Day of My Life:' 24 as Mirror Narrative of 9/11," in *Film and Television After 9/11*, ed. Wheeler Winston Dixon (Carbondale: Southern Illinois Press, 2004), 122.

4 Daniel Herbert, "Days and Hours of the Apocalypse: 24 and the Nuclear Narrative," in *Reading 24 Against the Clock*, ed. Steven Peacock (New York: I.B. Taurus, 2004), 93.

5 Lucia Bozzola, "The Palmer Effect: Has '24' Made the U.S. Safe for President Obama?," *The Simon*, January 30, 2007, http://www.thesimon.com/magazine/articles/canon_fodder/01316_the_palmer_effect_24_made_us_safe_president_obama.html.

6 Tony Bennett and Janet Woollacott, *Bond and Beyond: The Political Career of a Popular Hero* (New York: Methuen, 1987), 60–69.

7 Michael Curtin and Jane Shattuc, *The American Television Industry* (London: British Film Institute Press, 2009), 114.

8 Tom Regan "Does '24' Encourage US Interrogators to 'Torture' Detainees?" *Christian Science Monitor*, February 12, 2007, http://www.csmonitor.com/2007/0212/p99s01-duts.html.

9 Quoted in Alfred W. McCoy, *Torture and Impunity: The U.S. Doctrine of Coercive Interrogation* (Madison: University of Wisconsin Press, 2012), 170.

10 Mark Sample, "Sites of Pain and Telling," *Sample Reality Blog*, April 24, 2014, http://www.samplereality.com/2014/04/24/sites-of-pain-and-telling/.

11 James Castonguay, "Fictions of Terror: Complexity, Complicity and Insecurity in *Homeland*," *Cinema Journal* 54.4 (Summer 2015), 142–143.

12 Emily Nussbaum, "'Homeland:' The Antidote for '24,'" *The New Yorker*, November 29, 2011, http://www.newyorker.com/culture/culture-desk/homeland-the-antidote-for-24.

13 Lindsay Steenberg and Yvonne Tasker, "'Pledge Allegiance:' Gendered Surveillance, Crime Television, and *Homeland*," *Cinema Journal* 54.4 (Summer 2015), 133–134.

14 Steenberg and Tasker, "'Pledge Allegiance,'" 134.

15 James Castonguay, "Fictions of Terror," 143.

16 Linda Williams, *On The Wire*, 220.

17 Diane Negra and Jorie Lagerwey, "Analyzing *Homeland*: Introduction," 131.

CONCLUSION

As this guidebook has hopefully illustrated, political television is an incredibly flexible category, one that encompasses a wide variety of genres and viewpoints. More crucially, in a post-network era, in which viewers have an increasing diversity of choices, political TV has flourished, both in terms of popular success and critical acclaim, even while audiences are increasingly unlikely to watch the same shows at the same time. In fact, annual research by the consumer research group, Experian-Simmons, has consistently shown a chasm between liberals and conservatives with entertainment as well as political choices.[1] Thus, discussions of political polarization should take into account how these two categories of programming speak to each other and how media dispersion informs political fragmentation, and not just in the nonfictional worlds of cable news. In this sense, the narrative contrasts between two different national security melodramas, such as 24 and *Homeland*, might tell us quite a bit about how conservatives and liberals process the politics of counterterrorism and surveillance.

Further, as I have sought to argue, the boundary between entertainment and informational programming is becoming increasingly eradicated. TV shows such as *Scandal*, *House of Cards*, and 24 continue to be cited as reference points by politicians and pundits alike during debates about police brutality, political corruption, or torture, even while many public figures attempt to deny the legitimacy of these shows as depictions of the "real"

Washington. The increasingly fuzzy distinctions between news and entertainment became increasingly evident during the earliest stages of the 2016 Presidential election when real estate mogul and reality TV star Donald Trump began his run for the Oval Office, a circumstance that threatened to turn the Republican primary into something even more closely resembling a reality TV show, "Survivor: Washington, D.C." Trump himself seemed to reinforce this idea when he slipped and referred to his rival candidates as "contestants" during one of his many press interviews.[2] But in any case, Trump's presence in the election ended up opening up a number of questions about the role of the news media in participating in the creation of a political spectacle, in which candidates were pitted against each other in "challenges" that evoked reality television competitions.

As I argued in the news chapter, Trump's candidacy seemed to present a significant challenge for the Washington media consensus, in part because their attempts to police Trump's public statements often backfired and only seemed to make him more popular with voters who felt alienated by Washington's political culture, one that includes both elected officials and the media who cover them. But, at the same time, Trump's involvement in the election also served as a huge boon to these news channels, providing them with much larger audiences than might be expected for a primary debate, much less one that took place more than a year before the general election and several months before the first primary. In fact, the Fox News debate, which was watched by an estimated 24 million people, was the most widely viewed non-sports cable program ever by a significant margin. Even the so-called "Kids Table" debate that was broadcast at 5pm featuring the seven candidates with the lowest poll numbers, captured over six million viewers, which made even the afternoon event one of the most-watched primary debates of all time.[3] Thus, in addition to being an opportunity for the Republican candidates to perform on a national stage, it was also a chance for Fox News to promote its own brand, whether through its advancement of a conservative filter during the debate or through the performance of "toughness" by the debate's three hosts, Chris Wallace, Megyn Kelly, and Brett Baier.

Much of the Fox debate followed a reality TV competition that was structured around what Lance Bennett has called "candidate challenges," with debate moderators posing questions or identifying obstacles and

Figure C.1 Donald Trump gets singled out on the first Fox News debate

asking the contenders how they would overcome them, whether those obstacles were age, popularity, or some other external factor. The first question of the primetime debate asked the candidates to pledge to support the Republican nominee no matter what, a pledge that Trump refused to take, a question that allowed Fox to appear neutral—the question wasn't necessarily singling out Trump—even while knowing that he would be forced to explain the position he had taken publicly. Later in the debate, Megyn Kelly asked Trump to defend himself against accusations that Trump had repeatedly used sexist language in referring to women, reminding him that "You've called women you don't like fat, pigs, dogs, slobs and disgusting animals," at which point Trump interrupted her and said "Only Rosie O'Donnell," referring to the comedian and talk show host that he had insulted on Twitter on several occasions. Elaborating later, Trump accused Kelly of enforcing a false "political correctness" that got in the way of actually solving problems, a framing that again allowed him to espouse an anti-Washington establishment stance. Thus, by focusing primarily on these "candidate challenges" and what they said about the participants' personalities, the debate spent little time focusing on substantive issues, such as climate change, income inequality, and the Black Lives Matter movement, among other timely topics.

Within hours after the debate, Trump took to Twitter to attack Kelly and Fox News for what he perceived to be "unfair" questions. Ultimately, even while some media critics praised the Fox News hosts for asking tough questions, the debate exposed significant tensions within the cable news channel's brand, its attempt to encompass three contradictory purposes: its status as a profit-driven cable network, its claim to be a credible source for political news, and its role in promoting the Republican Party.[4] Thus, although Trump's participation in the Republican debate—and his appearances on other Fox News shows—were guaranteed to bring the network good ratings, the network's leadership was less interested in seeing Trump actually get the nomination, and during the post-debate analysis, many of its commentators promoted the idea that he had "lost" the debate, despite the fact that a number of polls showed that Trump's support held relatively steady; an illustration of the emergence of Trumpism, the often belligerent populism that sustained his presidential campaign. As a result, Trump spent several days feuding with Fox News, often by appearing on talk shows on rival networks, such as *Meet the Press* or *Morning Joe*, which were more than happy to reap the benefits of having the reality TV star as a guest on their show. But despite all this heated discussion, the biggest effect of the debate was simply the creation of "fireworks," of a political spectacle on a massive stage, one that would generate increased interest in cable news shows.

Somewhat overshadowed by the incredible heat generated by Trump's debate performance was the news that Jon Stewart was wrapping up his sixteen-year run as the host of *The Daily Show*. Stewart has, of course, been celebrated widely for his role as one of the most powerful media watchdogs of the post-network era. Few people pointed out the limitations of the political news media more effectively and more passionately, and yet, as Stewart's run ended, it was clear that he was exhausted from his efforts to fight back against what Jeffrey P. Jones called the "crass ideological propaganda and the overall anti-intellectualism" that he confronted on a daily basis.[5] Even though Stewart sought to assure his viewers during his final monologue that "the best defense against bullshit is vigilance," it wasn't hard to forget that the political media had changed little, as that evening's debate—and its aftermath—had illustrated. Instead, even if many of *The Daily Show*'s viewers had internalized many of Stewart's nightly lessons in media literacy, his departure left a significant void in the political media because of his visibility across television and social media. Thus, as Megan Garber powerfully argued, Stewart's departure indicated that hosting *The Daily Show* meant having "influence over the national soul."[6] In this sense, *The Daily Show*, perhaps more than any other television show, had served as a cultural and political institution comparable to the role that public affairs programming such as *Face the Nation* or *Meet the Press* might have had in the past. *The Daily Show* sharpened its viewers' media literacy skills, helping them to think through political messaging, often by showing how a particular idea or phrase might get repeated over time or by showing how politicians make statements that are clearly hypocritical or misleading. But even while Stewart was walking away from the conversation, new and updated forms of political satire continue to play a vital role in shaping cultural conversations. In particular, John Oliver has used the mode of comedic investigative journalism to address issues that are often ignored by the mainstream political news media, and in some cases modeled tangible forms of activism, as when he challenged his audience to leave comments on the FCC website asking the agency to uphold the concept of net neutrality. Meanwhile, Larry Wilmore's *Nightly Show* has transformed the comedic political forum show established by Bill Maher, creating a "barbershop" where the day's news events could be analyzed from an entertaining and enlightening point of view. Wilmore, in particular, provided a distinctive new voice on the issues of race and justice that might otherwise have gone unnoticed by Comedy Central's target audience. No matter what, these satirists have repeatedly proven that a comedic approach defined by critical intertextuality can go a long way toward dispelling and counteracting the political spectacle. And, in turn, they have helped make politics more engaging for audiences who feel disconnected from traditional news. That being said, these shows have not yet achieved the relatively cultural centrality associated with *The Daily Show*.

Finally, although fake news shows have received the most attention, political melodramas also play a vital role in helping audiences to make sense of complex issues, whether that involves an attempt to engage with our ambivalence about Washington's political culture or more local or issue-based subjects. While *The West Wing* demonstrated the potential for melodrama to engage with political issues, including how our elections are conducted, more recent shows, including *Scandal* and *The Good Wife* have addressed incredibly current topics, including voter fraud and campaign financing in ways that challenge viewers to rethink assumptions about how we define the "good" within our political system. Furthermore, *The Good Wife*, perhaps more than any show in recent memory, has used the multifaceted culture of Chicago city politics to develop suspenseful narratives that engage with the complexities of justice within the legal system. In all cases, these political entertainment shows enable that process of "working through" the raw material of the news, often by developing stories around major events. In fact, by looking across a range of melodramas, including *The Good Wife* and *Scandal*, and fake news shows, such as *The Daily Show* and *The Nightly Show*, we can begin to see how popular culture dealt with the issue of police brutality against African Americans in ways that opened up space for reflection and debate. And, even while these issues are being explored through a variety of genres and formats, debate about these shows spills out into the world of social media where fans and followers can talk with others, reacting to unexpected plot twists or, in some cases, sharing clips that reflect their beliefs or values.

These practices can play a valuable role in the cultivation of a mediated citizenship, in which citizen-audiences collaboratively engage in the challenging task of making sense of politics. These activities have profound implications for politics and media alike. As Henry Jenkins, Sam Ford, and Joshua Green have argued, "the everyday, often mundane decisions each of us makes about what to pass along, who to share it with, and the context under which we share that material is fundamentally altering the process of how media is circulated."[7] As a result, we as citizens play the role of media "curators," making choices about what to circulate and how to engage with that material. This is not a singular (or infrequent) task like voting that happens every two or four years. Instead, it is something that happens on a daily basis as we scan headlines on Facebook in the morning over coffee or as we live-tweet an episode of *Scandal* later that night. As Jenkins, Ford, and Green point out, sharing media can allow us to build community, as we connect with others who share our political beliefs or entertainment preferences.

The implications of these curatorial practices have not yet been decided. They can promote a more engaged and informed citizenry, as when smartphone users captured graphic images of police brutality and social media users circulated these images until the news media had little choice but to pay attention to these issues. They can also promote the dissemination of misinformation. They have almost certainly contributed to increased political polarization, especially as the sites where political media circulates become increasingly fragmented. This is not necessarily a call for political centrism or a return to a network-era model, in which newscasters operated from an illusory position of neutrality and objectivity, even while playing a powerful role in defining what counted as an important news story. Instead, I would welcome the emergence of more political media outlets that embraced their inner skeptics, especially when confronted with a political spectacle that presents either uncritical or transparently partisan analyses. At the same time, we must be attentive to the ways in which a political news media culture continues to privilege certain types of stories at the expense of others. Lost in the discussion of the first Republican debate was the fact that candidates barely touched on questions about climate change, income inequality, college tuition costs, or police brutality. Finally, all of these questions are being addressed in a political environment in which wealthy individuals can donate hundreds of millions of dollars to the candidates they support or pay for advocacy ads to promote policies that support their economic interests. But even while political donors spend millions on their chosen candidates, activists, many of them informed by satirical "news" stories on *The Colbert Report* and *Last Week Tonight*, have worked to turn public opinion against unlimited campaign spending.

Ultimately, questions about the role of political television in shaping mediated citizenship will continue to be debated for some time. The character of our political culture remains hotly contested—a debate that goes well beyond red versus blue, Republican versus Democrat—but instead focuses on questions of political power and inclusiveness. Thus, in many ways, Donald Trump, despite his status as a billionaire, proved to be a strangely powerful opponent of a "broken system," in which donors are able to buy access to the political process. Politics after *Citizens United* might seem to invite increasing political cynicism because it makes this situation even more visible. However, political entertainment, in both its comedic and melodramatic forms continues to hold out hope that a more transparent and responsive political system is still possible.

NOTES

1 See, for example, James Hibberd, "Republicans vs. Democrats Favorite TV Shows Revealed," *Entertainment Weekly*, November 3, 2014 http://www.ew.com/article/2014/11/03/republican-democrats-favorite-tv-shows and James Hibberd, "Republicans vs. Democrats TV: Lefties Want Comedy, Righties Like Work—Exclusive," *Entertainment Weekly*, December 6, 2011 http://www.ew.com/article/2011/12/06/republican-vs-democrat-tv.

2 Katie Wilson Berg, "Donald Trump Makes Rounds on the Morning Shows," *The Hollywood Reporter*, August 7, 2015 http://www.hollywoodreporter.com/news/donald-trump-morning-shows-debate-813850.

3 Andrew Prokop, "The Ratings for the First Republican Debate were Massive and Unprecedented," *Vox*, August 7, 2015 http://www.vox.com/2015/8/7/9117381/republican-debate-ratings.

4 Ezra Klein, "Donald Trump's Fight with Fox News and Megyn Kelly Explained," *Vox*, August 9, 2015 http://www.vox.com/2015/8/8/9121377/donald-trump-megyn-kelly.

5 Quoted in Thomas Seymat, "As 'Daily Show' Jon Stewart's Tenure Ends, Scholars Say Goodbye to Their Research Topic," *Euronews*, August 5, 2015 http://www.euronews.com/2015/08/05/as-daily-show-jon-stewarts-tenure-ends-scholars-say-goodbye-to-their-research/.

6 Megan Garber, "How Comedians Became Public Intellectuals," *The Atlantic*, May 28, 2015 http://www.theatlantic.com/entertainment/archive/2015/05/how-comedians-became-public-intellectuals/394277/.

7 Jenkins, Ford and Green, *Spreadable Media*, 304.

POLITICAL TV: QUESTIONS FOR DISCUSSION

CHAPTER 1

1. Discuss the implications of Citizens United on the United States electoral process.
2. What role has online video played in shaping political advertising? Especially consider how political activists have used video to influence elections.
3. Many critics have argued that negative political advertisements hurt our political culture. Based on the examples in this chapter, would you agree with that analysis?

CHAPTER 2

1. As Amanda Lotz has argued, television has undergone a dramatic shift from the network era through the multichannel transition to our current moment in the post-network era. How have these technological, cultural, and legal issues played a role in changing our expectations about political news?
2. Jeffrey P. Jones has suggested that cable news now functions as a form of "branded entertainment." What role does corporate branding play in shaping news programming?

3.   The political protests in Ferguson, Missouri, and Baltimore, Maryland, have challenged cable news to ask difficult questions about the issue of police brutality. How did their coverage affect perceptions of these pivotal events?

CHAPTER 3

1.   Fake news shows have played a vital role in challenging the authority of politicians and the media, often by mocking formats such as news magazine shows and primetime pundit programs. How have shows such as *TV Nation*, *The Daily Show*, and *The Colbert Report* adapted these formats in order to make more effective forms of political commentary?

2.   Many fake news shows start with the assumption that political media often fails to tell the truth—think of the concepts of "bullshit mountain" and wikiality. How effectively have these shows provided critical reading tools to lead us to a more authentic truth?

3.   Look at the web versions of some fake news shows. How do they use paratexts and other promotional materials to frame our interpretations of the show? To what extent do the online versions of these shows imagine an active viewer who might actually participate in political activity?

CHAPTER 4

1.   Many critics have suggested that *Saturday Night Live* does little more than mock the personality quirks of public figures, rather than engaging in more critical analyses of politics. What role does *Saturday Night Live* serve in commenting on the institutions associated with politics?

2.   To what extent does a show like *Tanner '88* anticipate not only the explosion of the political spectacle but also the emergence of reality TV as a genre?

3.   *Parks and Recreation* and *Veep* both function as workplace comedies that just happen to be set in governmental or political offices. How do these shows use their workplace settings to reflect on our perceptions of the role of government in our everyday lives?

CHAPTER 5

1. How might Linda Williams's updated interpretation of the melodrama help us to grasp the complexities of serialized political drama?

2. Several of the melodramas of political process prominently feature "debate episodes," in which the candidates themselves elect to ditch the rules for debates that have been established for them. How do these shows depict political debates and what do these depictions say about our beliefs about how elections are conducted?

3. One of the difficulties of depicting political shows is the idea of depicting everyday citizens or voters. How successfully do political melodramas depict "real" Americans? What groups do they tend to privilege when we see "real" Americans depicted on screen?

CHAPTER 6

1. Melodramas of national security have occasionally entered debates about the legality and morality of certain types of techniques such as torture and racial profiling. How effectively do these shows address these issues? In other words, does 24 explicitly endorse torture as a way of obtaining information? What techniques does it use to do this?

2. To what does Homeland seem critical of our national security institutions? Does it offer a more complicated portrait of counterterrorism than 24?

3. How might a show like The Americans, which treats Russian spies and U.S. FBI agents with equal sympathy, complicate our expectations about the national security melodrama?

A SELECT POLITICAL
TV VIDEOGRAPHY

The following list compiles the most prominent political TV shows distributed in the United States, as well as a small number of web resources and databases containing political TV content. Although this list is by no means exhaustive, it offers a relatively thorough compilation of important news and entertainment programs that prominently feature content depicting local or national political cultures. Where possible, I have included the production company and the initial broadcaster (although for many news programs, these companies are identical), as well as the program's creators. In some cases, I have included additional notes that explain significant changes in a show's title or production and distribution histories:

All In with Chris Hayes (2013–present). MSNBC. Hosted by Chris Hayes.
Alpha House (2013–present). Amazon Studios/Amazon. Created by Garry Trudeau.
Al punto (2007–present). Univision. Created by Jorge Ramos.
American Candidate (2004). Actual Reality Pictures/Showtime. Created by R. J. Cutler.
The Americans (2013–present). Amblin Television/FX. Created by Joe Weisberg.
The Awful Truth (1999–2000). Channel 4 Television/Bravo. Created by Michael Moore.
Bill Moyers Journal (1972–2010). WNET/PBS. Created by Bill Moyers.
Black Journal (1968–present). WNET and The Ford Foundation/PBS. Produced by Al Perlmutter and William Greaves. Renamed *Tony Brown's Black Journal*.

Borgen (2010–present). DR Fiktion/Danmarks Radio. Created by Adam Price.

Boss (2011–2012). Lionsgate Television/Starz. Created by Farhad Safinia.

Brick City (2009–2010). The Sundance Channel. Created by Mark Levin and Mark Benjamin.

Charlie Rose (1991–present). PBS. Hosted by Charlie Rose.

Chocolate News (2008). Generate/Comedy Central. Created by David Alan Grier.

The Colbert Report (2005–2014). Spartina Productions/Comedy Central. Created by Stephen Colbert, Ben Karlin, and Jon Stewart.

Commander in Chief (2005–2006). Steven Bochco Productions/ABC. Created by Rod Lurie.

Countdown with Keith Olbermann (2003–2012). MSNBC and Current TV. Hosted by Keith Olbermann.

Crossfire (1982–2005, 2013–2014). CNN. Created by Reese Schonfeld. Originally hosted by Pat Buchanan and Tom Braden.

The Daily Show (1996–present). Mad Cow Productions/Comedy Central. Created by Madeleine Smithberg and Lizz Winstead. Note: Retitled *The Daily Show with Jon Stewart* (1999–2015) and *The Daily Show with Trevor Noah* (2015–present).

D.C. Follies (1987–1989). Cannon Films/Syndicated by Access Syndication. Created by Sid and Marty Krofft.

D. L. Hughley Breaks the News (2008–2009). 3 Arts Entertainment/CNN. Created by D. L. Hughley.

Enfoque (2012). Telemundo. Created by Jose Diaz-Balart.

Face the Nation (1954–present). CBS News/CBS. Created by Frank Stanton.

Fareed Zakaria GPS (2008–present). CNN. Hosted by Fareed Zakaria.

Firing Line (1966–1999). RKO Television/NET and PBS. Created by William F. Buckley.

The First Family (2012–present). Entertainment Studios/syndicated. Created by Byron Allen.

48 Hours (1988–present). CBS. Created by Howard Stringer.

Fox & Friends (1998–present). Fox News. Hosted by Steve Doocey, Elisabeth Hasselbeck, and Brian Kilmeade.

Fox News Sunday (1996–present). Fox News. Created by Roger Ailes. Hosted by Chris Wallace.

Frontline (1983–present). WGBH–TV/PBS. Created by David Fanning.

The Glenn Beck Program (2006–present). Mercury Radio Arts/The Blaze. Previously broadcast on Headline News and Fox News.

The Good Wife (2009–present). Scott Free Productions/CBS. Created by Michelle King and Robert King.

Half Hour News Hour (2007). Twentieth Century Fox/Fox News. Created by Joel Surnow and Ned Rice.

Hannity (2009–present). Fox News. Hosted by Sean Hannity. Preceded by *Hannity & Colmes* (1996–2009).

Hardball with Chris Matthews (1997–present). CNBC and MSNBC. Hosted by Chris Matthews.

Hear It Now (1950–1951). CBS. Created by Edward R. Murrow and Fred Friendly. Hosted by Edward R. Murrow.

Hillary: The Movie (2008). Citizens United/Video–on–demand. Directed by Alan Peterson.

Homeland (2011–present). Teakwood Lanes Productions/Showtime. Developed by Howard Gordon and Alex Gansa.

House of Cards (2013–present). Media Rights Capital/Netflix. Created by Beau Willimon. Based on BBC series by Andrew Davies and Michael Dobbs.

Huckabee (2010–2014). Twentieth Century Fox/Fox News. Series directed by Peter Snyder.

K Street (2003). Section Eight/HBO. Created by Steven Soderbergh.

The Kelly File (2013–present). Fox News. Hosted by Megyn Kelly.

Larry King Live (1985–2010). CNN. Hosted by Larry King.

Last Week Tonight with John Oliver (2014–present). Avalon Television/HBO. Created by HBO.

The Living Room Candidate (online). Museum of the Moving Image. Online database of all presidential campaign advertisements 1952–present. Available at http://www.livingroomcandidate.org/.

Madam Secretary (2014–present). Revelations Entertainment/CBS. Created by Barbara Hall.

McLaughlin Group (1982–present). WTTW Productions/syndicated. Created by John McLaughlin.

Media Buzz (2013–present). Fox News. Hosted by Howard Kurtz.

Meet the Press (1947–present). NBC News/NBC. Created by Martha Rountree and Lawrence Spivak.

Morning Joe (2007–present). MSNBC. Created by Joe Scarborough, John Ridley, and Chris Licht. Hosted by Joe Scarborough and Mika Brzezinski.

Moyers & Company (2012–2015). Public Affairs Television and WNET/PBS. Created by Bill Moyers.

The Newsroom (2012–2014). HBO Entertainment/HBO. Created by Aaron Sorkin.

Nightline (1980–present). ABC. Created by Roone Arledge.

The Nightly Show with Larry Wilmore (2015–present). Busboy Productions/Comedy Central. Created by Jon Stewart.

Not Necessarily the News (1983–1990). Moffitt–Lee Productions/HBO.

The O'Reilly Factor (1996–present). Fox News. Created by Bill O'Reilly.

Parks and Recreation (2009–2015). Universal/NBC. Created by Greg Daniels and Michael Schur.

PBS News Hour (1975–present). WETA–TV/PBS. Created by Robert MacNeil and Jim Lehrer.

Person to Person (1953–1961; 2012–present). CBS. Hosted by Edward R. Murrow. Revival hosted by Charlie Rose and Lara Logan.

Political Animals (July–August 2012). Berlanti Entertainment/USA Network. Created by Greg Berlanti.

Politically Incorrect (1993–2002). Comedy Central Productions and Columbia TriStar Television/Comedy Central and ABC. Presented by Bill Maher.

Politics Nation with Al Sharpton (2011–present). MSNBC. Hosted by Al Sharpton.

The Rachel Maddow Show (2008–present). MSNBC. Hosted by Rachel Maddow.

Real Time with Bill Maher (2003–present). Brad Grey Television/HBO. Presented by Bill Maher.

Saturday Night Live (1975–present). NBC Studios and SNL Studios/NBC. Created by Lorne Michaels.

Say Brother (1968–present). WGBH/PBS. Produced by Henry Hampton. Renamed *Basic Black*.

Scandal (2012–present). ShondaLand/ABC. Created by Shonda Rhimes.

See It Now (1951–1958). CBS. Directed by Don Hewitt. Hosted by Edward R. Murrow.

Show Me a Hero (2015–present). Blown Deadline Productions/HBO. Created by David Simon.

1600 Penn (2012–2013). 20th Century Fox Television/NBC. Created by Josh Gad, John Lovett, and Jason Winer.

60 Minutes (1968–present). CBS. Created by Don Hewitt.

Spin City (1996–2002). Ubu Productions/ABC. Created by Gary David Goldberg and Bill Lawrence.

State of Affairs (2014–2015). Universal Television/NBC. Created by Alexi Hawley.

State of the Union (2009–present). CNN. Hosted by Jake Tapper.

Tanner '88 (February–August 1988). HBO entertainment/HBO. Created by Garry Trudeau. Directed by Robert Altman.

Tanner on Tanner (2004). Sandcastle 5 Productions/Sundance Channel. Created by Garry Trudeau and Robert Altman.

Tavis Smiley (2004–present). PBS. Hosted by Tavis Smiley.

That's My Bush (April–May 2001). Important Television/Comedy Central. Created by Trey Parker and Matt Stone.

That Was the Week that Was (1962–1963). British Broadcasting Company. Created by Ned Sherrin. Presented by David Frost.

The Thick of It (2005–2012). British Broadcasting Company. Created by Armando Iannucci.

This Hour Has 22 Minutes (1992–present). Halifax Film Company/CBC. Created by Mary Walsh.

This Week (1981–present). ABC News Productions/ABC. Created by Roone Arledge.

TV Nation (1994–1995). Dog Eat Dog Productions/NBC and Fox. Created by Michael Moore.

24 (2001–2010). Imagine Entertainment/Fox. Created by Robert Cochran and Joel Surnow.

24: Live Another Day (2014). Imagine Television/Fox. Created by Robert Cochran and Joel Surnow.

20/20 (1988–present). ABC News. Created by Roone Arledge.

Veep (2012–present). Dundee Productions/HBO. Created by Armando Iannucci.

The View (1997–present). Lincoln Square Productions/ABC. Created by Barbara Walters and Bill Geddie.

Washington Journal (1995–present). C–SPAN. Hosted by Steve Cully. Formerly hosted by Brian Lamb.

The West Wing (1999–2006). Warner Brothers Television/NBC. Created by Aaron Sorkin.

The X-Files (1993–2002). Ten Thirteen Productions/Fox. Created by Chris Carter.

Yes, Minister (1980–1988). BBC Two. Created by Antony Jay and Jonathan Lynn.

The Young Turks (2002–present). Current TV and YouTube. Hosted by Cenk Uygur.

A SELECT POLITICAL
TV BIBLIOGRAPHY

Arceneaux, Kevin and Martin Johnson. *Changing Minds or Changing Channels? Partisan News in an Age of Choice*. Chicago: University of Chicago Press, 2013.

Baumgartner, Jody and Jonathan S. Morris. "*The Daily Show* Effect: Candidate Evaluations, Efficacy, and American Youth." *American Political Research* 34.3 (2006): 341–367.

Baym, Geoffrey. "Political Media as Discursive Modes: A Comparative Analysis of Interviews with Ron Paul from *Meet the Press, Tonight, The Daily Show*, and *Hannity*." *International Journal of Communication* 7 (2013): 489–507.

———. *From Cronkite to Colbert: The Evolution of Broadcast News*. Boulder: Paradigm Publishers, 2010.

Beltrán, Mary. "SNL's 'Fauxbama' Debate: Facing Off Over Millennial (Mixed-) Race Impersonation," in Saturday Night Live & *American TV*, ed. Nick Marx, Matt Sienkiewicz and Ron Becker (Bloomington: Indiana University Press, 2013), 191–210.

Bennett, Tony and Janet Woollacott, *Bond and Beyond: The Political Career of a Popular Hero*. New York: Methuen, 1987.

Bennett, W. Lance. "Beyond Pseudoevents: Election News as Reality TV." *American Behavioral Scientist* 49.3 (2005): 364–378.

———. *News: The Politics of Illusion*, 9th ed. Boston: Longman, 2012.

Bennett, W. Lance, Regina G. Lawrence, and Steven Livingston. *When the Press Fails: Political Power and the News Media from Iraq to Katrina*. Chicago: The University of Chicago Press, 2007.

Boorstin, Daniel J. *The Image: A Guide to Pseudo-Events in America*. New York: Atheneum, 1987.

Caldwell, John Thornton. *Televisuality: Style, Crisis, and Authority in American Television*. New Brunswick: Rutgers University Press, 1995.

Castonguay, James. "Fictions of Terror: Complexity, Complicity and Insecurity in *Homeland*." *Cinema Journal* 54.4 (Summer 2015): 139–145.

Corner, John and Dick Pels. *Media and the Restyling of Politics*. London: Sage, 2003.

Curtin, Michael and Jane Shattuc, *The American Television Industry*. London: British Film Institute Press, 2009.

Day, Amber. *Satire and Dissent: Interventions in Contemporary Political Debate*. Bloomington: Indiana University Press, 2011.

Day, Amber and Ethan Thompson. "Live From New York, It's the Fake News! *Saturday Night Live* and the (Non)Politics of Parody," *Popular Communication* 10.1–2 (2012): 170–182.

Edwards, Richard L. and Chuck Tryon. "Political Video Mashups as Allegories of Citizen Empowerment." *First Monday* 14.10 (October 2009): http://firstmonday.org/article/view/2617/2305.

Elkins, Evan. "Michael O'Donoghue, Experimental Television Comedy, and *Saturday Night Live's* Authorship," in Saturday Night Live & *American TV* ed. Nick Marx, Matt Sienkiewicz and Ron Becker. Bloomington: Indiana University Press, 2013.

Ellis, John. "Television as Working-Through," in *Television and Common Knowledge*, ed. Jostein Gripsrud. London: Routledge, 1999, 55–70.

Epstein, Edward Jay. *News from Nowhere: Television and the News*. Chicago: Ivan R. Dee, 2000.

Gillan, Jennifer. *Television and New Media: Must-Click TV*. New York: Routledge, 2011.

Gitelman, Lisa. *Always Already New: Media, History, and the Data of Culture*. Cambridge: MIT Press, 2006.

Gray, Herman. "Remembering Civil Rights: Television, Memory, and the 1960s," in *The Revolution Wasn't Televised: Sixties Television and Social Conflict*, ed. Lynn Spigel and Michael Curtin. New York: Routledge, 1997, 349–358.

Gray, Jonathan. *Show Sold Separately: Promos, Spoilers, and Other Media Paratexts*. New York: New York University Press, 2010.

——. *Watching with The Simpsons: Television, Parody, and Intertextuality*. New York: Routledge, 2006.

Gurney, David. "Sketches Gone Viral: From Watercooler Talk to Participatory Comedy," in Saturday Night Live & *American TV*, ed. Nick Marx, Matt

Sienkiewicz and Ron Becker. Bloomington: Indiana University Press, 2013, 254–274.

Hall, Stuart, et al., *Policing the Crisis: Mugging, The State, and Law and Order*. New York: Holmes & Meier, 1978.

Hark, Ina Rae. "'Today is the Longest Day of My Life:' 24 as Mirror Narrative of 9/11," in *Film and Television After 9/11*, ed. Wheeler Winston Dixon. Carbondale: Southern Illinois Press, 2004, 121–141.

Hart, Roderick P. and E. Johanna Hartelius. "The Political Sins of Jon Stewart." *Critical Studies in Mass Communication* 24.3 (2007): 263–272.

Hendershot, Heather. "*Parks and Recreation*: The Cultural Forum," in *How to Watch Television*, ed. Ethan Thompson and Jason Mittell. New York: New York University Press, 2013, 204–212.

Herbert, Daniel. "Days and Hours of the Apocalypse: 24 and the Nuclear Narrative," in *Reading 24 Against the Clock*, ed. Steven Peacock. New York: I.B. Taurus, 2004, 85–95.

Hight, Craig. *Television Mockumentary: Reflexivity, Satire, and a Call to Play*. Manchester: Manchester University Press, 2010.

Holt, Jennifer. *Empires of Entertainment: Media Industries and the Politics of Deregulation, 1980–1996*. New Brunswick: Rutgers University Press, 2011.

Iyengar, Shanto. *Media Politics: A Citizen's Guide*, 2nd ed. New York: Norton, 2011.

Jameson, Fredric. "Realism and Utopia in *The Wire*." *Criticism* 52.3–4 (Summer & Fall 2010): 359–372.

Jamieson, Kathleen Hall and Joseph N. Cappella. *Echo Chamber: Rush Limbaugh and the Conservative Media Outlet*. Oxford: Oxford University Press, 2008.

Jamieson, Kathleen Hall and Paul Waldman. *The Press Effect: Politicians, Journalists and the Stories that Shape the Political World*. Oxford: Oxford University Press, 2003.

Jenkins, Henry. *Convergence Culture: Where Old and New Media Collide*. New York: New York University Press, 2006.

Jenkins, Henry, Sam Ford, and Joshua Green. *Spreadable Media: Creating Value and Meaning in a Networked Culture*. New York: New York University Press, 2013.

Jones, Jeffrey P. "A Cultural Approach to Mediated Citizenship." *Social Semiotics* 16.2 (June 2006): 366–383.

——. *Entertaining Politics: Satiric Television and Political Entertainment*, 2nd ed. Lanham: Rowman & Littlefield, 2010.

——. "I Want My Talk TV: Network Talk Shows in a Digital Universe," in *Beyond Prime Time: Television Programming in the Post-Network Era*, ed. Amanda D. Lotz. New York: Routledge, 2009, 14–36.

——. "Fox News and the Performance of Ideology." *Cinema Journal* 51.4 (Summer 2012): 178–185.

——. "Politics and the Brand: *Saturday Night Live's* Campaign Season Humor," in Saturday Night Live & *American TV*, ed. Nick Marx, Matt Sienkiewicz and Ron Becker. Bloomington: Indiana University Press, 2013.

——. "With All Due Respect: Satirizing Presidents from *Saturday Night Live* to Lil' Bush," in *Satire TV: Politics and Comedy in the Post-Network Era*. Ed. Jonathan Gray, Jeffrey P. Jones, and Ethan Thompson. New York: NYU Press, 2009, 37–63.

Kompare, Derek. "Publishing Flow: DVD Box Sets and the Reconception of Television." *Television and New Media* 7.4 (November 2006): 335–360.

Levendusky, Matthew. *How Partisan Media Polarize America*. Chicago: University of Chicago Press.

Levine, Elana. "Teaching the Politics of Television Culture in a Post-television Era." *Cinema Journal* 50.4 (Summer 2011): 177–182.

Lotz, Amanda D. *Redesigning Women: Television after the Network Era*. Urbana: University of Illinois Press, 2006.

——. *The Television Will Be Revolutionized*. New York: New York University Press, 2007.

McCabe, Janet. *The West Wing*. Detroit: Wayne State University Press, 2012.

McChesney, Robert. *The Problem of Media: U.S. Communication Politics in the Twenty-First Century*. New York: Monthly Review Press, 2004.

Minow, Newton N. "Television and the Public Interest," National Association of Broadcasters, Washington, DC, May 9, 1961.

Mittell, Jason. *Complex TV: The Poetics of Contemporary Television Storytelling*. New York: New York University Press, 2015.

——. *Genre and Television: From Cop Shows to Cartoons in American Culture*. New York: Routledge, 2004.

Negra, Diane and Jorie Lagerwey. "Analyzing *Homeland*: An Introduction." *Cinema Journal* 54.4 (Summer 2015): 126–131.

Newcomb, Horace. *TV: The Most Popular Art*. New York: Anchor, 1974.

Ouellette, Laurie. "Branding the Right: The Affective Economy of Sarah Palin." *Cinema Journal* 51.4 (Summer 2012), 185–191.

Parry-Giles, Shawn J. *Hillary Clinton in the News: Gender and Authenticity in American Politics*. Urbana: University of Illinois Press, 2014.

Parry-Giles, Trevor and Shawn Parry-Giles. *The Prime-Time Presidency: The West Wing and U.S. Nationalism*. Urbana: University of Illinois Press, 2006.

Pompper, Donnalyn. "The West Wing: White House Narratives that Journalism Cannot Tell," in The West Wing: The American Presidency as Television Drama, ed. Peter C. Rollins and John E. O'Connor. Syracuse: Syracuse University Press, 2003, 17–31.

Postman, Neal. Amusing Ourselves to Death: Public Discourse in the Age of Show Business. New York: Penguin, 1985.

Putnam, Robert. Bowling Alone: The Collapse and Revival of American Community. New York: Simon & Schuster, 2000.

Rosen, Jay. "Why Political Coverage is Broken." Press Think, August 26, 2011, http://pressthink.org/2011/08/why-political-coverage-is-broken/.

Scheuer, Jeffrey. The Sound Bite Society: Television and the American Mind. New York: Four Walls Eight Windows, 1999.

Steenberg, Lindsay and Yvonne Tasker. "'Pledge Allegiance:' Gendered Surveillance, Crime Television, and Homeland." Cinema Journal 54.4 (Summer 2015): 132–138.

Stroud, Natalie Jomini. Niche News: The Politics of News Choice. Oxford: Oxford University Press, 2011.

Tasker, Yvonne. "Television Crime Drama and Homeland Security: From Law & Order to 'Terror TV.'" Cinema Journal 51.4 (Summer 2012): 44–65.

Ethan Thompson, "Key and Peele: Identity, Shockingly Translated", Antenna: Responses to Media & Culture, February 7, 2012, http://blog.comments.wisc.edu/2012/02/07/key-and-peele-identity-shockingly-translated/

Tenenboim-Weinblatt, Keren. "'Where is Jack Bauer When You Need Him?' The Uses of Television Drama in Mediated Political Discourse" Political Communication 26.4 (2009), 367–387.

van Zoonen, Liesbet. Entertaining the Citizen: When Politics and Popular Culture Converge. Lanham, MD: Rowman & Littlefield, 2005.

Williams, Bruce A. and Michael X. Della Carpini. After Broadcast News: Media Regimes, Democracy, and the New Information Environment. Cambridge: Cambridge University Press, 2011.

Williams, Linda. "Mega-Melodrama! Vertical and Horizontal Suspense of the 'Classical.'" Modern Drama 55.4 (Winter 2012): 523–543.

———. On The Wire. Durham: Duke University Press, 2014.

INDEX